A THEOLOGY OF PASTORAL CARE

A THEOLOGY OF PASTORAL CARE

by Eduard Thurneysen

Basic translation by Jack A. Worthington and Thomas Wieser, assisted by a panel of advisers.

WIPF & STOCK · Eugene, Oregon

Wipf and Stock Publishers
199 W 8th Ave, Suite 3
Eugene, OR 97401

A Theology of Pastoral Care
By Thurneysen, Eduard and Worthington, Jack A.
Copyright©1962 by Thurneysen, Eduard
ISBN 13: 978-1-60899-582-0
Publication date 6/11/2010
Previously published by John Knox Press, 1962

In gratitude to the University of Aberdeen

Contents

		PAGE
	I THE BASIS OF PASTORAL CARE	
1	Pastoral Care in Theology and the Church	11
2	Pastoral Care as Church Discipline	32
3	The Soul of Man as the Object of Pastoral Care	54
4	The Struggle to Understand Man in Pastoral Care	68
	II THE NATURE AND PRACTICE OF PASTORAL CARE	
5	Pastoral Care as Conversation	101
6	The Form of Pastoral Conversation	115
7	The Breach in the Pastoral Conversation	131
8	The Content of Pastoral Conversation	147
9	Man's Responsiveness to the Forgiveness of Sins	179
10	Pastoral Care and Psychology	200
11	Pastoral Care and Psychotherapy	221
	III THE IMPLEMENTATION OF PASTORAL CARE	
12	Gospel and Law in Pastoral Care	255
13	Evangelical Repentance in Pastoral Care	274
14	Pastoral Care as Confession	284
15	Pastoral Care as Exorcism	315
16	The Pastoral Counselor	334

I *The Basis of Pastoral Care*

Pastoral care exists in the church as the communication of the Word of God to individuals. Like every legitimate function of the church, pastoral care springs from the living Word of God given to the church. This Word demands to be communicated in various ways.

1 Pastoral Care in Theology and the Church

Although pastoral care is recognized as a specific function within the church, nevertheless, its basis and continuance, its validity and practical formulation, seem rather uncertain. Instead of being practiced with unquestionable certainty and force, it has actually become a theological and ecclesiastical problem. Therefore, if we are concerned with a theology of pastoral care, we must begin with the question of its basis.

To put this inquiry on firm ground, we shall first establish the proper place of pastoral care within theology and the church. The theological textbooks unanimously place it within the discipline of *practical theology*. They therefore affirm that pastoral care is concerned with proclamation in the broadest sense of the word. For the act of proclamation or preaching is the proper subject of all practical theology.

The whole task of theology must be understood as the doctrine of the Word of God. As *historical theology* it has two aspects. First, it presents, in the form of exegesis, the Word of God on the basis of the record of his revelation in the testimony of the prophets and apostles. Second, it studies the history of the church and of dogma so as to trace the development, down through the centuries, of the understanding of the Word of God, and of the life of the Christian community which corresponds to such an understanding.

As *systematic theology* it is concerned with the content of the Word of God. It attempts to discover, in a concrete way, the

Christian truth contained in the Word of God, and to present this truth within the context in which it must be understood. This truth essentially is and inherently remains Word, Word of God, which means that it never exists except as an act, an event —namely, the event of its being spoken, the act of its going forth in the form of a living Word. Therefore, the record in which we encounter this truth is already a witness, the witness of those who first received and communicated it. This original witness is followed by a chain of continual witness in the church, repeating and renewing the testimony of the first witnesses. The history of the church is essentially the story of the various ways in which this testimony of the first witnesses was spread. Therefore, even systematic theology, if it is well advised, will, in spite of its name, studiously avoid presenting Christian truth in the form of a system. Rather, it will make certain in all of its affirmations, admittedly systematic in themselves, that what it presents is true only as it *becomes* true. It must correspond to the event of God's own speaking in the form of his living Word. To put it briefly, but not entirely without risk of misunderstanding: The truth of the Christian faith is a practical truth. That is to say, it is an "occurring truth," insofar as God ever anew makes it come true.

Practical theology exists, therefore, beside historical and systematic theology as a third form because this very act of continuing the witness must become the subject of special study and teaching.

We must remember that God's own act of speaking His Word will never under any circumstances be accessible to systematic study. But this event has its reflection or counterpart in human life since the Word of God is truly addressed by God to man. This counterpart is legitimately the subject of systematic teaching. It is the doctrine of the human proclamation which serves the divine Word and of the human acceptance which is effected by this Word. Practical theology deals with this doctrine. The witness continues today, and the act which serves this continuation must be examined responsibly. Here we confront the problem of preaching in the broadest sense. The subject of practical theology is neither the truth contained in preaching nor the source of the truth which is proclaimed. Nor does practical theology deal with the way in which the truth is obtained from its source. Rather, its subject is preaching itself, the communicating and the hearing of this truth as such, and all the functions of the church related to it.

The church's preaching is not a simple but a complex act. It is made up of a series of functions which are dealt with by a number of theological disciplines. The act of proclamation, which we know as preaching in the proper sense, remains central. *Homiletics*, the doctrine of preaching, corresponds to this. But preaching is indispensably and necessarily accompanied by the sacraments and by the prayer of the church. Why this is so shall concern us no further here.

Practical theology cannot be expected to provide an exegetically and systematically developed doctrine of prayer and of the sacraments, any more than a complete doctrine of the Word of God. This belongs in the province of systematic theology. But practical theology must indeed study and teach the practice of prayer as an act of the church and its relation to the preached Word. It must consider its right order and its manifestation in the life of the individual. This is the task of *liturgics*. It includes the doctrine of the worship of God as well as that of the right administration and distribution of the sacraments.

The Word of God is, however, not proclaimed only in the form of the sermon in worship. Truly effective proclamation requires preparation of the immature in every way. Specifically, this means Christian education of children and young people. Of course, this instruction cannot claim to be proclamation in the proper sense. It must instead be seen as a kind of preparatory school where those who have not yet been received into the adult congregation are introduced to the basic terms and the great themes to which Christian preaching refers. They gain access to and learn to trust the Holy Scripture, the basis for every sermon, so that they are enabled to listen to such a sermon. To be sure, proclamation is not absent in instruction. One cannot explain the Word of God without communicating it at the same time. Within practical theology, *religious education* focuses on this function of the church.

Further, the life of the Christian community takes on a definite form as a result of preaching and the sacraments. Man in his totality is grasped and moved by the Word of God. The sacraments of the church, baptism and holy communion, clearly express the fact that God claims man's whole life. And now, as if in response to the sacraments, the church erects further signs of a secondary and nonsacramental kind. These in turn indicate that Christ as the living Word of God grasps and sanctifies man's whole life. We think here of all the activities of the church in the fields of *home and foreign missions* and *social service*. We consider these as signs which point to preaching, baptism, and communion extending the proclamation into those parts of the world which are still untouched by the life of the church. These signs have the character of proclamation even if they do not involve preaching proper, provided that their connection with preaching and thus their character as signs within the community are clearly recognized and preserved. This means that the danger of secularization, especially of social service, must be averted. The church needs a body of teaching concerning all these functions, which must preserve and express their meaning and keep the church from going astray as it performs them. This is the teaching about missions and evangelism in the widest sense, including all the church's charitable activity. But we have not yet called attention to a more central realm: the formation of the Christian community itself which cares for preaching and instruction, for missions and social work. Again, the doctrine of the church as such is not the task of practical theology. But it must develop a doctrine of community, of its task, of its structure, and of the way in which it is to function. It is this part of practical theology which provides the framework for what we call pastoral care.

We shall still have to consider the significance and the content of pastoral care in detail. At this point we only establish in a quite preliminary way what is commonly and regularly understood by it: A specific communication to the individual of the message proclaimed in general (i.e., to all) in the sermon to the congregation. The concept of the individual in distinction from the whole of the Christian community appears in all definitions of pastoral care.

Theodosius Harnack says (*Praktische Theologie,* II, p. 296): "Usually the concept of pastoral care is defined so as to mean a spiritually edifying activity and influence relating to the individual." And his contemporary, Christian Palmer, states somewhat more animatedly (*Pastoral-theologie,* p. 356): "As preacher and liturgist, I do not deal with the individual; I do not even need to know the individuals to whom I speak." But he goes on to say that there is still needed an "access to the pastor, who must be open to each member all the time, so that the latter may tell him what impresses or stirs or tempts his heart and may receive comfort and counsel from him." (*Op. cit.,* p. 358.) And in more recent times, Hans Asmussen described pastoral care with special forcefulness (*Seelsorge,* pp. 15ff.) as the "proclamation of the Word of God from man to man" in the form of a conversation in which "the message is told to the individual face to face." There is a necessary distance, says Asmussen, between the preacher and the hearer. Pastoral care lessens this distance. "As pastor I am in the position to address my hearer at the point where he now stands."

This definition of an application and extension of proclamation depends on the existence of a Christian community which meets for worship. But as the message has gone out and continues to go out through the sermon and the sacraments, this community is in turn called to deliver it in the form of words communicated to the individual. Two dangers must here be pointed out.

First, pastoral care does not replace the sermon and the sacraments; it only accompanies them. Therefore, it ranks among those secondary signs which the community establishes in response to what it has received in sermon, baptism, and communion. The content of pastoral care is identical with that of public preaching, but here it assumes a private form. Among our forefathers, it is especially the Lutheran Wilhelm Löhe who has strongly and clearly pointed out this connection between preaching and pastoral care. Individual pastoral care, he thinks (*Der Evangelische Geistliche,* II, pp. 183ff.), occurs in preaching itself. "However," he adds, "it is an altogether too narrow delimitation of pastoral care when we merely continue with the public or general usage and think we are done as soon as we have preached, instructed, and worshiped and have administered the sacraments. To the general and public use of the Word must be added the special and extraordinary one which we summarize under the name of *private pastoral care."*

Second, it is not only the ordained preacher who has to carry on pastoral care. True, it is his duty in a special way, but basically, the whole community shares in it and is called to it. In order to find illustrations of this point, we must turn to the fathers and founders of our church. It is Bucer who, in his tract of 1538, *"Von der wahren Seelsorge,"* wrote concerning the Christian community: "It is the congregation and its community which are gathered from the world and agreed in Christ our Lord (thus by his Spirit and Word) that they are one body and members one of another, in which each has his office and work to the common betterment of the whole body and all its members." And it is Calvin who, influenced by Bucer, requires the institution of the visitation of homes, not only by the pastor but also by the elders. In short, pastoral care exists alongside preaching as the communication of the message to the individual in the form of a conversation by the preacher or by a member of the Christian community. Correspondingly, a special discipline within practical theology is concerned with this conversation, because it represents a special way of communicating the Christian message.

But this preliminary definition must strike us as purely pragmatic. While it establishes the fact of pastoral care and the existence of a corresponding doctrine, it does not establish their necessity within the life of the Christian community and within the whole of theological reflection. Is there nothing much to establish after all? Is the fact of pastoral care simply to be taken for granted without the possibility of classifying it and of making plain its inner justification? Furthermore, is such a proclamation from man to man necessary? Why and on what grounds do we call for such a special communication of the message to the individual? We are perhaps reminded of the inadequate pastoral care we ourselves have performed and received. We had the impression that under the name of pastoral care something took place in the church which was foreign to the church itself, perhaps even in conflict with it. Communication of the message to the individual—does this not involve an approach to the individual as individual? Does this not lead us into the sphere of purely human experience, of social phenomena, and of the reasoning appropriate to them? Is this still compatible with the Word of God and its communication? Is the category of the individual, which appears so dominant here, not suspect as such? In the congregation, does this individual exist before God? Certainly he does, but only as the individual who has become a member. But insofar as he is a member, what need has he of a special communication of the message? Is he as member not immediately directed to the general proclamation?

In the few theological definitions of pastoral care we have quoted, a certain basic reticence must strike us about their affirmation of the task of pastoral care. Moreover, they betray an almost complete failure to establish pastoral care in a total theological context. When Löhe speaks of an altogether too narrow delimitation of the function of the pastor insofar as he confines himself to the worship of God with sermon and liturgy, does he not add pastoral care to the sermon, the liturgy, and the sacraments on purely empirical grounds? Although he affirms the task of pastoral care, he is more interested in its limitation. This becomes clear when we read the following: "But on the other hand, it is also a great folly if one wants to make the extraordinary [pastoral care] into the ordinary, if one denies that sermon, instruction, and liturgy best effect pastoral care. Private pastoral care is something extraordinary, and its entire benefit is limited to him in whom the great means of general pastoral care have done their work. For unconverted people there is no other pastoral care than sermon and instruction, as one perceives so often at the sickbeds of the godless." (*Loc. cit.*)

Christian Palmer maintains that even if the preacher does not know the individuals, he still effects pastoral care by the sermon although indirectly rather than directly. The sermon—he says this as a child of the 19th century living in thoroughly bourgeois conceptions—may really be compared with a table talk, "the table talk during the banquet of the congregation at the table of the great King." But just as every such table talk must do, it occurs in the form of the thorough application of Scripture to the concrete situations of the hearers and could therefore be termed pastoral. (*Loc. cit.*) Palmer confines the individual pastoral conversation to the important instances of confession and the conversations which are legitimately open to the pastor on customary occasions.

Similarly, Asmussen relegates pastoral conversation primarily to these same occasions—preparation for baptism, preparation for marriage, and the visitation of the sick and dying. Then what shall we do with the multitude of people who seek the pastor out of some inner need which is related neither to marriage nor baptism nor death? Are all these conversations which might be called noncustomary illegitimate in terms of pastoral care? Are they therefore to be dismissed?

It almost seems so when one considers that Asmussen devoted a major section of his book on *Seelsorge* to the distinction between pastoral care and spiritual guidance. He maintains that besides pastoral care proper, which is the proclamation of the Word on the above mentioned specified occasions, there is the great area of "spiritual guidance." Under this term he subsumes everything which elsewhere he calls "education." It includes all the vital matters not related to the marriage ceremony, to baptism, and to death. A broader concept peculiar to Asmussen leads him to gather all this under the title "Pedagogical Questions" and to consider it as spiritual guidance even though it is to be accomplished within the community. This concept states that individual pastoral care consists of nothing else but the communication of the gospel and does in no way include the communication of the law. "Pastoral care really has to do with the gospel, but spiritual guidance is a matter of the law and therefore a work foreign to the pastor." (*Loc. cit.*) Furthermore, according to Asmussen, only the pastor himself can practice pastoral care since he alone can speak the Word of the forgiveness of sins. Is this really not the limitation rather than the establishment and building up of pastoral care?

In quite another way, the French theologian J. D. Benoît presents a division between actual pastoral care (in the case of baptism, marriage, and death) and a "spiritual guidance" to be separated from it and no longer to be called pastoral care. (Cf. his comprehensive work, *Direction Spirituelle et Protestantisme*, Paris, 1940.) However, while Asmussen lays every stress upon individual pastoral care and the proclamation of the Word through which it is to be practiced, Benoît emphasizes free pastoral counseling, which shall be concerned not so much with the proclamation of the Word as rather with instruction and direction, in part moral, in part intellectual and apologetic, and in part what he calls "religious," whereby the empathic ability of the spiritual guide (*directeur spirituel*) plays the decisive role. With Asmussen, Benoît explicitly rejects the idea that confession and the forgiveness of sins have to stand in the center of spiritual guidance. This may be the concern of pastoral care in the narrower sense, but the latter is given only a subordinate place beside the spiritual guidance which Benoît presents and develops. It is the voice of an outspoken Protestant modernism which is heard here. In characteristic fashion, Benoît refers extensively to the Roman Catholic teaching and practice of spiritual guidance, which likewise is not bound to the Word of God. Catholic doctrine has replaced the Word of God with the authority of the priest, but Benoît is forced even to reject the latter.

Asmussen's distinction between pastoral care and spiritual guidance merely represents an older tradition of the Lutheran

Church. I refer to August Vilmar, who (in his *Lehrbuch der Pastoraltheologie*) likewise confines pastoral care to the office of the pastor and the church elders, and defines the occasions for pastoral care so as to include the fostering of church discipline in the family and the congregation at large. Finally, it is still to be noted that in our forefathers there is an almost universal reticence and aversion toward all spontaneous acts of pastoral care. They confine pastoral care to the office-bearer and what might be called the duty-prescribed occasions of pastoral care. One should not seek out such encounters. Of Löhe it is said that he made a single exception to his rule against spontaneous visits to the members of the congregation, at a time when the pastor was due to make a collection of Easter eggs. And Steinmeyer says bluntly that the air of private houses is not suited for the unfolding of the glory of the office; Elijah's mantle falls from the shoulders of the pastor when he makes private visits.

We shall beware of making the reproach to this older generation that it did not know about individual pastoral care. That would be wholly wrong. Wilhelm Löhe himself carried on an enormous amount of pastoral care. Not without good reason was he a center for renewal of the Lutheran Church in the last century. But as he intimates, he mainly practiced his pastoral care through his preaching, by asking for confession prior to holy communion, and through his spiritually powerful prayer. But we must ask whether what he himself called the "extraordinary work of pastoral care" is already contained in the functions he performed, or whether we must still look for it elsewhere. But where? Is the reticence which he himself felt toward this extraordinary work nonetheless finally justified? Is this work, which he calls "private pastoral care" and which goes beyond preaching, confession before communion, and prayer, perhaps not a really legitimate work and therefore not to be defended any longer?

In this connection we must also refer to Claus Harms, a somewhat older contemporary of Löhe. He distinguished between three roles in his famous *Pastoraltheologie:* Those of the preacher, the priest, and the pastor. But this third role turns out to be relatively slight in comparison to the treatment of preaching and the administration of the sacrament. Also, he likewise confines the occasions of pastoral care primarily to conversation with those "who need or expect a special encouragement because of special incidents of a mournful or joyful kind."

But along with men like Löhe and Vilmar, we must consider their opponents on the side of Pietism. The extraordinary work of private pastoral care was pursued quite extensively in the form of pietistic pastoral care. In fact, the reticence of a Löhe and a Vilmar is directed precisely against this form. In Pietism, this reticence toward all noncustomary pastoral care is quite freely abandoned. Pietism is characterized by the impetuous desire for "private pastoral care." The whole task of the pastor and of the church seems to be directed toward this end. Pietism even evaluates the sermon and the distribution of the sacraments on the basis of the extent to which they address the individual as individual.

For Löhe and Vilmar the Christian community is the comprehensive concept, the realm, so to speak, in which the individual is lifted up and confirmed as a member in his individuality. He actually exists only insofar as he is a member of the community. But the opposite for Pietism: the individual awakened and converted by Christ is at the fore. What makes him a Christian is not his being baptized, but his being awakened; not his membership in the community, but his private believing. His membership in the communal fellowship only follows this. The Christian community does not so much confirm; it exists only as the sum of these awakened and converted Christians. The word "private" in the concept "private pastoral care" is preponderant. One can actually conceive of Pietism, already in Spener and in Francke, but especially in Zinzendorf, as a movement of pastoral care, as the impetuous desire in the church for the nurture of the individual soul through conversation or by addressing a personal call to him. This concern had always been in the church. But Pietism is unique in placing exclusive emphasis on it. The function which Löhe still designated as the extraordinary work of the pastor overrides and excludes all other work. It becomes the ordinary work.

Löhe states this very strikingly in the following manner:

> Here, then, is the problem of that particular application of the divine Word which we call private pastoral care: If one reads an old Lutheran pastoral theology, the rubric of private pastoral care may be lacking completely. In the writings of these men, the rubrics of a preacher and pastor seem generally meager and his duties unimportant. On the other hand, if one reads a Gottfried Arnold, a Baxter: Ah, what duties, what responsibility, what an intolerable need, so that one might cry a thousand times with Chrysostom: *'Mirum, si sacerdos, salvetur!'* But what new means of pastoral care do Arnold, Baxter, etc., know? Have previously hidden treasures been revealed to them? No, they have what their forebears have, but in a special way, in a particularly specialized use. What was taken as self-evident is now stressed; what should be an occasional activity is emphasized above moderation. The old pastoral doctrines in their simplicity know how to place the spiritual weapons into the hand of the beginner as a firm guidance and to give him courage to use them and to give credit to the good Spirit, that he may have power, endurance, and general experience. Today, we are given such a detailed description of the work and the responsibility of the pastor that it makes us shudder. This legalistic manner humiliates a man deeply, but it also takes away courage and gladness. . . . The simple rule is this: Use the old means in old ways and continue in teaching, learning, and experiencing, in temptation and prayer until you ripen into a pastor. You will be able to approach your parishioners publicly and individually, perhaps in a hundred or a thousand ways, but never overdo it in any way, with any method, with any gift. Do your job in simplicity. Use the time-honored means prayerfully in every way that is indicated, and let God worry about how it may turn out. You can make visits to the houses or not, go called and sometimes uncalled to the sick, do this and that or don't do it, as you consider it best after calm consideration of all the circumstances before God. But make nothing into a fetter and burden of conscience. Avoid every methodism! (Löhe, *Der Evangelische Geistliche*, II, pp. 187 ff.)

We can say that Pietism, solely because of this basic preponderance of pastoral care, brought about a whole new conception of pastoral service. A new type of pastor and of church life emerged, corresponding to this conception. The pastor's frequent visitation in the homes of the members of the congregation, carried out without particular outward occasion, but also the return visit by the members of the congregation to the pastor, and the individual conversation connected with both, for the first time became central to the pastor's labor in the congregation. Besides individual conversation, pastoral care through correspondence and the wider conversation in the form of the private assembly, the so-called conventicle, are among the special marks of Pietism. The letter-writing, so much practiced in Pietism, may clearly be regarded as only a wider use of private pastoral care for the distant individual.

An eminent example of this kind of pastoral care is preserved for us in the letters of Gerhard Tersteegen. Tersteegen practiced this pastoral care through daily correspondence in the hours left after his writing of books, his prayer, and his meditation. One is tempted to say that he did it systematically. He certainly would not have spent so much time on it if he had not thought of it as a completely decisive means of spiritual efficacy and one to which he was called.

But even the assembly, the conventicle, is essentially nothing but an occasion where this individual conversation—the interchange of individual converts with one another—is practiced. Of course, this is not done without the study of the Word of God, but it is mainly by means of the conversation so that all the participants have a chance to speak. Even when the Bible is interpreted, this serves essentially as the exchange of personal experiences which the awakened and converted have had with the Word, rather than the proclamation of the Word of God as such. It is a deliberate and conscious effort to transform the public proclamation of the Christian community into a private conversation. It relates the proclamation to the individual. Here it becomes clear that it is the individual who is the bearer of the Christian community. A congregation is considered dead if it does not include the gathering of awakened individuals. They constitute its core and are therefore willingly called the core-community.

What distinguishes this community from the gathering in worship of the total congregation is its exclusive emphasis on pastoral care.

This newly emerging image of the pietistic pastor and of the life of his congregation is reflected above all in the biographies of the great pietistic pastor-curates. Even the existence of these biographies themselves is an integral part of the success of the whole pietistic movement in pastoral care. The writing and reading of the numerous lives is nothing less than an especially effective means of pastoral care. It is the exercise of influence by an individual upon another individual. Since biography presents the picture of such an individual—the picture of his spiritual method and experience—that individual awakens other individuals no less than if he still existed and could converse with them. Furthermore, these biographies reveal that it was the basic intention of pietistic pastoral care to influence the individual. This explains the completely pastoral character of its preaching as well as the fact that it was not merely accompanied by but overarched by conversation and correspondence and the gathering of the awakened into the conventicle. We also frequently detect a polemical attitude toward ordinary preaching of the church.

I cite the life of Ludwig Hofacker as an especially penetrating example of this whole new attitude. He represents one of the purest and most spiritually powerful exponents of the Pietism of southern Germany. Perhaps his purity and power are related to the fact that he died still in the springtime of his work (1798-1828), and thus in his youth. Consequently, he had not yet made a name for himself. He died as the village pastor of Rielinghausen, while others, like his brother Wilhelm Hofacker, made careers in city and even in court pulpits, which did not always prove to be an unqualified advantage and blessing. Incidentally, Ludwig Hofacker was a preacher of great stature. But his preaching strongly reveals the characteristic urgency of the personal appeal for the awakening and conversion of individuals. Furthermore, his pastoral work is also distinguished by the fact that beyond his preaching he was deeply involved in private pastoral care. Above all, he was a pastor to his own soul. This also is a characteristic sign of the pietistic movement in pastoral care. Out of ceaseless introspection and internal conversation with himself and with God (in which it is not always clear where the conversation with oneself stops and the conversation with God begins), he earned for himself his whole, intimate knowledge of the spiritual life and set it down for others in diaries and memoirs. On the basis of this self-knowledge, he then sought to lead the members of his congregation to the same self-examination. To be sure, this always involved the confrontation with the cross of Christ. But before a person could be reckoned as really believing, he had to analyze or almost to assimilate the cross of Christ as the Word of God. The individual had to receive it entirely as his own possession.

There is a strong concentration on Jesus and his cross in the life of Hofacker and of those whom he awakened, a concentration which we must certainly respect; but it primarily focuses on the individual who makes this salutary fact a part of his spiritual experience. The affective power of this spiritual experience is shown by the following sentence from one of his letters: "Weep if you can, until you feel in your heart something of the revelation of Jesus' name, which is an out-poured spikenard, something of the transfiguration of his redemption; thus will you become a poor, penitent, forgiven lover of Jesus before you are prepared for it yourself; you will marvel at what the Spirit of truth will kindle in your heart." Note the expressions: weeping, feeling transfiguration in him, becoming a lover of Jesus, getting something revealed in his heart. This shows what is meant and understood here by successful pastoral care. And the letter writer continues immediately and in characteristic manner:

> Dear brother, we intend to write to one another still more about such matters. There often reigns among blood brothers such a dumb bashfulness that they, when they meet, are afraid to let a Christian word fall between them, and if it does happen, it happens in a learned or jesting tone, so that no one will notice that the proud Adam is subject to a Saviour. (Albert Knapp, *Leben von Ludwig Hofacker*, p. 262.)

Again, not a word is to be said against the idea that, as Hofacker says, a "Christian word" should fall between the members of the congregation. But we must remember that it was precisely the word of Christian self-confession which the pietist meant and only this. That special meetings were needed for this is easy to understand. For in the sermon this Christian word could only appear on the fringe illegally, so to speak. Therefore, there was need for conversation, for letters, and for conventicles. Also, it is said of Ludwig Hofacker: "He rightly devoted a special, loving care to the nurture of the souls of the awakened so as to cultivate a solid core of living souls in the congregation. So he fed with tender love, like a faithful shepherd, those who desired life and peace." This is pietistic nurture of souls: the implanting of the core-community into the congregation by special pastoral care for the awakened. These are called the really living members, to whom the unawakened are opposed as dead. The sharply polemic attitude toward the unawakened and their pastors is clearly revealed by the following sentence from the biography of Ludwig Hofacker:

> How different was Hofacker from many of the rigidly orthodox or heartless hirelings who immediately inflict with the convenient title "Pietism" every bud of the new birth, every earnest question about Jesus to a spiritual friend, and who often with obstinate anger watch the ducklings, not even hatched by them, go into the water, while they walk around on the shore, not like motherly, worrying, clucking hens, but like proud, comfortable, crowing cocks; and concerning those in whom there is a desire for eternal life, they scarcely do more than perhaps offer an intentionally evil or, along with the sermon, a satirical cockcrow, a testimony to the fact that they themselves cannot swim. (Knapp, *op. cit.*, p. 263.)

We have already seen in the example of Löhe that there were not only the rigidly orthodox or the hirelings, but true preachers of the Word of free grace, who had a critical word to say against this whole method of pietistic pastoral care. Even more strongly than in Löhe, the warning against individual pietistic pastoral care is sounded by August Vilmar. He strongly complains in his

Pastoraltheologie about the "pietistic preoccupation of many, especially young awakened pastors, with their own spiritual experiences, so that they speak to others of these experiences and perceptions with great partiality. They use a personal example with delight. They glory in the confidence of the congregation. This can easily dissolve the pastor's spiritual life into catchwords and lies." (Vilmar, *Lehrbuch der Pastoraltheologie*, p. 156.)

Vilmar continues:

> Above all, the pastor has to show proof of the *aepios einai*, of gentleness and earnestness. Don't urge or twist. Don't force anybody to reveal his thoughts (this, at any rate, is pedantry); the majority of our people are melancholic and phlegmatic. They become angry, and being forced to speak is harmful to them! One must wait until the conversation opens up by itself. We must know that the great majority of those who are entrusted to our nurture remain *vocati*, and we must be satisfied with that. The ability to wait at this point is among the pastor's most important virtues. He should not think that he can produce the Christian community overnight, that he can make all alike into awakened Christians. The awakened merit a special attentiveness. They plunge easily into all kinds of brooding, become *curiosi*, and seek their own way. The sanguine and choleric, in contrast, act rashly when they are awakened. They think that their spiritual life is already perfect. They always desire the strongest incentives, such as sentimental hymns, because they cannot stand the evangelical hymns of the church. Thus, about ten years ago, "Fairest Lord Jesus" was preferred to all other hymns in awakened circles. They also very often drift into fancied holiness (to be children of God, who bear the seal on their foreheads). They no longer know of the *regressus ad baptismum* and even maintain, in quite Catholic fashion, that they can now commit only sins of infirmity. The pastor is no longer good enough for either the phlegmatic or the choleric among the awakened; yes, the simple, dry Word of God no longer satisfies them; they oppose the pastor and turn themselves into a sect. (Vilmar, *op. cit.*, pp. 154ff.)

Claus Harms should also be cited here again. However much his *Pastoraltheologie* may reflect the new movement of awakening on the soil of the Lutheran Church, he still lays considerable stress upon Word and sacrament, upon the pastor as preacher and priest. In his third part, which deals with the shepherd and pastor, he at one place warns explicitly against participation in special activities in the church:

> But concerning the holding of conventicles, whether it be in ours or in another's house, I must warn against it. The pure profit of such hours seems to me to involve much disadvantage which cannot easily be kept out. If a conventicle is formed by itself in your congregation, then let it develop! But let your participation in it be confined to what is lawful; see the regulations of 1741. I would rather advise an increase of the public worship. For it is true that our souls are touched too seldom, especially in places where family devotions have not become customary. Still, what is to be gained from further public devotions when there is so little participation in the already existing ones? (Harms, *Pastoraltheologie*, III, 5th Speech.)

We note from this criticism: It certainly does not reject pastoral care in general, but it does reject the displacement of emphasis to conversations about the state of the soul, to spiritual pressure, and to self-made holiness. And, what is certainly still more important, it is feared lest the things which were previously decisive be made secondary: the "time-honored means," as Löhe calls them, Word and sacrament, the old hymns of the church, and the simple Scripture interpretation in the Sunday sermon. The issue is joined: Pietism emphatically pushes the concern for pastoral care into the foreground. But the church on its part (and not only the really dead orthodox) is reticent about it. Of course, it is not denied that an important problem has been raised which might have been overlooked for a long time. But the distinctive way in which Pietism carries on pastoral care is rejected. The attacking side exhibits a strong consciousness that it has for the first time found the true way by which to revive the church. The defense exhibits a certain insecurity, as if wondering how to react to the new movement with its appeal for a church which at last would exercise genuine pastoral care.

In the words quoted from Claus Harms, the insecurity which pervades ecclesiastical circles is plainly perceptible: "For it is true that our souls are touched too seldom!" he says himself, but at the same time he warns against participation in pietistic conventicles, in which there actually is such touching of souls. Basically, he prohibits no one from it and recommends instead increased public worship of God, but he himself adds that even this is not much needed since the already existing ones were poorly attended. It is no wonder that such opposition to the attacking party could easily be outdistanced. Here, then, arises with all urgency the question concerning the valid basis of genuine pastoral care within the Evangelical Church. It can be broken down into the following sub-questions: Is the reticence of the church justified with regard to the use of pietistic pastoral care? If so, must it be a general reticence, that is, is reticence in order toward pastoral care generally and in every form? Or does this apply only to pietistic pastoral care? Is there a legitimate form of individual pastoral care? There would have to be a pastoral care which has its basis and its validity in the Word of God and which would therefore be indisputably in order within the church which is based on the Word. What does the basis and form of such a pastoral care look like? This must be our question.

As we take the Word of God as our measure, we confront the decisive criterion which must be operative. In the controversy between the pietists and their critics this criterion was not fully applied. This may account for the weakness of all the attempts to set up a clear doctrine of pastoral care, partly attacking the pietists, partly defending them. We can detect the criterion in their formulations: Something was wrong with pietistic pastoral care for Löhe, for Vilmar, even for Claus Harms because the Word of God alone can feed and nurture the soul, can awaken it and preserve its life. The self-sufficiency of the Word seemed endangered in pietistic pastoral care. What else does Löhe mean when he speaks of the "time-honored means" to which one has to be faithful, or Vilmar, when he speaks a little awkwardly of the "simple and dry Word of God" which is too little for these modern men? What else do both mean when they mistrust the private gatherings with their spiritual conversations and when they recommend the ordinary congregational assemblies? Pastoral care?—Yes, we hear them say, but pastoral care through the Word and its proclamation! Even pastoral care to individuals?—Yes, certainly also to them! But even where the individual is privately addressed, it must happen through the Word!

But is not then the Word of God and belief in it also the one and only thing on which Pietism depends? For it was precisely Pietism which combated Rationalism, by opening the Bible anew and placing it in the center of faith as the sole source of all knowledge of God. But in Pietism, the Word of God revealed in the Bible no longer stands in the center as the great, objective vis-à-vis before which believers always have to remain hearers, like students before their teacher. Rather, Pietism depends precisely on the removal of this objectivity, on its transformation into the subjectivity of human piety. It no longer depends so much on the Word as such, its sovereign speech, and the hearing which it sovereignly affects. Rather, it depends more on the individual's consumption and apprehension of the Word. It depends on whether this Word can be experienced, on the manner and method in which its hearer adopts the Word as it enters into him, as it first awakens him to the true life, as it flashes up in his soul and begins to burn. The Word of God, made into the possession of the man who grasps it—this is the focus of interest in Pietism.

This transition of the Word and its possession by the soul which longs for it presuppose, however, a capacity (or as one liked to say in the 18th century, a "faculty") on the side of man to ascertain the Word and to apprehend it. Consequently one can teach the way of taking the Word into possession, give instruction in it, and cultivate the capacity for it. This is, in fact, the essence of the pietistic teaching of pastoral care. It intends to cultivate men who engender and exemplify spiritual life by virtue of their possession of the Word and its content. But this means that the Christian community and the Word entrusted to it are no longer the primary context. The main focus is on the spiritual individual—the individual awakened by the Word—and his piety.

It is understandable that misgivings about this idea and rejection of it should be voiced by all those who feared that the independence of the Word could be obscured by it. But the question remains: Can these misgivings settle the whole problem of pastoral care, in which Pietism excelled? When the pietistic form of pastoral care is called into question, is pastoral care as such questionable? Did not the church of the Reformation, for which the objectivity of the Word was paramount, also know and practice pastoral care? We think at the moment simply of the fact that the Reformation itself grew directly out of care for the salvation of the soul and that it was thus nothing else but a pastoral care movement. If this is true, how could pastoral care be incompatible with the Word of God? The conclusion is unavoidable that pastoral care must be practiced. But it must be pastoral care in which the Word of God retains its self-sufficiency and stands over against all human piety and in which man does not cease to be its pupil.

Since God certainly will not abandon the individual, pastoral care is a means of leading that individual to sermon and sacrament and thus to the Word of God, of incorporating him into the Christian community, and of preserving him in it. So understood, it is an act of sanctification and of discipline by which the visible form of the community is constituted and kept alive and by which the individual is redeemed and preserved in spite of his degeneration and corruption.

2 Pastoral Care as Church Discipline

In order to define the nature and purpose of pastoral care, based on the Word of God, we now take up the concept of *church discipline* and the concern to which it points. As we do this, we reach far back beyond Löhe and Vilmar, on one side, and their opponents in Pietism on the other, to the founders and fathers of our church. It is primarily the fathers of the *Reformed Church* who took over church discipline from the medieval church, but completely reinterpreted and reshaped it. Calvin encountered the problem during his residence in Strassburg. In Bucer he saw church discipline used as the great means by which the community which gathers around Word and sacrament would be kept alive and pure. How much importance he later attributed to it is clear from his discussion in the Fourth Book of the Institutes of 1559. He writes there (Ch. XII, 1):

> But as some have such a hatred of discipline, as to abhor the very name, they should attend to the following consideration: That if no society, and even no house, though containing only a small family, can be preserved in a proper state without discipline, this is far more necessary in the Church, the state of which ought to be the most orderly of all. As the saving doctrine of Christ is the soul of the Church, so discipline forms the ligaments which connect the members together, and keep each in its proper place. Whoever, therefore, either desire the abolition of

all discipline, or obstruct its restoration, whether they act from design or inadvertency, they certainly promote the entire dissolution of the Church. For what will be the consequence, if every man be at liberty to follow his own inclinations? But such would be the case, unless the preaching of the doctrine were accompanied with private admonitions, reproofs, and other means to enforce the doctrine, and prevent it from being altogether ineffectual. Discipline, therefore, serves as a bridle to curb and restrain the refractory, who resist the doctrine of Christ; or as a spur to stimulate the inactive; and sometimes as a father's rod, with which those who have grievously fallen may be chastised in mercy, and with the gentleness of the Spirit of Christ. Now, when we see the approach of certain beginnings of a dreadful desolation in the Church, since there is no solicitude or means to keep the people in obedience to our Lord, necessity itself proclaims the want of a remedy; and this is the only remedy which has been commanded by Christ, or which has ever been adopted among believers. (7th American Edition, Philadelphia, 1936.)

The definition of the nature of church discipline as the personal admonition of the individual coincides fairly closely with what we have already conceived as pastoral care. This is very sharply and clearly distinguished from what Calvin calls the teaching of Christ, which means the sermon for him (it is self-evident for Calvin that the sacraments teach Christ). This teaching of Christ (the word of God and its distribution in sermon and sacrament), says Calvin, is the soul of the church. He means by this what Löhe calls "the time-honored and ordinary means" of the church. But they do not suffice. Rather, they inherently demand the additional step of the personal admonition of the individual. The church, says Calvin, would immediately disintegrate if this individual admonition were lacking. Not only the basic bond between the members of the congregation, but also their being rooted in the Word, depends upon the presence of this individual admonition—or we now say, this pastoral care. Already in his time, Calvin perceived the lack of it as a deep crisis that cried urgently for relief.

Must we not say (of course with allowances for the differences in times and men) that here the concern of Pietism is actually taken up already, that here Spener's *pia desideria* were voiced ahead of time? But it likewise takes account of the concern of Löhe and Vilmar, in that it clearly represents the idea that the soul of the church is and remains the Word, the Word alone. Here pastoral care is called for which is wholly related to the Word, required by and grounded in the Word, and oriented toward the Word. Here the concern is not with some fostering of piety, but with preserving the Christian community as a community of the Word, as a community guided by "the teaching of Christ."

We find here the concern for a community which appears in visible order and in greatest possible purity. When we read these words of Calvin's, we can visualize people marching in straight formations. A moment ago it was a wild and disorderly rabble, but now, as if by command, it becomes like a well-ordered army, starting on its advance. The command proceeds from the Word of God. But in order to emphasize this Word, in order to make it effective, the individual needs to be encouraged and addressed, disciplined and admonished, so that he might actually enroll and place himself under the Word with his whole life.

But we must never overlook or forget the fact that this visibly emerging and marching community really is and remains the community of the Word and of grace. Pastoral care (church discipline) does not replace the Word. It is itself awakened and supported by the Word; it enforces it; it gives it its full weight, so that the individual really submits to it, really becomes obedient to the Word with his life and so partakes of the grace of the Word. The community is not at all based on and established by this visible deployment, this order effected by church discipline (pastoral care), but it is based on the fact that God has called it together and continues to call it together. It has its basis in the free election of his grace. God and God alone is in Jesus Christ the builder of his community. Because it pleases him not to abandon his own, individuals are gathered into the community by his Word.

We like to call attention at this point to the comprehensive presentation of the doctrine of election by Karl Barth, *Church Dogmatics* II, 2, ch. 7: "The Election of God," especially the sections concerning "The Election of the Community" and "The Election of the Individual." We shall be kept from all sorts of missteps and degeneracies in the doctrine and practice of pastoral care only if we continuously keep in mind that the Christian community, as well as the salvation of the individual, is grounded in the gracious election of God in Jesus Christ.

There is a certain distinction between Calvin and Luther. More strongly than Calvin, more strongly even than Zwingli, more onesidedly than both of them, Luther emphasizes the idea that God and only God builds his community. Word and faith —and only Word and faith—are the foundation of the church and its sole content. Of course, Calvin says this no less strongly and unequivocally; when he speaks of the foundation of the church, he also spells out the *sola fide,* through faith alone. But just as resolutely and unequivocally, he sees and says that this faith in the Word and in its preaching is actually the foundation of the church as a visible organization and institution which gathers men and preserves them in the faith. With Luther, one has the impression over and over again that he is oriented almost exclusively toward the invisibility of the church, toward grace, penetrating from above like a ray, as the Word of God, while with Calvin—and this is his strength and his peculiarity—the actual penetration of the rays in the horizontal plane of human life and its reality appears at least as important. Calvin is constantly concerned about grace (and the election grounded in it) becoming a reality in a visibly emerging community. He also knows that the true church rests completely and exclusively upon Word and grace, but that as it rests upon Word and grace, it is truly and visibly the church. Thus, he conceives of a dual movement: first toward the Word and then, just because of the Word, toward the gathering and building of a holy community, obedient to the Word and actually belonging to and serving God. For him the second is not merely added to the first. For him, too, grace includes everything, but he understands it as an actively intervening and molding power which does not consider it below its dignity to shape for itself a visible body in the form of a community being built up here on earth.

Luther says (in a sermon of 1521): "We men can indeed consecrate bishops and make parsons, but the Holy Spirit alone makes true preachers. If He does not do it, it is not done." Calvin could have said it in exactly this way. But he would have added: For just that reason, we shall go now and actually intend to be such preachers and call others to it. Such true preachers, who are born of the Spirit, shall now be found among us. And they shall really gather the true community around them. And we shall do everything in our power to bring it into being. For Calvin, the work of the Spirit, who accomplishes everything, and the service of man awakened by this Spirit were not opposed to each other. For him the complete transcendence of grace and election was the very possibility and the sufficient basis for us to take sure and certain steps of our own toward the building of the Christian community. The church, precisely on account of its transcendent anchorage, is anything but a merely ideal, spiritual, airy, and imagined entity. On the contrary, a church worthy of its name will at any cost want to assume a form on earth. The building up of such a community means to tread a narrow ridge between the Catholic and the modern spiritualistic church forms. And we have to ask ourselves: Do we realize that just this church, born out of what is invisible, out of the Word of God, will not be passive and unshaped at all, that instead it will be very active, very maneuverable? Calvin's church certainly was, because it was built on the Word and out of grace, but it also was visible in its tangible order.

In order that the church may thus appear, in order that a community representing the church may begin to emerge, the visible institutions of the preaching office and of the distribution of the sacrament must firmly be established. The gathering of the congregation for worship, the event of baptism, the offer of communion as the feeding of the people of God, all of these visible acts must repeatedly occur. They indicate that here is the church, that here the Word does its work, and that men let themselves be called by it. But both signs—sermon and sacraments—instituted by God himself in his Word, demand certain further measures. They can actually be effective only when they do not remain alone. They do impinge upon the real lives of the men they call. But this is expressed, as we have seen, in a series of further signs of a secondary and nonsacramental kind, which are established in the church and which alone give the church its full and actual form. Church discipline is the first sign of this kind and includes all of those still to follow.

Church discipline is to be understood in this way: The church sees to it that the power proceeding from the Word and sacrament actually becomes effective in the members of the church. It cannot simply look on, when Word and sacrament exist without evidence of the life which should proceed from them. It cannot tolerate that individuals who are members of the community drop out of the living relation to the community, or that those who are called to become members fail to enter into the community. These people run around wild, so to speak, without living within the order of the community. It attempts to deal with them in "individual admonition," as Calvin calls it, to fetch them back or bring them in for the first time, and to engraft them more fully into the body of the community. It calls out of the world the men it addresses—always in the power of the Word. It singles them out and seizes them for God. This is not different from what happens in preaching, but now it is done by means of a sustained individual appeal. It sanctifies them. Of course, this does not mean that some pastoral measure could make men sinless, but it does mean that in a very concrete way they as sinners are subjected to the Word, which directly concerns and meets them and reckons them as God's in spite of their sin. In this encounter which is of the essence of pastoral church discipline, they are put into a process of "dying to sin" and of "awakening to a new life." We use here formulations from the Heidelberg Catechism, but they are already found in Calvin. We also find this idea no less clearly in Luther. If we consider only the wording of his first thesis, we see that the word "daily," set before the word "penitence," indicates like an exclamation mark that he spoke and thought of the power of grace, working in life, no less emphatically than did Calvin later.

The church establishes pastoral discipline because of this relation between the Word of God and the life of men. This discipline represents a sort of cross-questioning of man in view of the proclamation of the gospel. Because the church proclaims the gospel in its preaching and in the administration of baptism and communion, it inquires from its members about their sanctification, which is nothing else than the fruit produced by Word and sacrament. The church does not pretend that it can effect true sanctification or repentance through its own discipline. This is produced only by the Word itself. But the church indeed contends that it holds in honor the Word given to it and proclaimed by it, by inquiring from the members of the community about their repentance and sanctification by means of individual admonition.

We quote here the famous definition of the church in Article VII of the Augsburg Confession: *"Est autem ecclesia congregatio sanctorum, in qua evangelium pure docetur et recte administrantur sacramenta."* ("It is also taught that at all times there is to exist and to continue one holy Christian church, which is the congregation of believers, among whom the gospel is purely preached and the holy sacraments are administered in accord with the gospel.") Both modifiers, *"pure"* and *"recte"* ("purely" and "in accord with the gospel"), signify that the gospel is truly to be taught without admixture, that is, on the basis of its inherent power and importance, and that the sacraments are not to be administered arbitrarily, but (contrary to the Mass) in obedience to the Word of Christ. Only in this way are they empowered to call men to and preserve them in the community. Thus, church discipline denotes what might be called the underscoring and enforcing of this *"pure"* and this *"recte."* It signifies the communication to the individual of the Word of Christ which is heard in the church. Discipline in the church is designed to bring about the true gathering of the community around Word and sacrament, the establishment of the *"cité de Dieu,"* appearing as the visible form of the invisible church.

Calvin's intention in establishing church discipline has repeatedly been interpreted as if this meant the realization of the Kingdom of God in this world. Nothing could be further from the truth. Of course the community will distinguish itself from the world by virtue of its discipline of confession, which means that forgiveness and sanctification have become a reality in its midst. But this is not to be confused with some conception of holy community as the Anabaptists or the Romanists understand it. On the other hand, church discipline will prove impossible the existence of a community that actually had Word and sacrament, but gave no evidence in its life of their presence. Preaching, communion, and baptism awaken life, or they are not what they should be.

In this sense Calvin concretely established the discipline of confession in the church and defined it in the following way: The true members of the community are to be known by the fact (1) that they confess the true faith, (2) that their conduct is in accordance with their faith, and (3) that they are strengthened ever anew in this conduct by regularly attending not only the sermon but also the Lord's Supper. We see in this summary that no further action is needed besides the action of Word and sacrament, as if sermon and sacrament depended on it in order to become a vital force; rather, through church discipline the power of sermon and sacrament to reform life and convert men shall actually penetrate the life of the members of the community.

Martin Luther comes to Calvin's support in a passage from the Schmalkald Articles which today are again receiving attention. He says: ". . . God is superabundantly rich in his grace. First, through the spoken Word, by which the forgiveness of sins is preached in the whole world. . . . Secondly, through baptism. Thirdly, through the holy sacrament of the altar. Fourthly, through the power of the keys, and also *per mutuum colloquium et consolationem fratrum.*" (Part 3, IV, "Of the Gospel," St.

Louis, 1952.) It is quite clear that Word and sacrament are mentioned along with the other ordinances, including the discipline of the church. Even so, it is equally clear that they are not only placed first, but that they stand over against all others, having their own order and dignity. Church discipline is described quite clearly as pastoral conversation among the members of the community for the purpose of consolation. For Luther it points to the forgiveness of sins. It is joined to Word and sacrament for the purpose of concretely offering the forgiveness of sins given in Word and sacrament to the individual members of the community. Here, Luther, too, requires what Löhe calls the "extraordinary work" of pastoral care.

We have now determined the place of pastoral church discipline—below Word and sacrament, so to speak. It is clear that it may not gain some kind of false independence of Word and sacrament. Under no circumstances can it be cut loose from the ordinary means by which God through his Son builds the community. A congregation would be unthinkable in which only pastoral care would be practiced at the expense of sermon and communion. Furthermore, the principal interest must never be centered on pastoral care as if the *"mutuum colloquium,"* the "conversation of man with man," were more important in the congregation than sermon and communion.

This view is supported by the sharp polemic which Luther, as well as Calvin, conducted against the institution of penance in the Catholic Church. In the Catholic Church, pastoral care occurs fundamentally and essentially in the form of *confession*, which the church has developed into an institution. Each pastoral conversation which the priest has in daily life actually has its origin and its end in the confessional. But the priest's action in the confessional as the center of all pastoral care is itself a sacrament on a level with the sacrifice of the Mass, and above the sermon which has no special dignity and power since it is not considered a sacrament. One will accordingly have to say that in the Catholic Church the community is built quite directly by pastoral care itself. This cannot be said of evangelical church discipline. For true repentance, the proper action for salvation, rests exclusively with the Word and with the sacraments of baptism and communion. Forgiving sins is what only God in Jesus Christ can do, and he does it through his Word and his sacraments. Church discipline is to be strictly distinguished from such an action. It is no doubt an indispensable means, but still only a means.

Calvin called the preaching of the gospel "the soul of the church," but likened discipline in the church to the "ligaments" which connect and unite the members of the body. Luther too—again in the Schmalkald Articles (Part 3, VII, "Of the Keys")—says the following: "The keys are an office and power given by Christ to the church for binding and loosing sin, not only the gross and well-known sins, but also the subtle, hidden, which are known only to God." However, we also must remember that the decisive passage in the *Augsburg Confession* (Article VII), already quoted, where the church is defined, does not even mention the power of the keys as something separate from the Word and sacrament. Rather, it is included as self-evident in Word and sacrament, which are the decisive foundations of the church.

Again, Löhe and Vilmar both simply say that pastoral care occurs primarily in preaching, not because they wish to exclude individual conversation, but because they think of this as only an underscoring and enforcing of the Word offered to the whole community. Luther, upon whom they both depend, also means the same thing when he says very concretely: "Where you see someone publicly or privately forgiving or reproving sins in people, know that God must be there." And further: "For where God's people is not, the keys are not, and where the keys are not, God's people is not." (WA 50, 632; Z 10ff.) Thus church discipline, the office of the keys, is demanded throughout. Where it is lacking, where sermon and sacrament stand alone without church discipline, without the individual conversation of pastoral care, the true church does not exist at all. On the other hand, church discipline, the office of the keys, also has no independence for Luther. Pastoral care which is urged here is no doubt indispensable, but it is simply the sign for true preaching and hearing. It is not of the same rank and dignity as sermon and communion. It must exist where God's Word is rightly preached and heard, as a sign that may not be absent, for "where the keys are not, God's Word is not." Yet it exists only as this sign which points to the center. The center itself is the forgiveness of sins through the Word of God. Insofar as pastoral church discipline serves this fact, it has a right to exist as "an aid and consolation against sin and a bad conscience" and "ought by no means to be abolished in the church." (Schmalkald Articles, Part 3, VIII, "Of Confession.") This much is explicitly affirmed. But because Luther saw forgiveness and consolation extremely endangered in the confessional practice of the Roman Church, he turned forcefully against the continuation of the sacrament of penance. For instead of comforting and giving peace to the conscience by pointing to the Word of Christ, it threatens man with despair and uncertainty. "Here, too, there was no faith nor Christ, and the power of the absolution was not declared to him, but upon his enumeration of sins and his self-abasement depended his consolation." And "men hoped by their own works to overcome and blot out sins before God," where yet "neither can the satisfaction be uncertain, because it is not our uncertain, sinful work, but it is the suffering and blood of the innocent Lamb of God who taketh away the sin of the world." (*Loc. cit.*, III, "Of Repentance.") We can stand securely solely on the basis of this message.

Following the trail blazed by Luther, Calvin (already in the *Institutes* of 1536 in the section, *"De Falsis Sacramentis,"* under the title *"De Poenitentia"*) grimly attacks the idea that penitence is an individual sacramental act which as such effects forgiveness of sins. "One can say," he writes, "that the life of a Christian man is constant and tedious striving to mortify the flesh until it has entirely passed away." Thereby we are not to be absorbed in our own contrition, but to learn how to direct both eyes to the mercy of God, *in sua humilitate dare Deo gloriam*. But auricular confession—this is explicitly demanded—must go; thus the abolition of the institution of the Catholic confessional on the basis: Against God only have we sinned; God alone can help us; to him alone can and shall we make our confession.

"He is a physician," says Calvin, "to him, then, let us discover our wounds. He is injured and offended; let us pray to him for peace. He is the searcher of hearts, and privy to all thoughts; let us hasten to pour out our hearts before him. Finally, it is he who calls sinners; let us not delay to approach him." (Bk. III, Ch. IV, ix.) These sentences deserve consideration today when some would like to reintroduce the institution of confession in the form of the mutual confession of sins. According to Calvin, the authority to loose and to bind rests solely with the Word of God in the preaching of the gospel, in which God makes himself known, in which we hear him pronouncing his Word of judgment and of grace. All the conceptions of a sacramental authority of the priest who can bestow forgiveness out of the treasure of the church are erroneous human inventions. It is not disputed that penitence is an act that must certainly occur; it is even demanded, but it is no sacrament. The true sacrament of penance is baptism, which together with the communion is sufficient as consolation for the penitent.

Thus, according to the opinion of the Reformers, pastoral church discipline is an order which the church must and will establish in some form, whenever it has heard the Word of its Lord. According to Luther, it is valid as "an aid and comfort against sin and a bad conscience." For Calvin its purpose is to expel the manifest evil-doer from the Christian community, to protect good members from corruption, to lead sinners to shame and repentance. Thereby, Calvin immediately set certain limits. He asked for the church discipline which he required to be practiced with great discretion and reticence. It certainly should not restrain the sovereignty of divine mercy. Thus, for example, one may in no case equate the exclusion of the unworthy from communion which is ordered in the course of the exercise of church discipline, with the condemnation of those so excluded, with their very exclusion from the Kingdom and the grace of God himself.

Here we see clearly how the removal of the sacramental character of church discipline practically results in its transformation from a spiritually judgmental act into a strictly pastoral one. This will also be important with respect to what we shall consider to be the contemporary significance of pastoral care. It must never be allowed to deteriorate into pharisaical or clerical interference which, in the end, is entirely unspiritual.

Admittedly, it cannot be denied that in the practice of Reformed pastoral care, such violations and transgressions of the boundaries at this point have occurred over and over again. Catholic pastoral care with its sacramental unlocking and locking of the Kingdom of heaven in the confessional was still all too near; the need and corruption of the church, indicated by Calvin, were too great and too threatening. The violation that was to be avoided under all circumstances takes place when church discipline is no longer simply that resource, that *remedium* which may well accompany the offer of Word and sacrament, but when it suddenly takes over the function of Word and sacrament. The whole opposition of the Reformation had raged against just this danger—which had developed over the misuse of the power of confession by the priest. Yet the Evangelical Church was and still is guilty of practicing this misuse.

A trace of such misuse is found even in the Heidelberg Catechism. It declares plainly and incontestably in Question 84 that the Kingdom of heaven is unlocked and locked only by the preaching of the holy gospel. The Word and only the Word is here judged to have the whole power of forgiveness or condemnation. This certainly does not exclude church discipline, does not exclude pastoral care, as we have seen, but includes it. This clear recognition is placed in question and obscured by the following Question 85: *"How is the kingdom of heaven shut and opened by Church Discipline?"* If we understand correctly, it is now no longer "shut and opened by the holy gospel," but "by *Church Discipline*"! Notice that here at the close of the whole second division of the catechism, in which Word and sacrament have been so competently set before us, church discipline is now treated. In itself, of course, this is significant and important; this corresponds wholly to the Calvinistic insight that a church resting on Word and sacrament cannot do without church discipline.

It is evidence of the systematic strength of the Heidelberg Catechism that it explicitly speaks of such discipline here and that it presents discipline in the manner of an aid to, an underscoring of, the power of Word and sacrament, which are to become effective in the sanctification of the Christian community. It is by all means in order when, prior to the discussion of church discipline, Question 84 establishes once and for all that only the preaching of the gospel communicates the forgiveness of sins. However, in Question 85, when this forgiveness is also ascribed in the same way to Christian discipline, the boundary is violated that sets apart church discipline as a mere *remedium*, as a mere resource of the means of forgiveness proper. And this damage is even clearer when we consider the answer which is given to this question. It reads: "In this way: that according to the command of Christ, if any under the Christian name show themselves unsound either in doctrine or life, and after repeated brotherly admonition refuse to turn from their errors or evil ways, they are complained of to the church or to its proper officers, and, if they neglect to hear them also, are by them excluded from the Holy Sacraments and the Christian communion, and by God Himself from the kingdom of Christ . . ." We notice that it is within the frame and province of church discipline to exclude individuals from the communion, but at the same time to exclude them from the Kingdom of Christ itself! Thus not only the function of conferring but also of refusing forgiveness is ascribed to church discipline as such. This is what must not happen! In view of this problem we should in general have deep reservations against the refusal of communion as a means of punishment within church discipline. Admittedly, the Heidelberg Catechism was not first in proposing this extreme measure; we have already heard that it stems from Calvin himself, who recommended it in the *Institutes* and in the *Discipline Ecclésiastique* of 1539. But we must regard such a denial of the offer by a human measure of repentance and grace in the sacrament, even when it is supported by Calvin, as a regression into the Catholic confessional practice.

The Heidelberg Catechism here refers explicitly and verbally to the "command of Christ," as found in Matthew 18:15ff., "Of Behavior Toward Brothers Who Have Sinned." No doubt in this passage we have before us the fundamental text upon which all church discipline rests. And we see here the conversation of two or three within the community as the basic form of church discipline. But the final purpose of such discipline is gaining (vs. 15); thus its purpose is to open the ears of a brother for the message of repentance and forgiveness. The parable of the pardon of the debt of ten thousand talents by the mercy of the King follows immediately afterward, laying the basis for forgiveness (vss. 21-27). It is to be remembered that the action under discussion is wholly borne by Christ himself (he is indeed the merciful King of the parable) and is conferred upon his apostles (it is they who exercise discipline). The apostles and the community based on them are thus pictured as the place where repentance and forgiveness are to be communicated in definitive terms to the individual. This in no way means practicing exclusion, but ever more urgently offering grace to the unrepentant. Nevertheless, the possibility is allowed for that the result may be the refusal of the forgiving Word and a hardening (vss. 28-35). But such hardening then proceeds from the Word itself. The Word as such excludes. Man can believe in it or be hardened against it. This is what is meant by the loosing and binding which is conferred upon the community of Christ on earth (vs. 18). Furthermore, insofar as a man is hardened against the message, the text asserts that he is to be considered "as a Gentile and a tax collector" (vs. 17).

This certainly means that such a man is excluded from the Christian community with his hardness. But in the context of the whole New Testament message and especially of Matthew 18, it can certainly not mean that we are to exclude him "from the Kingdom of Christ." Rather, the "Gentile and tax collector" is primarily and properly the subject of a new offer of forgiveness, the message of the Kingdom of Christ, which goes out to him again and again (vss. 21ff.). Therefore, what is commanded is not just exclusion, but a renewed and still more urgent offer of grace. The final separation of the tares from the wheat within the community is withheld from us. Incidentally, even the Heidelberg Catechism itself has somehow understood this. For the last sentence of that answer to Question 85 reads: "If they neglect to hear them also, they are by them excluded from the Holy Sacraments and the Christian communion, and by God Himself from the kingdom of Christ; and if they promise and show real amendment, they are again received as members of Christ and His Church." This causes us to suspect that the refusal of forgiveness, the actual exclusion from the community and Kingdom of Christ, was not meant quite so seriously after all. If so, we should not threaten people with the possibility as if we could effect this exclusion by the power of human church discipline. It would only be a simulated exclusion.

We shall have to keep in mind this dangerous extension of the authority of penitential discipline throughout our further discussion of the nature of pastoral care. Insofar as for us church discipline and pastoral care coincide, it must be strictly maintained that pastoral care does not possess authority either to forgive sins or to refuse forgiveness, except insofar as it points or leads man to the Word of God. Belief or hardening will occur in the confrontation with that Word.

This limit is well observed in the Second Helvetic Confession by Bullinger. It states: "Many fancy things are said about the keys of the Kingdom of God, which were handed over to the apostles by the Lord. People forge from them swords, spears, scepters, and crowns and gain omnipotence over the greatest kingdoms, as well as over body and soul. Our opinion about this is based simply on the Word of the Lord, and we say that all properly called servants of the church possess the keys of the Kingdom of heaven and exercise the power of the keys when they proclaim the gospel." We cannot say it better than it is stated here: The power to forgive sins or to harden rests in the proclaimed Word itself. The preacher is only the servant who communicates the Word, and as this is done, the unlocking or locking of the Kingdom of heaven is accomplished. In this sense, he exercises the power of the keys in the sermon. Church discipline, however, is clearly distinguished from that. It is a measure which is incumbent upon "the servant of the church . . . since discipline must be in the church." Although it is ordered in great reticence, it may be the duty of the servant to make use of discipline for the edification of the community, depending on the circumstances of the times and of public life. Yet—it is explicitly added—"the Lord himself has forbidden him to pull the tares out of the field because there is a danger that he may pull up wheat as well."

We summarize: Our discussion of the Reformers' position leads us to the conclusion that for them the Christian community, gathering around Word and sacrament, exhibits that realm which they called "church discipline," thereby using the language of the ancient and medieval church. They do not consider it as something accidental which could be lacking, but as something necessary which must under no circumstances be lacking. If there were no church discipline, there would be no real community. Church discipline is actually to be understood as the shape or the external form which the community assumes if it is constituted by the Word and the sacraments as the people obedient to Christ their King. We think once more of the deployment of an army that must march not as a wild, unordered rabble, but in rank and file. We have used the term "sign" for this form, shape, and order that may not be lacking. That is to say, discipline has no value in itself; it does not guarantee the victory of this army; nor can it provide by itself the meaning and the motivating force for this whole deployment. Victory, meaning, and force of the gathered community lie entirely elsewhere than in its orders. They are solely rooted in the Word of God around which it gathers, in Jesus Christ himself who is this Word solely and exclusively. However, gathering around this Word cannot happen without this order appearing and being heeded. Therefore, the Reformers expressly deal with this order and the measures corresponding to it. It is the order in which the teachers, preachers, and servants of the community are appointed and exercise their office; the order in which the members of the community rally around their teachers and preachers. They deal with the positive and negative characteristics by which one can perceive whether the community actually meets as one that is holy and well-pleasing to God. The community itself is summoned to establish these ordinances and rules and to observe them, as it were, as a response to what God offers in his Word. This means that the community must have a constitution, and that it must be concerned about the confession of the true faith. It means further that it watches over the choice and installation of its ministers, and that it cares for the outward and inward well-being of every individual member. Once again, none of this is important in itself; it is important only as an appendix. None of this makes the community what it is. But if it is what it should be, it will not lack this. All of this is important only insofar as it is related to the forgiveness of sins and its establishment and communication in sermon and sacrament. But in this relationship it is important!

Finally, it is of utmost interest for our subject that this order is established through repeated inquiries to be directed to the individual in the form of conversations "from man to man." These conversations focus on the responsibility of the individual toward the orders established by the community, or better, toward the proclamation of the Christian message, which the orders serve by attempting to ensure its true reception. Thus, for example, the preacher of the Word is required to testify by the sign of obedient conduct that he actually stands in the power of the forgiveness of sins. He will be asked about it and have to answer for it. Or: The member of the community is required to testify by the sign of participation in prayer and in the reading of Scripture that he belongs to the community of the Word. He will be asked about prayer and the reading of Scripture and be responsible for them. Or: We are required to support the poor and oppressed within the community. The individual is asked about it, and he has to answer for it. Only then can the order of charity remain in force as a sign that we live in the community which enjoys the great charity of God and which therefore must in turn be merciful. Or quite simply: Granted that there is preaching, baptizing, and the offering of communion, do those who enjoy these great benefits really know what confronts them here, and what it means to be a part of it? They will be asked about it and be held responsible for it in order that they may actually become true recipients of the Word in all its forms. There are also the indifferent and the rebellious who turn to heresies and strive against the Word; they will have to be asked about their conduct lest they be lost. This is what it means to practice church discipline, what it means to be a living community that really and truly cares for its members.

We have proposed the term "pastoral care" for this aspect of the church's life. Or rather, we have defined and interpreted the concept of "pastoral care" by the concept of "church discipline." It is obvious that the latter is the more comprehensive. Not all that is to be understood under church discipline is described by the words "pastoral care." But church discipline indicates the context in which pastoral care can meaningfully be carried on. We undertook the definition of this context because the concept of pastoral care was at first somewhat vague and undefined. At first sight, it means simply that a conversation takes place between the pastor and a person to whom he is to minister, a conversation concerning God and divine things for his salvation. But this definition does not contain anything about the legitimacy and nature of this conversation. This conversation hangs, so to speak, in the air; at least in the usage of modern Christianity, the concept of pastoral care does not make clear that the presuppositions of this conversation are the Word of God and the congregation. Therefore, without further definition it is ambiguous to speak here about the soul and the care of the soul. Above all, we do not know what is to make up the substance of the conversation in which this care of the soul shall satisfactorily be carried out.

Reflection upon the teaching of the Reformers, however, has given us a firm footing in this matter, a ground upon which pastoral care in the church of Jesus Christ can stand and must stand if it is to proceed properly. We have perceived this ground to be what the Reformers called church discipline. Here the whole vagueness which at first surrounded our concept vanishes; here it is filled with a specific content which makes it a means of proclamation. This presupposes a clear relationship between those who render pastoral care and those who receive it, since both are seen within the context of the church. This makes possible the delimitations that protect pastoral care from being confused with the nurture of souls carried on by means of modern psychology or common sense. Now we can make clear what we mean by "soul" and by "care" for the soul. Now we are on firm ground.

The term "discipline" in the phrase "church discipline" may at first appear to us irrelevant for the concept of pastoral care. But we must remember that this term is derived from the word *"disciplina,"* which means "school." Pastoral care would thus consist in teaching and learning. But within the context of the church, the teacher whose pupils we may be and by whose teaching our souls are cared for can be none other than Holy Scripture. This removes from the outset any moralizing connotation from the word "discipline." We become pupils of the Word of God who may receive what it addresses to us. This means for us to be addressed by the Lord of the church, and therefore to come under the care and protection of this Lord. Should this be objectionable? Is this not really pastoral care in the best and deepest sense of the Word?

It may further be pointed out that the Reformers based their teaching about *disciplina*, about discipline, on Holy Scripture. They refer to Scripture when they discuss the call directed to the individual privately and in public proclamation, be it the sick or dying, be it the fallible and erring, be it the authorities or any other part of society—even the clergy itself! (We think, for example, of Calvin's pastoral care of pastors through his letters; cf. Kolfhaus, *Calvin als Seelsorger*.) Among these scriptural references we find all those numerous passages from the Old Testament where the prophetic warning is sounded, all those special conversations in which the individual was subjected to God's truth and justice. Here we are referred, for example, to Nathan's rebuke of David (II Samuel 12) to Elijah's of Ahab (I Kings 21), and to all the pronouncements over king and people by the Old Testament prophets. In addition, all the passages from the New Testament are mentioned which deal in particular with warning or consolation.

It is not possible here to cite these Scripture passages individually. But they remind us that where God's Word goes forth through his prophets and apostles, such a call is continually addressed to individuals or groups. It is clear, therefore, that such admonition and consolation are of the essence of the Word of God. Consequently, insofar as it contains this consolation and warning, pastoral care is by no means exceptional and dispensable, but it is essentially based on the Word of God itself. Indeed, the Word continually and explicitly reveals the need for this individual act. It underscores and especially emphasizes what is already contained generally in the Word of God. And when the Reformers placed the special institution of church discipline beside the general proclamation of the Word, with its inherent call to man, they performed an act of obedience in which they echoed in their own words this emphasizing and underscoring to be found in the Word of God itself.

Finally, this means that in regard to its content pastoral care can be nothing else than a communication of the Word of God in a particular form. Hence, pastoral care can be concerned with nothing else than the proclamation of forgiveness and the sanctification of man for God. But in characteristic distinction from Catholic doctrine, pastoral care can lay claim to no sort of sacramental character. We must insist that pastoral care in no way become a reintroduction of the Catholic sacrament of penance. God alone, not the pastor, forgives sins or retains sins by the power of his Word. Pastoral care serves this Word as it leads to the Word and its communication through preaching and communion.

Consequently, pastoral care occurs within the realm of the church. It proceeds from the Word and leads back to the Word. It presupposes membership in the body of Christ, or it has this membership as its purpose. It can be practiced by the appointed bearer of the office of proclamation and must be included among his indisputable duties. However, it can also be exercised by the members of the church for each other. For, even in the case of the office-bearer, membership in the body of the church and not merely his special office is the essential presupposition of his pastoral care. He, too, practices it as brother to brother. It will be one among the signs of a vital congregation that such pastoral care is voluntarily offered and received by all of its members.

The ultimate presupposition here as elsewhere when we are concerned with the Word of God is the *Pneuma*, the Spirit of God, who alone gives life to the Word. The goal, however, is to win men for the Kingdom of Christ and for his church on earth.

Pastoral care is care for the soul of man. The human soul with which pastoral care is concerned, however, is not simply the psychic element in man, but soul is to be understood according to Holy Scripture as the totality of man's personal existence in body, "soul," and spirit under the claim of God. The knowledge of man's existence before God has its basis in the incarnation of Jesus Christ. Accordingly, the task of pastoral care is to be defined as the sanctification of the whole man for God.

3 The Soul of Man as the Object of Pastoral Care

Pastoral care means and is care for the soul of man. But what is to be understood by this human soul, both with regard to the concept of soul and with regard to the caring for this soul?

When we inquire about man's soul in the context of pastoral care, we are concerned neither with scientific anthropology (whether biological or psychological) nor with philosophical anthropology (whether materialistic or idealistic), but our inquiry is a purely theological one. We therefore proceed from the passage in Holy Scripture that is basic for our concept: Genesis 2:7. It reads in the King James Version: "And the LORD God formed man of the dust of the ground, and breathed into his nostrils the breath of life; and man became a living soul." Here it is simply and fundamentally stated that man consists of body and soul in such a way that the soul makes him who he is—man. The meaning is this: A physical being is constituted, but it is still not man as "living soul." For him to become this, a further and special work of God is needed: He "breathed into his nostrils the breath of life." Only now does he become a living human being, a "living soul." Man thus lives his life as man only in terms of this soul by which he actually comes into existence. But he also lives it as the one and complete life that is given him in body and soul.

The distinction of body and soul and the totality in which they are related to one another are equally important here. The soul is an independent, sovereign entity standing over against the body; it is no mere function of the body. But the body is also an essential part of man; it is nothing secondary, not simply an appendage nor a mere lodging, even less a prison, in which man lives as a soul. His humanity depends just as much on his body as it does on his soul, even though it is defined by his soul. But both soul and body are to be conceived as a unity, which makes up the totality of his life as well as each individual act. Man is not simply a being who has a body and a soul, but as God breathes into him the breath of life, he *becomes* man, who in body and soul is one whole.

The nature of man thus rests upon nothing isolated, neither certain characteristics nor certain instincts of body or soul, but it rests upon the relationship in which all characteristics and instincts of body and soul stand to the act of God, this inbreathing of his breath. This breath or Spirit of God (in the Hebrew the one word *ruach* is used for both terms) penetrates everything. All characteristics and instincts participate in it and are marked and defined by this participation. It is this which constitutes this being as human. If only for a moment one disregards this inbreathing and leaves it aside, everything disintegrates. The relative dualism of body and soul becomes absolute, and man no longer exists as a whole. Something may still exist which we call "body" and something "psychic" besides, but there is no longer a human existence, a human organism based on God's inbreathing. Therefore, when we speak of the soul of man, we have to understand it to mean the whole man, man's unity and totality in the duality of his body and soul.

The first insight, then, to be gained from the Bible expresses the idea that the reality of man exhibits a double aspect, an inner and an outer, a visible and an invisible one. Although man is united in himself, he lives as a citizen of two worlds, one physical and visible and the other psychic and invisible. This thesis contradicts neither scientific nor philosophical anthropology. Rather, it is simply the statement of a fact which every conceivable anthropology has to describe and which it will attempt to interpret and to comprehend in its own particular way.

The second conclusion from our Scripture passage is this: The inbreathing of the Spirit, by virtue of which man becomes a living soul, is an act of God. "God breathed into his nostrils the breath of life." By this act of God, man in body and soul is what he is. The act of God animates him. Thus, through God and only through God does man become man. He lives his life as a life borrowed from God. This is the *creatureliness* of man. Man has God as Creator; that is, man is created, he is creature. Again, this createdness of his, his creatureliness, is to be related to the totality of his existence; it pertains to body and soul. Our passage says explicitly that his body is created out of earth: "The LORD God formed man of the dust of the ground." But the soul is also created. "God breathed into his nostrils the breath of life; and man became a living soul." Thus, the soul is not of divine nature; it is no emanation of God. It is also creature. Even between the soul and God stands the act of creation from which the soul derives its life.

This does not preclude the *immortality* of the soul. But its immortality is neither the first nor the last word. The immortality of the soul remains far below the eternity of God. But it does exist. One must not deny it simply because Platonism asserts it. Even though the soul must be considered as a creature, it must as such be considered imperishable. But what does the imperishability of the soul mean? The word imperishable—immortal—characterizes here simply the invisible spiritual reality to which man belongs, in addition to and beyond his physical reality. That the soul cannot die still does not mean, however, that man possesses the eternal life of God. Man is man only so long as he lives in the unity and totality of body and soul. If the body decays in death, then man, even if his soul is immortal, is completely called into question. If the body dies, then the soul also is no longer man. Neither the corpse that remains behind nor the soul that takes off is man. First Corinthians 15:53 declares that "this mortal nature" (i.e., man in his unity of body *and* soul!) "puts on immortality" (i.e., *eternal* life!). If this does not happen, if there is no *resurrection* of man (i.e., of the *whole* man in body and soul), then we confront in death the annihilation of man in spite of the immortality of his soul. Such an immortality cannot help but be uncanny and evil.

In the third place, man is not the only created being. He coexists with all other creatures. Together with every other creature he is placed within that realm of life which we call "nature." Thus, with respect to his creatureliness, he is on equal level with the animals. He finds himself in the hand of the Creator, in which he is no more but also no less than a sparrow, which may live in this hand joyously and without anxiety. The animals, too, live the lives proper to them, by the "breath" of God, as the psalm expresses it (Psalm 104:29ff.): "Thou takest away their breath, they die, and return to their dust. Thou sendest forth thy spirit, they are created." Biblically expressed, man, too, is "flesh," including even his soul. But now the problem arises: Both man and animals are indeed created beings; yet man is not to be placed on a par with the animal. Again, the passage in Genesis 2:7 points to this difference when it states that the inbreathing of the breath of life by which man becomes a "living soul" represents a new, special act of God: God forms man out of the dust of the earth and breathes into him his breath of life, and thus man becomes a living soul. It is not an animal, but man that is created here, man in the particularity of his being, man who indeed stands before God and lives by his Spirit like all other creatures and yet in a quite different way. God is creating here as there, man as well as the animal, but it is totally different here from there.

Wherein does the difference lie? What is it that distinguishes man basically and finally from the animal? We refer here to the words in a prior passage in Genesis, 1:26ff.: "And God said, 'Let us make man in our image, after our likeness' . . . So God created man in his own image, in the image of God he created him." Here something is said of man which is true of no other creature. Man is indeed created, but he (only he!) is created in the *image of God*. But what does this mean? What is to be understood by image, the image of God?

We can say formally that image is not the same as an ideal after which I am to strive, not the same as a law which I am to fulfill, a goal which I have to achieve. But let us recall again that man stands before God. Image is thus a status in which I find myself and an attitude corresponding to this status. To be sure, we shall never be able to conceive of this status and attitude in physical, biological, historical, or psychological terms. For it is the status and attitude of the image of God, the *archestatus*, which is here at issue. Thus, it is the reality of man before God pre-dating all natural or historical reality. But it is nonetheless a reality, it is *the* reality by virtue of which man is what he is.

But how are we to define the *content* of this status and this attitude? Can they be thought of otherwise than that man, through his being created, receives something from God which recalls God himself? As God creates man, he endows him with the likeness of something that only God himself is and possesses. According to Holy Scripture, however, God is the totally sovereign, personal God; his name is "I am." And now, God, according to his gracious pleasure, grants to man what he grants to no other creature; as he breathes his breath of life into him, he also gives him that impress of personhood which makes him "similar" to God; only then is he actually man. God is the mighty "I am," but now man also may become the "I" that encounters God so as to understand God and to become obedient to him. Therefore, we are more than sparrows. God wants to have intercourse with us as "I" to "Thou." And this means that God wants to be known by us. No matter how it is with the other creatures, man as a creature shall not live a dull and unconscious life; he *knows* what it means to be a creature before God. He knows himself as the point of creation where God's purpose for his creation is exposed and evident. This is what distinguishes man as "living soul" from all other creatures.

We can call this pecularity of man, this knowledge of his about

God and about himself, his "freedom." But we must not interpret this term as if man by his freedom may himself become a little god who can do and not do what he pleases. He remains God's creature even in his freedom. For he does not have it so as to be free *from* God. Rather, he has it so as to be free *for* God. If he misuses it—and he will misuse it—then he loses it, and a new intervention by God is needed in order to redeem him from the misery caused by this misuse. Actually, a new creation is needed. The "second Adam," Jesus Christ, must come into the world in his incarnation and recreate depraved man.

This God-appointed intercourse of man with him finds its ultimate expression in the intercourse through his Word and in his Word. God breathes his Spirit into man. But the decisive act of this Spirit is the Word. Thus God creates man by *his Word.* God's creating is not a mechanical making nor an emanation nor a mere contriving and imagining; rather, it is his speaking. The whole creation story attests to this. God said: "Let it be!" And it was! God's knowing and willing become event when they are comprehended in his Word. In this creative Word of God, "all things" are created, "all things" have their duration. So it is said also of the creation of man: God *said,* "Let us make man!" But man is not "a thing." In the Word of God that creates him, man is enabled to respond. That is, God not only calls him into being, but by calling him into being he summons him. He not only speaks over him his "Let it be!", but when he speaks over him, he also speaks to him, he addresses him. And how could he address him if man were not allowed to hear him and were not able to answer him! Thus, God creates man not only *by* the Word; he creates him also *for* the Word. When God addresses him, man recognizes himself as created so as to hear God and to recognize him as God. He lives in the call and summons of God as one addressed by him and speaking to him. This is how God brings about his *intercourse* with man in the *Word.* The whole mystery of our life, the mystery of our personhood before God, is included in the miracle of the Word which God speaks to us and in the Word which he confers upon us.

But the point in man at which he is met by this call of God is again his soul. We have already seen that it is created, that it is nothing else than the inner nature of man. But as it is created, it is prepared and defined by God himself to the end that this intercourse with the Word may come about wherein man first awakes to his true life. God's Spirit, "the miraculous finger of God," touches him, and now he may stand up, although he is only a creature no better than some worm, and meet his Creator in the totality of his existence in body and soul so as to belong to him and serve him like no other creature. Therefore, the soul of man is ultimately to be understood as the mystery of his personal existence, being called before God by his Word. We can, must, and may say of ourselves, I—body and soul—am called to stand before God as his man listening to him.

It may be asked whether, besides the terms body and soul used thus far, we ought not to introduce the term *pneuma* or spirit to denote in particular this responsible personhood of man before God. Pneuma or spirit would then be the proper term for the call of God and the responsible attitude of man before God based on it; but by "soul" would be designated the creaturely point in man where this calling and responding takes place. There are passages in Holy Scripture in which the existence of man is described in this trichotomous or threefold way. (Cf. I Thessalonians 5:23; I Corinthians 2:14ff., where a distinction is made between the psychic man and the spiritual man and where it is explicitly stated that the [merely] psychic man understands nothing of the Word of God; insofar as he is not touched by God's Spirit, he lives a [merely] fleshly life.) Besides, other passages are found where the word "soul" is used for this standing of man before God. "Soul," then, would have the same meaning as "spirit." (For example, Jesus speaks of the incomparable worth of the human soul, in Matthew 16:24-26, and uses the word "soul" to mean the man who stands before God with his whole life and knows that he loses this life of his and suffers eternal loss when he becomes untrue to the call of God. God can, as he says in another passage [Matthew 10:28], "destroy body and soul in hell.") But a threefold conception is basic even to those passages which speak only of the "soul" and not of the "spirit." The inner and outer nature, soul and body, stand beside one another, with the soul superordinate to the body; but the action of God stands over against both as a third element which affects soul and body. Even when it remains unexpressed, this third is God's Spirit and Word. For God always acts toward us by addressing us in the Spirit.

Biblical-theological anthropology shares with all merely natural, biological, and psychological knowledge of human nature the recognition of the duality of human existence. It agrees with biological-psychological anthropology in distinguishing body and soul, an outer and inner realm of human existence. However, it is new and distinct from them in that it does not stop at this duality, but proceeds to ask whether or not man—in and with his inner and outer nature, in and with his body and soul—lives under God's call. This question alone is decisive for his manhood. If he lives under it, then he has become the spiritual (pneumatic) man in the totality of his existence in body and soul. If he does not live under it, then he is, again in body and soul, the fleshly man who does not fulfill his destiny. His personality and humanity, his manhood, lose all meaning. Like a promise that is not kept, his existence remains unfulfilled. Natural anthropology either does not know this antithesis between flesh and spirit at all, or if it knows it, it confines it to the interior of human existence itself. Within human nature, it distinguishes spirit and drive, intellect and emotion, a divine and a demonic realm, between which man is forced to choose. This is connected with a value system which superordinates or subordinates the one to the other.

Biblical-theological anthropology also makes such distinctions within human nature. But because it also knows of that wholly other distinction, of the great transcendence of the Word and Spirit of God, before which man stands with his whole life, it cannot consider those immanent distinctions of body and soul, of spirit and drive, of a divine and a demonic realm within human nature as representing the last word. As with all things human, it understands not only this duality and contradictory character of man's nature but also the overarching unity of his personhood, on the basis of the action of God who does not cease to summon and to address his creation. Biblical-theological anthropology is thus confronted with the same data as every natural anthropology. But since it relates these data to the Word of God, it sheds the light of a new understanding of man upon them.

Natural knowledge of human nature lacks this light. It seeks to understand and to interpret man from within himself. We must doubt whether this can succeed. How, on the basis of its immanental presuppositions and without the light of the Word of God, can it conclusively deal with the phenomenon of human nature, which harbors such deep riddles in its distinction of body and soul and the simultaneous unity of its personal structure? At best, it will be able to present and unfold this phenomenon in its complete mysteriousness, only to face a secret which points beyond itself and which by its methodology it is unable to unravel any further.

But in no case may we manufacture a synthesis of natural and spiritual knowledge in which the strict transcendence of the Word and Spirit of God is dissolved and divine and human things are confused. The nature of man, of course, exhibits great heights and depths, but it always remains immiscibly divorced from the nature of God by the boundary of creatureliness. Even the highest spirituality in man is not so high and his deepest psychic process not so deep as to reach beyond this boundary, so that man would cease to be creature and become one with his Creator. The biblical concept of the image of God in man must never be construed to mean this. Man is and remains below, and God stands above him as one whom he can neither reach nor move. He is flesh even in his greatest potentialities and achievements and continues to be dependent on the Spirit and Word of God, from whom alone he receives and lives his life.

There is, to be sure, *one* synthesis between man and God; but it lies no longer within the compass of human possibility, neither within the natural nor the supernatural; it is in no sense our deed; it is the deed of God himself. Therefore, we had better not call it a synthesis. It is given, but also concluded at the point of the incarnation of the Son of God. In him, in *Jesus Christ,* man and God became one. Here human nature really took part in the nature of God, but not of itself; this happened solely in Jesus Christ as the incarnate Word of God. But there the boundary between Creator and creature is protected; in Jesus Christ, God remains God and man remains man. Jesus Christ is therefore the first and last Word of all real knowledge of human nature.

We cannot speak of the uniting of God with man in Jesus Christ, however, without encountering a fourth and last way in which the Word of God defines man. It is summarized in the one word "grace." Grace conclusively expresses once more the fact that God calls man and that through this call man is placed before God, but now in such a way that he stands before God as the sinner who receives forgiveness. Again, grace means that man has intercourse with God as his image, but this image is no longer the original one of his first status; it is the image restored in Christ. Since we forsook it, the original status lies behind, being irreparably lost to us. Grace includes the idea that we are indeed God's creatures, but corrupted and therefore divorced from him not only by the boundary of creation but by the even more severe boundary of our fall from God. Between us and God stands not only the act of creation—that act which unites us with God just as much as it withdraws us from God—but between us and God stands the dark riddle of our *sin,* by which we have destroyed God's creation and with it our union with God.

The corruption of sin consists in the fact that man, who was destined to know God and to live in communion with him, no longer fulfills this destiny of his. The light of the Word of God, in which and for which he was created, has become for him the darkness in which, being without God, he falls into corruption. But what then is left of man? Indeed he still exists, but exists in the night of his sin, an "I" to whom the "Thou" of God has become strange. He leads a meaningless life, the life of the flesh without the Spirit, a life that is torn by severe conflicts. He decays, the body being given into death, and the soul to its dreary immortality.

Grace, however, means that the Word of God remains in force for this man and is directly concerned with him. Grace means that it goes out to him anew. And now man continues to be summoned before God in spite of his sin. His misery is brought to an end. He is once more addressed; God repeats his promise; God remains faithful to man. Man may once again arise as at his creation and become obedient to his God and serve as man whom God accepts in his sin. Now it becomes clear that everything we had to say about the creating Word of God, which called man to life, stands under the promise of the grace of Christ. God's Word is from the beginning and by nature the Word of grace to the sinner; God's Spirit is the Spirit of grace, who from on high accepts man below and has mercy on him. And it becomes clear also that everything we had to say about the existence of man, not only about his creatureliness in body and soul but also about his being made in the image of God and his personhood before God, stands under the mark of sin, which surrounds and covers his whole existence and which he himself cannot cast aside, but which is now cast aside by the action of God in Jesus Christ. God's total concern for man is focused on the act of God which was once and for all: the *forgiveness of sins*. In the forgiveness of sins through the gracious Word of God, man lives his life as one summoned of God in body and soul, thus fulfilling his destiny.

This means, however, that our whole knowledge of man is *knowledge of grace*. We cannot draw it from some natural exploration and experience of our life, but whatever we know about man, we know through *Jesus Christ*, in whom God's gracious Word goes out to us. That I stand as a sinner before God and that I not only stand before him, but that I can stand before him as a being of worth—this I do not know of myself. Such knowledge—knowledge that is neither speculation nor reverie nor human fantasy!—exists only in the realm of grace, the realm

The Soul of Man as the Object of Pastoral Care 65

of Jesus Christ. Jesus Christ in his incarnation is the true, original "image of the invisible God" (Colossians 1:15). As this image of God, he is the second Adam by whom God has newly formed us into his image after the misuse of our freedom. Therefore, biblical-theological anthropology is always and exclusively christological anthropology.

The foundation and development of a theological anthropology is one of the most important tasks of all theology. It includes its differentiation not only from scientific and philosophical anthropologies, but also from Catholic anthropology, which rests upon that synthesis between natural and spiritual knowledge; the latter is always suspect, and especially when it is presented with all the refinement and shrewdness characteristic of Catholic theology. This task, newly recognized today, has already been begun. We refer to the attempts to state a doctrine of man in Emil Brunner's *Man in Revolt* and also in Schlink's *Der Mensch in der Verkündigung der Kirche*. But above all Karl Barth must be mentioned; in his *Church Dogmatics* III, he develops the doctrine of creation and in this connection presents for the first time in recent years a strictly christological doctrine of man and thereby establishes the necessary clarifications and delimitations on all sides.

We summarize: We have presented the view of man as the image of God, created by the Word of his grace in Jesus Christ. We have approached it with a view to pastoral care. Because this man is the object of pastoral care, we had to deal with him. And we had to deal with him in detail since the basis, the content, and the goal of pastoral care can be determined and later practiced only when its object is before us in complete clarity. Pastoral care is only possible on the basis of the true knowledge of man. Therefore, true knowledge of man is the necessary starting point for a true doctrine of pastoral care. The development of pastoral care must be in conformity with its object.

But what a highly esteemed object man is! The greatness of his divine creation and calling as well as the depth of his fall and above all the power of the grace of God, which governs this fallen man, must continually amaze us. Indeed, if the whole pastoral action is not born by this amazement, it will not be rightly performed. Therefore, as pastors we can never really fathom the depth of the *mystery of man*. How shall we care for his soul without ever again exploring and penetrating this mystery of his? Tell me what you think of man, and I will tell you what kind of pastor you are! All confusions in pastoral care have their root in a distorted or false understanding of man. For the doctrine of pastoral care a differentiation from all other kinds of understanding of man becomes absolutely necessary.

Furthermore, true perception of man is to be gained only from Holy Scripture. Man is created by the Word of God; thus, he can only be perceived in faith through the Word of God. Here the spiritual and the purely natural knowledge of human nature part ways. True pastoral care must be *biblical*. Let it beware of deviating from this! It proceeds from faith, but it also leads to faith. For man is created not only by the Word, but also for the sake of the Word. It follows that our care for man can consist in nothing else than in announcing the Word to him. To care for man means to provide him with this Word. Proclamation of the Word is therefore the beginning and the end of all true pastoral care. Being created for the sake of the Word, however, means that man exists as an "I" who hears the Word of his God. Personhood is the category of his existence as man. Therefore, the proclamation goes out to mankind not only in general, but it also proceeds from person to person. When it carries the proclamation, which addresses everyone, into the life of the individual, it becomes pastoral care. Here it assumes the *form of a conversation* that continually seeks, and shows concern for, the individual man. Pastoral care that did not know this care for the individual, that did not know of the immeasurable worth even of his soul before God, would be no genuine pastoral care. None must be lost; each is to be striven for in conversation since he, too, is one called of God and is to become certain of this call. Therefore, a doctrine of pastoral care that knows its business will have thoroughly to investigate the right form of this conversation and its implementation.

For the sinner, the content of the Word of God is the Word of grace. Therefore, the content of the proclamation of pastoral care can be no other than the *forgiveness of sins* through Jesus Christ. God's absolving grace must be communicated in pastoral care. But because man is not simply soul without body, because his person is the center of a whole, physical existence, grace must be so communicated that man is seized by it in the totality of his life. The *power* of forgiveness consists precisely in the fact that man is reclaimed for God, in body and soul, and brought under his hand, just as truly as sin seized his whole existence down to its last psychophysical depths. True pastoral care does not rest until it has carried the forgiving Word into these depths in the strength of the Spirit and of prayer and has really and completely brought man again under the healing power of grace. The conversation in pastoral care therefore is a *controversy;* the pastor is doing battle for God's Kingdom and affairs among men. Again, it will be the task of a theology of pastoral care to present what it means rightly to conduct this conversation. It will find it necessary seriously to concern itself with the psychophysical nature of man as the scene where the forgiving Word engages in battle with sin and death. It will thus have to enter into discussion with the psychology and pathology of human life.

Finally, we can sum up under the term "sanctification" the recovery of man from the realm of sin and death into the realm of the grace of Christ. Sanctification means: In the forgiveness of sin, man is claimed for God in his total existence. He again becomes what even in sin he had never ceased to be—God's own. God's Word in forgiveness is powerful and effective liberation. In it man receives a new life. This new life is expressed in his acceptance of God's Word as a command which calls him to fight against sin. To practice pastoral care, therefore, always means to proclaim God's command and to call man to obedience. The doctrine of pastoral care will have to deal with repentance and with the keeping of God's commandments as they emerge in pastoral conversation for the salvation of man.

This is why the nature of true pastoral care must result from the true knowledge of man as its object.

The understanding of the existence of man before God as based on Holy Scripture is contested. Other views of man contradict it. Yet the underlying understanding of man will determine the form of the theory and practice of pastoral care. The understanding of man thus determines the nature of pastoral care.

4 The Struggle to Understand Man in Pastoral Care

In order to complete the concept of man we have just gained and to deepen the comprehension of the true nature of pastoral care derived from it, we now seek to sharply outline an understanding of man and a corresponding comprehension of pastoral care as they result when one deviates from the biblical perception.

First, we mention once more that which can be summarized under the name of pietistic pastoral care. Pietism is understood as that whole movement of awakening which flanked and attacked orthodoxy in the course of the 16th and 17th centuries in various waves and under various leaders. Historically, it presents a very complex structure, but still contains a certain unity. In distinction from the contemporary movement of Rationalism, it did not question orthodox doctrine as such, but sought to breathe new life into it. In the center of orthodoxy stands the doctrine of justification.

The pietistic awakening has the merit of having accepted the central truth of the forgiveness of sins through the blood of Christ as given in the doctrine of justification and of having preserved it amid the flood of the rationalistic emasculations. But Pietism did not rescue this truth without making a deep and far-reaching alteration in the substance of it and thus endangering it. Orthodoxy had understood justification as God's claim on sinful man. This claim is made in God's act of judgment in Jesus Christ which sets man free. God in Jesus Christ declares the sinner justified and thus recreates him. Everything depends on God's kingly Word of absolution. Everything depends on the fact that the Son of God does for us what we could never do for ourselves: He carries our sins away as he suffers and dies in our stead and gives us new life in his resurrection.

Pietism in no way wants to question this absolution by God; on the contrary, it would speak of nothing else. But speaking of it in a new way, it shifts the emphasis from the act of God in Christ onto man in whom this act occurs. The sole effectiveness and freedom of grace is no longer central as the exclusive subject; man, as the receiver of this grace, moves into the center. All interest plainly lies in sanctification, in this acceptance of man, much more strongly than in the act of justification whereby man in his sin is accepted as a child of God and is sanctified. Of course, it is recognized that God asserts his own glory in Jesus Christ by the absolution of the sinner, that he asserts it before man and among men, that man remains who he is, a sinner sentenced to die over whose existence the word "life" is now written, that this is a life from God in spite of sin and death, and that man may now walk in the power of this promise, and become a new creature, and thank God—all this recedes behind the fact that it is *man* who *experiences* it. It is not so much God's work in him as man's work, his awakening to a new life, which is emphasized. Man's function in the act of forgiveness is highlighted at the expense of the consideration that even this function of man, his penitence and repentance (which certainly must not be absent), is again only the work of God and his grace. Sanctification becomes an independent subject, a secondary matter, an act of man, in addition to the act of God in Christ. It is not enough to emphasize the fact that justification actually takes hold of the life of man, bringing about repentance and remorse; sanctification stands, alongside justification, for a specific new act whose subject is now man, an act not already contained in justification, but added to it as something new. The conjunction "and" between justification and sanctification receives a strange, uncanny importance far beyond what is warranted. Hence the interest shifts from God to man and his acts. We think of Zinzendorf's famous formulation: "This I did for thee"—namely, the forgiveness of sins through the blood of Christ—"What dost thou for me?"—namely, sanctification as a work of man. The movement that effected this shift in emphasis is what we have referred to here, for simplicity's sake, as "Pietism": the idea that the piety of man accompanies and even precedes the work of God in Christ.

Pietism hoped to breathe new life into the harsh and cold orthodox doctrine. But has it not awakened something quite different from the actual truth of justification, something that would have better remained unawakened?

Since Pietism, as we have seen, accepted pastoral care as its main concern (pastoral care is related to sanctification in a special way), this shift of emphasis is particularly manifest in its pastoral care. Pietistic pastoral care is indeed the special place in which this shift occurs. This is evident in the particular way in which pietistic pastoral care becomes increasingly independent; it is true that it is not unrelated to the proclamation of the Word in sermon and sacrament, but it assumes an extreme importance of its own which puts it at least on a level with the proclamation.

At this point we are again confronted with the objection which the confessional Lutherans Löhe and Vilmar raised against the Pietism of their day. What they attacked was just this independence of pastoral care from what they called the "ordinary means of proclamation." They sensed in this preferential treatment of pastoral care among the activities of the minister a defection from the Word of God and its essential contents. Such a defection actually occurred: The pietists no doubt continued to speak fervently and sincerely of the work of the grace of Christ in man. But they spoke of it in such a way that this work of grace tended, perhaps unwittingly and unconsciously, to be transformed into a work of man even though it never quite reached that point. They surely knew that sanctification can be nothing but the act of becoming God's own, and that this act must be done not only by the spirit of man, but by the Holy Spirit himself; yet this work of the Spirit appears in the disguise of a very elaborately portrayed work of man.

Understand me correctly: There is indeed an act of man even in the reception of grace; the work of sanctification has its distinctly human side. This must not be denied. We must also speak of this. The death of the old man and the awakening of the new man of which the Catechism speaks quite certainly occurs only in such a way that man with all his powers shares in it with the totality of his existence—body and soul. Sanctification is actually to be understood as this sharing of man, his full participation in the work of grace. It is *my* accepting of grace, *my* hearing, *my* receiving of the Word, and as a result *my* penitence and repentance which here are very seriously and very really at stake. Indeed, I may and I shall do works, even good works. My own willing and acting are concerned. But who is this man who may now emerge as an acting subject, as one who, as it is said in the Sermon on the Mount, lets his light shine in his own good works? It is precisely the man who is created and recreated by the Spirit of God. Thus sanctification itself is again concerned not with me, but with God and his work in me.

Seen in this perspective, I am even at the moment I act the recipient who can do nothing of himself but rather lives entirely in the certainty of the words of Jesus: "Apart from me you can do nothing" (John 15:5). Again, my participation in Christ is of course *my* participation, but my participation *in him* is all that counts. The whole truth is stated only if Jesus Christ and his work are not lost to sight for a moment. Everything I may and I can do is, so to speak, only a mark of his work in me. He is and remains, even where I act, the subject from whom everything proceeds. Everything must be so seen and said that it does not get that misplaced importance of its own which Pietism stands in constant danger of giving it. Thus as is true in any valid pastoral care, we may and must quite certainly consider and express all kinds of things, including a great deal that is human and psychological, i.e., related to our acts. But it must be done in such a way as to make manifest at every moment the fundamental breach which separates and discards all my works, everything merely human and psychological, from what Jesus Christ is and does. Through this breach all light then falls on the one fact which is decisive here: that my sins are forgiven through the blood of Jesus Christ. If anything else is said of sanctification, if it is presented as a separate addition to the forgiveness of sins, something that I have to add to forgiveness as a second thing, then the work which God's sovereign Word will do in me is shoved aside, perhaps even replaced or at least completed, by a work that somehow originates with me.

This shift of emphasis toward the side of man and his works will immediately have a fatal consequence. As soon as we get down to specifics, we cannot speak of sanctification except in terms of a battle between the power of forgiveness and the power of sin. If the stress is laid on man, we will have to represent this battle as a conflict within man himself between the higher aspirations and the lower instincts, the forces of the spirit and those of the flesh, or whatever one may call it. But then we no longer understand the opposition between flesh and spirit as the opposition which involves the totality of man who with his higher aspirations and his lower instincts, with his good and his evil doings, lives without God, yet who on the other hand, in body and soul, with his good and his evil, in life and in death, has become the property of Jesus Christ through God's absolving Word.

Understand me well: Even in the perspective of grace there will be a battle in man, a battle between higher and lower powers, between mind and drive, between good and evil, between spirit and flesh. This conflict will necessarily arise in man as the result of grace. What the Catechism calls dying to sin, hating and turning away from it, cannot occur except in the form of such a conflict within man. We must take this conflict very seriously. It is important—but only relatively so. That is to say, this fight has its importance in the fact that it is related to an entirely different fight—namely, that fight which man does not wage since it is the fight between what is actually above and what is actually below, the fight which Jesus Christ has waged and decided for us, the fight between him and the power of darkness. The inner battle of man is, so to speak, only the reflection of this real battle, which was decided on Golgotha and on Easter morning. Apart from that it cannot really be fought. If this real battle is disregarded, if it is equated with the inner battle in man, if it is actually removed from the cross to the heart of man, then Jesus Christ is pushed aside. He and his work are then identified with man's own doing. What is really above and below, as manifest at the cross, is projected into what is above and below within the human mind. The work of forgiveness is psychologized—and thereby emptied.

Pietistic pastoral care is continually in danger of doing this. Sanctification is conceived of as an inner process of progressive perfection in man; and when it is so understood, all serious discussion of justification disappears. Its proper content, the forgiveness of sins, resembles an open door through which one enters, only to leave it behind. For in the unique act of the experience of forgiveness we enter the way of progressive perfection considered to be the proper goal of the Christian life. As leader and guide, the pastor has the task of bringing about and supervising this process in his parishioners.

The fathers of our church standing in the Reformed line have seen this in quite another way. For them, the sinner does not cease to be a sinner even after he is forgiven. Rather, he recognizes himself ever anew as a sinner in constant need of forgiveness. Hence, to make progress in the Christian life, to grow in sanctification, will actually mean to gain an ever deeper and more real knowledge of one's sinfulness, yet at the same time of the knowledge of the power of grace. Sanctification is then nothing but making concrete this knowledge: I experience in my own life that when sin increases, grace abounds all the more. I am privileged to know and experience the fact that I live by grace and only by grace since I am the sinner for whom Jesus Christ died, as Luther declared it in the interpretation of the second article of the creed, or as the Heidelberg Catechism did in its first question and answer in very personal terms. True, this includes and gives rise to the battle man has to fight in himself against his sin. However, this battle is not a secondary thing which only follows forgiveness and completes it, but it is, as it were, the form in which forgiveness is clothed, the sign that it has been granted to me. Taking up this battle is my obedience effected by grace. For grace never comes to me without placing me under God's commandment. Standing under this commandment, and thus under grace, I recognize myself as a sinner who is forgiven, but who for this very reason must hate and avoid sin in the power of forgiveness.

The commandment of grace discloses my sin, yet in such a way as to confront me with Jesus Christ, who fulfills the commands and forgives. Forgiveness and the concomitant knowledge of sin can therefore never be used as a mere stepping stone on the way toward progressive perfection. The only perfection we really know is perfection through Jesus Christ, who has carried away all our offenses on the cross. Then we understand sanctification as the battle for increasingly accepting the forgiveness that alone sanctifies. This is the way, through continually accepting forgiveness, to avoid and hate sin. This is also the way to be again and again victorious over concrete sins. But such victory is certainly not a sign of my own progressive perfection, but a sign of the forgiveness of all sins in Jesus Christ.

This at last makes understandable the rejection of pietistic pastoral care by an orthodox theology in the good sense—that is, one based on the doctrine of the Reformers—as it is found in Löhe and Vilmar. Löhe and Vilmar objected to this transformation of justification into a perfection in pietistic pastoral care. They were aware of the seriousness of sin and of the greatness of the liberating grace which are lost in the pietistic view of grace and sin, in spite of all the consuming zeal thrown into the inner battlefield.

This may be clarified by two examples. The first is a passage from one of the letters of Gerhard Tersteegen to a woman who was in his pastoral care:

We see, possess, love, and even hold on to ourselves, and this is the source of all pain and misery. Blessedness lies only in letting go and losing. The soul may seek ever so sincerely to serve God; it may seek it in many ways, but it will never be wholly satisfied or actually find God if it cannot resolve to sacrifice everything which belongs to us and is in us, and to renounce our own willfulness and obstinacy. The slightest look at ourselves disturbs our full rest in God, who is our only goal, our only rest, and our only blessedness. I know that this is deep and can be expected more through waiting than doing, but the Lord encounters each with his call according to the condition and nature of each. If we take to heart this call by remaining with him and following him inwardly, we shall learn how his divine love leads us step by step into the depths of letting go and losing. Individuality is afraid of this nakedness. It yearns either for natural or spiritual life and nourishment, but pure love pitilessly cuts it off from all this, however spiritual or divine it may appear. And if this pure love inspires us, we do not even desire it otherwise. We do not flee this consuming fire of love, for we know from experience that the more we let go of ourselves and what we possess individually, the more God and his blessedness can communicate to us. This explains why we feel in the depth of our hearts incessantly drawn onward and upward if the pure love of God really meets and leads our spirits. If the soul is gathered up and surrenders blindly to this tug, then it will become alien to and released from itself and all creatures, thus approaching God and its own rest. (Tersteegen, *Briefe in Auswahl*, Basel, 1889, p. 144.)

We notice how remarkably close this description of the progressive self-denial of the soul and of the increasing rest and inner mortification comes to Catholic mysticism as well as to the whole Catholic pastoral direction. An inner affinity between the Pietism of Tersteegen and Catholic pastoral care cannot really be contested. Substantially, a concept of the soul appears that no longer corresponds to the totality of the biblical understanding of man as described by us. The soul is here seen as a depth within man himself; in this depth and by virtue of it man is united and one with God in a particular way (and this means even apart from grace). This depth in us is our proper nature, as opposed to man's lower, sensual nature. And now the battle rages in us where this deep nature of the soul fights against the lower nature. Inwardly, we are to let go of the world insofar as it resides and lodges in us and clings to us. The heart must be awakened to the upward tug that never again deserts us and leads us away from everything creaturely toward God. Nothing but events within man are described here, and no reference is made to Holy Scripture, no word of the victory over the world wrought in Jesus Christ. Tersteegen's whole discussion in this letter turns out to be remarkably legalistic and therefore of remarkably little comfort; it cannot be otherwise in the absence of a clear relation to the Word of God and his grace and in spite of all the fervor and affection with which the author admonishes and counsels. His words are punctuated with a truly tragic seriousness surrounding these inner events as if the decisive turn were to be expected from them. His admonitions have a hollow ring since no end of this inner battle is in sight. This is because the outlook lacks the end already given long ago in the victory of Christ. No real reference to the Word and the sacraments is made, and therefore everything proceeds according to intellectual and psychological categories, instead of these categories being overcome by the proclamation of grace in Jesus Christ. Man is fundamentally left alone with himself and his psychic experience.

As a contrast may be cited a counsel that Wilhelm Löhe gave to a deeply troubled woman. It is found in a small, rare book which A. von Harless, a Lutheran, edited under the title *Krankheit und Heilung* (Brandenburg, 1864). It tells of the journey of a Franconian woman who made up her mind after many struggles to seek the help of Christoph Blumhardt, Sr., in her severe sickness. But even before she came into contact with Blumhardt, Löhe, who was a contemporary of Blumhardt's almost to the year, had given her pastoral counsel. Her suffering consisted of severe temptations of a demonic nature which exhausted her even physically to such an extent that she was completely given up by the physicians. Her mother writes of her: "She has the most sinful, heinous thoughts and fancies day and night about divine things and feels the most dreadful things, yet cannot escape them. Her lamentation most severely affects her body; she is again as miserable as ever. God have mercy!" She now turned to Löhe, and he answered her as follows:

> The grace of the Lord Jesus Christ our Saviour be with you. Although I gathered only accidental news of your suffering in recent months, I still remembered you and your heavy afflictions. Now I remember you all the more since I have news of you through your mother. As we celebrated holy communion with one another last Sunday, we—even if we did not call names—remembered your suffering and your misery and implored the God of mercy for your final release from the blazing oven of temptation.
> How gladly would I have written you some words of brotherly sympathy last Sunday if this were so easily done. I have a great deal to preach, to call, to stand by the sick and dying these days. Nevertheless, I have no rest; out of the midst of my toil I must call a few words to you way over the hills and forests. However, I foresee that, if I intend to serve you, I must engage in a fight with you. You will not admit I am right, and I can and must not admit you are right. I maintain and I know that Christ is your Lord, the Christ who has said: No one can snatch my sheep out of my hand.
> But you fear the adversary, Satan, is mighty in you. Why do you maintain this, my co-redeemed sister? Partly because you feel your physical suffering, but partly also—and this not the least part—because you look more at yourself than at him the crucified, in whom a sea of grace and mercy flows to us. Yes, yes, if one is tempted by the devil, one is tormented to the bottom of one's soul. For what are we? How easily can the Evil One find in us a hundred thousand sins; ah, and how one must become anxious and afraid unto death if one cannot defend oneself and go, quite poor and empty, to him who alone quickens the weary and heavy-laden.
> How different is he who gives himself completely, just as he is, to the Lord Christ, and says to him: You are my righteousness and my joy! If you have nothing left, but leave yourself to Jesus, who can drive you out of your fortress? As one who is tempted, you must throw off the last remnant of Pietism and of your own righteousness, and as St. Peter admonishes, set your hope entirely upon grace. Those who are not tempted do not know this, but you, in the oven of your affliction, can experience what a comfort and a rest of the soul, indeed, what a strength

against all devils flows to him who dares to speak without ever looking at himself and his own circumstances: "Since you have come to the salvation and comfort of all the poor and miserable, you are also my salvation and comfort, you with your deep wounds. And since you can take away all hardships, call all the weary and heavy-laden to rest, so I come also; the Devil may make exceptions; you, Lord, make none, for you say: All, all who labor—here I am! Here I am!

It is true I am not your pastor, but still a brother in Christ Jesus; and I can and must say to you what I am about to say. All your torment, your doubt, your terrors, your fears, your fancies, your reminiscence on the sins of your youth, your affirmation to be inhabited by the sin against the Holy Spirit—all these things are partly illness, partly temptation, and like most temptations are pure lie and deceit. The truth is that God in Jesus Christ is merciful unto you. Man against man! My word against yours! Why should you be right in your highly troubled situation? I admonish you in the name of the Lord Jesus Christ to set your hope entirely in grace, to disregard yourself, and you will find in the tumult of your soul a secure position in the battle, peace and successive victories. Your healing lies in the righteousness by grace alone.

This is written to you with the heart-felt sympathy of your fellow pilgrim and fellow combatant, W. Löhe. (*Krankheit und Heilung*, pp. 82 ff.)

What happens in this letter? Löhe comforts the tempted woman by saying to her: Do not despair, for you are a member of Christ's people. He remembers her in the Sunday service, above all when communion is distributed. She shall know that the congregation joins with her in this hour of worship in prayer and in the hearing of the Word, and brings her concern before God. A completely different note than in Tersteegen! The tormented, sick woman is referred not to her own inner conflict, in which she is already immersed deeply and hopelessly enough, but to the Christian community, to her membership in it by virtue of her baptism, to the power of the Word of God, and above all of holy communion, which is significant for her even though she herself cannot participate in it.

Löhe then makes it clear to her that she is bound to fail in her own conflict. Hers is a conflict not to be waged with flesh and blood, since Satan and his spirits are engaged, and which, therefore, only Christ can decide. In this connection he can say to her bluntly: Stop all your own attempts to control the adversary; also leave behind the last remnant of Pietism! Trust in grace alone! Here lies the whole difference: The conflict concerns not only the inner life of man, much as this inner life may be affected by it and may even become a battlefield. This battlefield is the scene of a conflict which is fought entirely from above and in which only the Word and grace can conquer.

When we consider this, we understand why this woman went from Löhe to Christoph Blumhardt, who in his own remarkable way professes the same knowledge. Blumhardt's significance lies precisely in the fact that he stepped completely outside the line of Pietism in his pastoral care. This he did because his experiences in Möttlingen gave him a vision of the battle of Christ with the spirits from below. He relies solely on the fact that the decision fell at the Cross and at Easter and is valid even for our own inner conflicts. This view comes much closer to the doctrine and the belief of the Reformers than to the pietistic mysticism of Tersteegen. Löhe, too, is concerned with the totality of man, who in body and soul falls prey to sin and death and shall become free in body and soul by grace in the Word of forgiveness.

We have already referred to the inner affinity between the pietistic conception of man and the corresponding pastoral care, and the Catholic conception of pastoral direction and the understanding of man in which it is rooted. In the Catholic understanding, man is essentially thought of in terms of the dichotomy of soul and body, perhaps even the triad of soul, body, and spirit. This psychic or mental part in man, in spite of the sin to which his whole life has been chained, appears as not entirely cut off from the divine life which man enjoyed before the Fall. Sin is taken seriously, yet not so seriously that, to speak metaphorically, the door which leads to God in the soul of man is fully locked. It is indeed shut, yet not so fully that it could not again be opened by man, from below, when grace seizes him from above.

This incomplete closure of man before God, this capacity of man to turn to God, as it was granted in creation and now continues even through sinfulness, is the point where the Catholic doctrine of grace parts from the Reformed doctrine. The essence of Catholic thinking about God and man lies in the continuity of God's gracious presence in man. This continuity is no doubt interrupted by sin, yet not so completely as to rule out a successful establishment of contact by grace with the nature of man. Hence man is endowed with a positive, original capacity to know God, a capacity not entirely destroyed even by the Fall; true, man assuredly has the "faculty" to approach God of his own will, through a great deal of earnest penitence. Man still retains the faculty, the possibility of moving toward grace from below. Sin has not entirely permeated the nature of man; a remnant of creation has remained intact. The connection between God and man has indeed been impaired by the Fall, but it has not been severed. We refer here to the Catholic doctrine of the *analogia entis*, according to which an analogy with God is present in all being, a similarity of all being to God which no sin eliminates, and with this the possibility for man to appeal to it and rely upon it.

The seat of this faculty, its location in man, is precisely the deepest and most powerful part of the human being, called "soul" or "spirit." The task of all pastoral care is thereby clearly given; it shall awaken this slumbering capacity in man; it has to kindle this spark of the soul; it has to initiate the inner conflict by activating man's innate faculty, arousing him to battle against flesh and sin and to elevate his "soul" toward God and his grace.

It becomes clear that this is what is meant when one studies the Catholic doctrine of pastoral care in its classical expression, the *Exercises* of Ignatius Loyola. His whole pastoral guidance is based on the concept of the soul just described. For Loyola, man's soul is what is opposed to his body and flesh. This soul is assumed to be equipped with a faculty to rise above its co-ordinate, lower nature. It can and it shall—this is the meaning of all counsels and manipulations by the pastoral guide—renounce the instinctual inclinations that pull man down; it can and it shall seek after and find the will of God and thereby reach salvation. The soul is man's potentiality of gaining life and redemption through his own inner activity. Ignatius, of course, takes the power of grace seriously, just as seriously as he takes the power of hell and damnation. But grace is scarcely mentioned as objective power. It is presupposed, as the sacrament of grace in the Mass is truly presupposed, as the goal of all penitential practices to which pastoral care leads. But all interest centers exclusively in the inner occurrences of awakening penitence and of stimulating the soul to decide, to make the "choice" between what is above and what is below, between Christ and corruption. Whatever the role of grace, the soul and its possibility and power of deciding for grace is the true subject of the *Exercises*. The soul can and shall be "conditioned" to make the decision. Pastoral direction is concerned with this conditioning. This is its whole content, and the activation of the potentiality resting in the soul is its whole purpose. There is a definite preparation and guidance to be given to man by virtue of which the soul is truly conditioned. The soul is man's potentiality for God, and exploration of conscience, meditation and reflection upon appointed passages of Scripture and above all on the suffering of Jesus, together with continuous prayer guided by the counselor, are the means which can be used for the realization of this potentiality.

This matter is seen quite differently by the fathers of a church based on the Word. Such an activating of the soul on the basis of a presupposed natural possibility and faculty is unthinkable with Luther as well as with Calvin. It is unthinkable because a fundamentally different understanding of man prevails with them. They, too, know about the double nature of man, about the duality of body and soul, of flesh and spirit, of something below and something above in us. But they see man entirely—"both body and soul, in life and death," as the Catechism says—subject to the power of sin. Man no longer has any self-control in the presence of sin; he has completely succumbed to it. Sin is for them not simply an impediment in man's inner life, incapable of extinguishing and obliterating the true essence of being and of the soul, that "image" of God in us. They have recognized the evil in themselves as not simply a part of their nature standing over against another part. They recognize themselves, everything they are and have, as fallen prey to evil (and it is the Evil *One* whom they perceive in the evil!). Since they understand the word sin and all it stands for in utmost and illusionless seriousness, all exits close on them, and there is left only the awful night of an inescapable, eternal separation from God. There is no bridge, no "faculty," no "point of contact" within us which would lead from us to God! Yet is not even this radically sinful man still a creature of God? Does not the "living soul," that self by virtue of which he becomes man in the first place, continue to subsist in him? Admittedly, the soul lives, but the depth of the misery and torment of sin consists precisely in the fact that this man, created by God and made responsible to him, has fallen away from God and now is rejected. That man, called to perceive God's power in the things that have been made (cf. Romans 1:20), *fails* to perceive God's power and only intensifies the horror of his addiction to the opposing power of evil.

Luther can speak of this ineffaceable knowledge about God in man only with extreme horror: Save for this knowledge, the "conscience" as he calls it, this "evil beast and evil demon," this "hellish fury," were "it not alive, hell would have neither fire nor torment; this wild animal, however, kindles and strengthens death and hell and arms the whole creation against us." When this knowledge holds a man captive, God is "a consuming fire and zealous God, such a fire that does not rest, but devours and consumes, and a God who is zealous still." (W. A. 44, 500ff.) What help is all natural knowledge of God, what help is all reference to a faculty of the soul in man if *this* is man's predicament?

There is only one help left: the Word of God, that absolves man and calls him in the totality of his life, again "in body and soul, in life and in death" to where he "is no longer his own, but belongs to his faithful Saviour Jesus Christ, who completely paid for all his sins with his precious blood and redeemed him from all power of the devil." Now it becomes clear why Luther and Calvin removed the redemption of man's soul entirely from man and his inner possibilities, occurrences, and experiences, and transferred it to the Word of God and to that alone. Now it becomes clear that dwelling upon this gracious Word of God must signify the true and final opening of the door from man to God by God himself. It is the act which comforts and redeems man. No, God does not establish contact from within man. Even Mary and all the saints are no "points of contact," no bridgehead for the grace of God. Man as a being who in God's sight need not (as Luther says) be "devoured and consumed" in the heat of his wrath—this man no longer exists at all. God does not establish contact—he recreates. He calls from death to life. The man whom he calls and recreates is the same man whom he should judge and destroy; yet he does not judge him, but absolves him, accepts him, calls him his child. This is not establishing contact; this is God's free and incomprehensible grace. Now it becomes clear what pastoral care alone means and can be: It can no longer mean and be anything but the work of communicating this absolving, gracious Word to the individual.

We must now glance at the broad field of modern psychotherapy. Of an essentially secular nature, it develops outside the church, yet reaches into it. As a rule, modern man as we find him both inside and outside the church is far from ignorant of what pastoral care means. Even if he has never come into contact with any kind of pastoral care in the church, he already brings with him a quite definite concept of what it is. It will be an important requirement for our pastoral care toward him that we know about his concept and his expectation of pastoral care, and understand his concern in order to meet him in the right way. Untold pastoral efforts end in failure because the partners in the conversation never meet on common ground. At best, the pastor stands on the ground of the Word and the church, while the parishioner whom he wants to help proceeds from very different presuppositions, speaks an entirely different language, and gives an entirely different meaning to the spiritual counsels and words used by the pastor. Or at worst, the pastor stands with his partner in conversation on the ground of modern psychotherapy, detached from the Word of God. No real pastoral care is possible from this ground; only some secular form of common sense, personality development, or psychology can be practiced.

It may at first be surprising to hear modern psychotherapy mentioned at all. We usually outline a very different picture when talking of the life of modern man. It is the picture of a human society almost totally devoid of any kind of pastoral counseling. There exists, it is maintained, a complete vacuum with regard to personal counseling and help. As to his emotional problems, present-day man is uncared for and has to go his way unaided. Now that this fact has been rediscovered, the call for pastoral care, it is said, arises with new urgency.

There is doubtless some truth in this. Modern man, at least in the European and American civilization, has become a mass-man. Around the beginning of the 19th century, all civilized countries underwent an unparalleled increase in population. How small were our cities at the beginning of this period of time! How easily could their inhabitants be reached! As compared with our time family, school, church, and society could give much more attention to the individual. The loss of grasp on the environment everywhere is the one factor in the manifest deterioration of the inner life of present-day man. The other factor is the modern industrialization and mechanization of all realms of life and the resulting materialism in philosophy of life and way of life. The life of man's mind and soul is no longer understood, valued, or even seen at all; or if seen at all, it is treated as a more or less irrelevant, if not fictitious, quantity.

We may cite the statement of a leading psychologist and psychotherapist. C. G. Jung writes (in *Die Beziehung der Psychotherapie zur Seelsorge*, Zurich, 1932, p. 4): "In the course of the 19th century, medicine had become in method and theory one of the disciplines of natural science and paid tribute to the same philosophical presuppositions, namely, Causalism and Materialism. The soul as a spiritual substance did not exist for it; likewise, experimental psychology endeavored as much as possible to be a psychology without soul." Jung says this of medicine and psychology, those two disciplines that today should be most apt to be concerned with man and thus also with the life of his soul.

The church has continually tried to turn the tide of this deterioration of man's inner life. However highly valued its impact may have been, it does not greatly count because hand in hand with the collectivization and materialization of modern civilized man, an unprecedented decay of church life had also set in, a veritable flight from the church. The deterioration finally became so appalling that remedy had to be sought. Toward the end of the century, the call arose for deeper knowledge of the inner life, for pastoral care and counseling. Since it possesses a great deal of validity it has not been silenced to this day. The soul in its needs was, so to speak, newly discovered. It truly compelled men to this rediscovery, because it took revenge for being neglected by turning into a cause of sickness. It is the psychologists (again C. G. Jung, but already before him, Sigmund Freud) who hit upon the simple conclusion: "It seems to me that parallel to the decline of religious life the neuroses increased considerably." (Jung, op. cit., p. 14.) This intends to confirm that the common liability in the inner life of modern man, his nervousness, his philosophical confusion and bewilderment, and the resulting severe disturbances are rooted in a deep deficiency in the inner support, the clarity and strength of his life.

Long before these psychologists, an expert on human life who saw as deeply as Christoph Blumhardt, Sr., had expressed the truth that "the roots of many illnesses lie in unforgiven sin." We observe the difference in the formulation of the pastoral counselor and of the modern psychiatrist. Both Blumhardt and Jung are obviously concerned about the same problem: the inwardly broken, sick man of their time. But while Jung speaks of neuroses and considers "the soul as spiritual substance," Blumhardt speaks of unforgiven sin and sees man in body and soul in the totality of his alienation from God. He sees the connection between *sickness* and *sin*. He, too, knows that man has an inner life and that this life of the soul, neglected as it is, has become the cause and seat of a sickness. But he knows in addition that this sickness of the soul is only the symptom of quite another "sickness," of sin-sickness. He knows, therefore, that one cannot ultimately help man by seeking simply to cure his mental suffering, but that one helps him only by placing the whole man—man in body and soul, man in the totality of his existence—under the forgiveness of sin.

Although in the 19th century not only the world but even the church failed to appropriate this deep insight of the elder Blumhardt, there was a widespread awareness of this illness of man's soul. In a rather mild way a psychiatrist describes the situation of modern man as follows (I quote again C. G. Jung, *op. cit.*, p. 14): "I know one thing for certain: The spiritual condition of the European nearly everywhere shows a critical deficiency in equilibrium. Among my international clientele, made up without exception from the highly educated classes, I have a not inconsiderable number of patients who sought me out not because they suffered from a neurosis, but because they found no meaning in their life or were beset with problems for which our philosophy or religion had no answer. Some thought perhaps I knew a magic word, but I soon had to explain to them that I have no answer either." This leading psychiatrist is himself the best evidence for the fact that as a result of the distress prevailing in this perplexed and mentally ill world a very comprehensive movement has begun which at least makes the attempt to find a remedy. This is the first point to be made here. As the wave of materialistic and naturalistic world view began to ebb, a very intensive preoccupation with the problems of the psychic life set in. Modern psychology, psychiatry, and psychotherapy are the best evidence for this.

The exploration of psychoneuroses more than anything else, was of decisive impact here. It led to the almost obvious insight that the neuroses cannot be explained by physiology, e.g., neither by bacterial infection nor by disturbances of the glandular functions, as much as these contribute their part. Rather, they must be explained by psychic processes. Healing must be sought not only through somatic or pharmaceutical treatment but through psychotherapy, by some manner of psychic conditioning. This gave rise to the broadly ramified and deeply grounded *modern psychotherapy*. And men flocked to the psychiatrists. Later we shall have to define our position, as based on our interpretation of pastoral care, with regard to psychiatric treatment of disturbed people. At this point we only want to state that a multitude of those with whom we have to deal as pastors of local congregations have undergone or are undergoing such treatment; they come out of the consulting room of the psychiatrist to us, the pastors. It is most certainly not irrelevant to ask what kind of presuppositions underlay that consultation. It is not irrelevant precisely because of conversation into which we now enter with them on the basis of our presuppositions. We are not to lead a conversation without presuppositions; other conversations about psychic things, based on different philosophical assumptions, have already preceded ours, and we have to reckon with them. If a person seeks pastoral counsel he brings with him his own view of his predicament, which does not easily conform to the biblical view we espouse.

However, psychiatry in the narrower sense has no monopoly in dealing with the psychic disturbances of present-day man. There are a multitude of personal counselors in the broader sense. We may mention the numerous philosophical and religious leaders, thinkers, counselors, and advisors who, alongside the genuine psychiatrists, offer their services in the form of books or some kind of practice. There is scarcely a person who has not come in touch with some such counselor or physician of the soul. If we wanted to count them all, we would never end. Therefore, I name only two here, who are of special interest to us within the church because of their particular significance and influence: Johannes Müller and Rudolf Steiner.

Johannes Müller (besides his other writings, consult the two volumes of his autobiography, *Vom Geheimnis des Lebens*, Deutsche Verlagsanstalt, 1937-38) has reached a point where his influence is declining. But the powerful impact he exercised as a pastoral guide and counselor is not to be denied. He originally was firmly rooted in the church. He was himself a theologian, and one cannot avoid the impression that at least during his earlier years in a certain way he sensed and accepted something of the vital power of the Word of God. Throughout the rest of his life, he was driven again and again to ambitious attempts at interpreting and applying the Scriptures. But he was induced by the discovery of great psychic distress in his contemporaries, and also seduced by a certain innate magic power in the use of words and the concomitant power of psychic influence, to adapt the knowledge which he had originally gained from the Bible more and more to pure psychology. He developed his insights in the direction of a way of life, and he consciously brought this way of life—not to say technique of life—into opposition to the church. In the spirit of the commercialized century in which he lived, he knew how to build up something like a giant religious enterprise of pastoral counseling. He had numerous lesser imitators and supporters. He may in any case be cited as proof of the abundant supply of personal counseling and guidance in his time.

Is not Rudolf Steiner, the founder of Anthroposophy, and all his work ultimately to be understood in the same way? He freely presents himself as the great diagnostician who has recognized the sickness of the time in all realms of life and has now come, indeed has been sent, to offer the great remedy. This remedy is excellently designed as spiritual guidance and education aiming at forming a truly new man, who will then create a new world. Thus again the age is to be helped from within, by awakening a spiritual man in us. And again there are countless people in every land who in their perplexity and their afflictions listen to this call and expect Anthroposophy to usher in the decisive change in the inner and outer situation of their lives.

These two spokesmen help us to comprehend once more that the great presupposition from which guidance of man's spiritual life proceeds is again a definite understanding of what the "soul" is, a definite perception of man in general. Again the manner and nature of this modern guidance is contingent upon the underlying anthropology. Again its main point of departure is in some explicit or implicit way the view of the divine soul-part imbedded in man. We reiterate that the duality of man, the higher forces and the lower forces in him, flesh and spirit, soul and body, certainly including his mental and emotional life, is relatively right. But the question is what use we make of this immanent, double nature of man. Do the higher forces in man already in and of themselves mean his belonging to God? Or, on the contrary, has not the whole man—including all his good, spiritual powers and possibilities—fallen prey to sin and therefore been separated from God, so that even the awakening of the "divine soul-part" in him cannot help him? As a contrast, we recall the revival of the whole man by the Spirit of God of which the Holy Scripture speaks and which Christoph Blumhardt meant when he spoke of the forgiveness of sins as the true salvation of man, a salvation which is not only spiritual but also reaches into the sphere of physical life.

We can discern in Johannes Müller great psychological and practical knowledge of life, experience of life, even mastery of life. According to the picture which he sketches of himself in his autobiography, he may be called a truly wise man, versed in the art of living, able to give pastoral help out of the fullness of his knowledge of people to countless individuals of his time who could no longer find their way. But one thing cannot be said of him: that he rightly knew what was man's sin and the forgiveness of sins through the death and resurrection of Jesus Christ. He consistently interpreted the divine life—of which he speaks incessantly and which in his own way he found in the testimony of the Bible—as a human possibility. Each of us has this potentiality; it is admittedly buried in us all, yet can be awakened and set in motion by certain exercises—he himself occasionally called them "tricks." He built upon this view a whole technique of shaping human life—he calls it "nurture of personal life"—and thereby obtained that great success to which he testifies just before the outbreak of the Second World War in the comprehensive autobiography referred to.

The same may be said about Rudolf Steiner, only more saliently. The spiritual man he wants to awaken slumbers in every man. He has in himself an intellectual capacity, thought of as a sublime, materialized essence. This capacity must come to life. Then the spiritual man begins to rise as our own higher nature. We establish contact with the higher worlds, whose powers begin to flow into us and become available to us. We may well concede that Steiner knows about things that are right in their proper context, even though they do not become perceptible and tangible in Steiner's largely fantastic presentation. These feelings at any rate cannot be verified on the basis of our contemporary knowledge of man and his subconscious. Steiner's anthropology is essentially a high-flown projection of the immanent, double nature of man into a metaphysical upper and lower world. Its reality does not need to be argued. The decisive objection again is that the realm of sin and grace as it is announced and proclaimed in Holy Scripture still lies beyond all the worlds in between and above of which Steiner speaks. Even Steiner's spiritual man, rising to the heights of the worlds of the stars and suns, is and remains a sinner. Nothing at all helps him if the real Jesus Christ—so often invoked, yet fundamentally misunderstood by Steiner—and the forgiveness of sins he wrought do not become his portion. Everything Steiner tells us about this ascent of the spiritual man is ultimately utterly irrelevant for faith. However, insofar as faith in Jesus Christ, as proclaimed in Holy Scripture and the confession of the church is hidden by broadly inflated knowledge about the mystery of human existence—and this happens in Anthroposophy in the form of an overriding of faith by the metaphysics of man's supernature called "spiritual science"—Anthroposophy with its whole store of spiritual guidance and redemption is to be judged as a dangerous aberration. Georg Merz is right when he sees in it a revival of the mysteries and *gnosis* which arose in opposition to the Christian faith in its earliest days. (Georg Merz in *Kirchliche Verkündigung und moderne Bildung*, Munich, 1931, pp. 121ff.)

The basic view of the double nature of man as exposed here is actually a dogma that currently almost universally determines and governs the thinking about human affairs, and thus pastoral care as well. It can be expressed in various ways. Sometimes the higher nature, what is "above" in us, is represented as a "religious disposition" by virtue of which we are able to perceive God, as a capacity of man for divine things; sometimes it appears simply as a kind of divine substance which remains unimpaired in us and which can be brought to life by definite training—perhaps by mystic contemplation, mental concentration, or by active moral purification. But whatever view prevails, this "divine" part resides within man, comparable—and this comparison is very ancient—to a spark to be kindled into flame. Pastoral care based upon this assumption is therefore the effort to kindle and awaken one's own self, which in its deepest meaning is divine. Furthermore, it is quite clear that on these grounds understanding the power of the Word of God and a pastoral care based on it is, and must be, impossible. Pastoral care based on the Word is concerned with bringing about the real encounter—initiated and ever again granted by God himself—of the total man with his God, apart from any personal guidance in which man remains alone. We think again of Luther, who said that everything divine in him did not bring him peace, that, on the contrary, the very voice of God in his conscience made the fury of accusation all the more frightening. What helped him was solely the liberating Word of God fetching him out of this hell. This answered his question: "How can I find a merciful God?" His soul was finally "cared for."

Contemporary man, however, as a rule does not have this understanding of sin and grace as it is disclosed in the Word of God; rather, he has that self-understanding according to which his soul as the divine part in him is to be awakened. There will scarcely be a single pastoral conversation with people outside the church in which we shall not come across the expectation of personal help from moralistic, mystic, or intellectual endeavors. This is to say that he who asks for help does not reckon with sin as that total fact which completely imprisons him; nor does he long for the forgiving Word as the only effective remedy. He yearns for the nurture of his psychic life, for a way in which he may bypass grace and seek to walk on his own. For this he is perhaps prepared to make great efforts and sacrifices. But he insists that we, so to speak, believe in him and his inner resources and possibilities, awaken and strengthen this faith in him in turn. He wants a way without grace.

It is all-important that we do not give in, but rather block this road for him. We cannot help disappointing and offending him. We shall certainly take pains to understand from a psychological and human point of view everything that can be so understood about his situation. Yet our counseling will not draw only from the psychological realm. At one point there will be a breach in our conversation. We shall do everything to transfer his concerns from the human and psychological realm into the quite different realm disclosed by the Word of God. We shall refer him to the Holy Scriptures and to prayer. *How* this is to happen, *how* this breach and referral are to be accomplished is yet to be dealt with in detail. *That* it must happen is indispensable, is the basic requirement. It will determine the worth or worthlessness of our pastoral care. We must be perfectly clear that if we evade this breach, we deviate from our line, be it only by a hair's breadth. If we join the counselee—perhaps only tentatively and experimentally—on the ground from which he first comes, we base our pastoral care not on the Word but on a secular understanding of man and on a corresponding "natural theology." We may subsequently, perhaps very searchingly and earnestly, speak of sin and grace and Jesus Christ—even the anthroposophists also speak of them!—but fundamentally, our efforts will be lost. For our partner in conversation will fill all our words, even the highest and last words of faith, with a mystic or moralistic or philosophical content dissolving them from within. From his point of departure he cannot do otherwise. But he will not really be able to hear that his sins are forgiven in Jesus Christ.

In his critical evaluation of "natural theology," Karl Barth convincingly demonstrates that such a tentative adoption of a viewpoint foreign to Holy Scriptures and the Christian faith and the resulting pastoral counseling with mental reservations can actually harden a man's heart (*Church Dogmatics* II, 1, 26). He says among other things: "The partner in the conversation discovers that faith is trying to use the well-known artifice of dialectic in relation to him. We are not taking him seriously because we withhold from him what we really want to say and represent. It is only in appearance that we devote ourselves to him, and therefore what we say to him is only an apparent and unreal statement. What will happen then? Well, not without justice—although misconstruing the friendly intention which perhaps motivates us—he will see himself despised and deceived, and indeed doubly despised and deceived. He will shut himself up and harden himself against the faith which does not speak out frankly, which deserts its own standpoint and merely pretends to take up the contrary standpoint of unbelief. What use to unbelief is a faith which obviously knows different? And how shocking for unbelief is a faith which only pretends to take up with unbelief a common position."

We have yet to make one more statement. This understanding of man, contested by the Scriptures, has entered not only the modern world but also the *modern church*. I am referring here to the devastating impact of the invasion of natural theology into the realm of the church and the local congregation. It is the thought and the "faith" corresponding to it which claims to be able to draw its knowledge of God from two sources, revelation *and* reason, the Holy Scriptures *and* man's innate capacity to think, learn, and experience. It will immediately be clear that this second source can mean nothing but the "higher powers" in man, whatever they designate, his spiritual, or even "divine" nature. Furthermore, it will also be clear that any natural theology represents some form of the anthropology we reject because it stands for the double nature of man seen without grace. Pastoral care fights against this duality. Indeed, this anthropology makes up the fundamental substance of natural theology. Natural theology so understood has always been the adversary of all thought and faith in the church as bound by the Scriptures and conditioned by revelation. It is present in our time in what we call *Liberalism*. Liberalism and natural theology are one and the same thing. Inasmuch as we have seen that all natural theology is characterized by that fateful interpretation of man, indeed presupposes and engenders it, the pastoral care corresponding to it is bound to be, in principle and in practice, an essentially mystic or moralistic pastoral guidance. Not allied with the Word and not bound by Scriptures, it is no genuine pastoral care.

Such a pastoral guidance tending toward natural theology and not necessarily bound by the Word can be examined in the voluminous work of Jean-Daniel Benoît already referred to, *Direction Spirituelle et Protestantisme*. In spite of many worthwhile references and studies, it cannot be spared the reproach of evading the distinction between faithfulness to the Word and natural theology demanded here, and thus errs from the start. Its search for a biblical basis of pastoral guidance cannot alter this fact. The result is a dangerous inclination toward the Catholic pastoral guidance which permeates the whole book. In contrast, we may refer once again to the comprehensive critique of all natural theology in Karl Barth's *Church Dogmatics* (II, 1). It is not possible to ignore this presentation whenever the problem of natural theology is discussed. Natural theology in various forms penetrates all ecclesiastical and theological thought and action; it is the presupposition upon which is based the thought and speech of the members of our congregations, and indeed of modern man in general. No preacher and no missionary who has to deal with this man of today, above all no counselor, should therefore neglect to acquaint himself with Barth's conclusive inquiry into the roots and nature of all natural theology and its immanent contradiction to all scriptural and revealed faith. Pastoral counseling can be safely entered into and carried out only when we are informed and warned about the continual threat from natural theology that menaces even the thoughts and words of the counselor himself, and are thrown back to the Word of God. The importance of sound doctrine for the practical task can hardly be more evident than at this point.

In fact, the church should offer the utmost resistance to natural theology and its understanding of man. Opposition indeed has not been lacking. We have already mentioned Wilhelm Löhe, August Vilmar, Claus Harms, and both Blumhardts. They are the ones who in modern times have sought and held the strict, biblical line in pastoral care against any Liberal temptation.

Others who have stood unfalteringly on this good and sound line as pastoral counselors deserve to be mentioned. There was Hermann Bezzel, the successor to Löhe in the direction of the work of the deaconesses of Neuendettelsau and later President of the Church of Bavaria; his writings testify to genuine pastoral care in word and deed. There was Hermann Friedrich Kohlbrügge, Löhe's contemporary, strictly Reformed, who as preacher and counselor built up his Dutch Reformed congregation in Elberfeld by faithful adherence to the Heidelberg Catechism (cf. his collected writings and the biography by H. Klugkist-Hesse describing him as pastor of the congregation). Lastly there was P. Geyser, his successor in the pastorate of Elberfeld; a little book *Besuche bei Sterbenden* (Visitation with the Dying) (Elberfeld, 1892) bears witness to his pastoral care as rooted in the Bible and the Catechism. Above all, we need to say that the church has never entirely lacked pastors who quietly stood on the ground of the Word and led their congregations in the right direction.

But on the whole, the spirit of Liberalism has made its conquest even in pastoral care. Is not the fabulous rise of the theologian Friedrich Schleiermacher at the beginning of the 19th century a sign of this? Liberalism is not quite wrong in harking back to him as one of its fathers even though "natural theology" is presented in Schleiermacher in an extraordinarily refined and balanced, indeed genial, way. And is not Albrecht Ritschl, his adversary in the middle of the century, also on the way of a softening of scriptural theology?

Neither in the school of Schleiermacher nor in that of Ritschl is theory and practice of pastoral care lacking. However, it no longer emerges strictly from Scripture and Catechism, but from that pious consciousness and life of the congregation which Schleiermacher took for granted. Contentwise, it is no longer exclusively related to the proclamation of the forgiveness of sins, as the Catechism of Luther as well as the Heidelberg Catechism had taught it. The pastors of this persuasion hold the truth of justification to be too doctrinal and, under the slogan that life is more important than doctrine, turn more and more to matters of Christian experience and philosophy of life. Their pastoral care becomes art of living and apologetics. At best, it offers guidance in the earnest, though legalistic, exploration of conscience, the awakening of an inner-directed, personal piety.

It must never be said that under the influence of Liberalism numerous pastors and members of the Christian community did not become willing and eager to practice pastoral care and were not seriously and fondly devoted to it. But in spite of all its seriousness and personal zeal, this pastoral care shows a marked deficiency in substance. In countless biographies of leading personalities, primarily among the educated classes of that time, we notice how little they were touched and grasped by the message of the church, as proclaimed either in its instruction and preaching or in its pastoral care. On the other hand, there was a growing confidence in personal counseling outside the church. There existed a real need for advice and guidance, but instead of looking to the pastor from whom so little relevant help came people sought out psychologists, even psychiatrists. This is understandable. If even the church and its pastoral care are concerned only with elucidating the inner life with psychological and philosophical instruction, then I may just as well or even better turn for advice from the pastor to the expert, the psychiatrist or the philosopher.

We most certainly have no reason for belittling the work and service of the psychiatrist or the philosopher. We shall highly esteem them at the proper place. It is one thing to carry through a psychiatric treatment or philosophical clarification. It is quite another thing to communicate the forgiveness of sins. Today the psychiatrists themselves are again aware of this. There are those who do not wish to have the forgiving Word withheld from their patients and who therefore refer the patient back to the pastor. But for just this reason, everything now depends on the pastor's proclaiming nothing but this Word. Then a pastoral care would again exist in the church which focused on the Word of Christ and on it alone.

Let me conclude quite concretely: We need a pastoral care which sees man in the perspective of *baptism*. For baptism is the sign that man in and with his whole double nature, his conscious and his unconscious, in short his totality or, to quote once more from the Catechism, "With body and soul, both in life and death, is not his own, but belongs to his faithful Saviour Jesus Christ." To proclaim this to the individual, to make it relevant to his life, to do this on the basis of the preaching of the church—this is the task of evangelical pastoral care.

II *The Nature and Practice of Pastoral Care*

Pastoral care is accomplished in the form of a conversation which proceeds from the Word of God and leads to its proclamation in the church. In pastoral conversation as in all human speech within the church, man's natural articulateness must be put in the service of the Holy Spirit, in order that the Word of God may address man.

5 Pastoral Care as Conversation

We have dealt with the *necessity* of pastoral care, with the proper basis on which it can be practiced, and with man as the object of pastoral care. We now turn to *the nature and form of true pastoral care*.

We remember once again that, rightly understood, the *whole* function of the church can be seen as care for the soul of man. Sermon and sacrament also serve pastoral care. Nevertheless, the specific use of the concept of pastoral care as an extraordinary function alongside preaching and the administration of the sacraments seems now justified.

We have already found this special use in Calvin's *"admonitio privata,"* the personal admonition of the individual; we have found it explicitly mentioned by Luther, as the *"mutuum colloquium et consolatio fratrum,"* the mutual, brotherly conversation and consolation; we have found it reinforced in Bucer; and we have seen how Pietism actually made this special function the center of church activity, but also how its opponents—we have become well acquainted with them in Vilmar and Löhe—acknowledged this function and made use of it themselves. A history of pastoral care would demonstrate these connections and show the accuracy of the fundamental insight which we present here: Pastoral care based on the presuppositions of the founders and fathers of our church is truly that legitimate, extraordinary means or sign which the church is compelled to use if it rightly administers Word and sacrament, since Word and sacrament require the use of this means.

Our first affirmation is that pastoral care so established and required is accomplished in the form of a conversation. This form is not accidental, but constitutes the very nature of this means. It is conversation both formally and materially. Let us consider what this means.

We begin with a statement about speech which is found in the *Zwölf Reden über die Beredsamkeit* which the romanticist philosopher Adam Müller delivered in Vienna in 1812. He said:

> The soul itself is no more distinguished nor any greater than speech. Rather, speech is the divine seal which alone makes serious and genuine all the singular and diffuse thoughts of the individual. What the soul cherishes as its most precious possession remains mere vision and dream, without influence on the world and so without amicable impact, until it can be expressed, i.e., until it is confirmed by speech. Speech is an exuberant substance in which all ages and all generations, even the poorest, have handed down the most beautiful treasures of their lives. Thought becomes thought by the same token as man becomes man. In short, as with every other property, that of the soul cannot be secure until it has become common property— and it becomes this by speech. (Quoted by Hofmannsthal, *Deutsches Lesebuch,* 2nd Part, p. 132.)

Müller also points out that flight from clear and popular speech may debase public life. And what he says of the use of speech in philosophy is also true for theology and the church:

> At one moment, we treat speech despotically and arrogantly as if it were something contrived, a kind of cipher or code which one alters arbitrarily if the key has fallen into the hand of the enemy; the next moment, speech instead handles us, controls our thoughts against our will, domesticates and tames them.

One can hardly express more beautifully and with more inspiration how great and life-giving the speaking of man to man is. Adam Müller has a vision of the magnitude and power of the human psyche and now directs the question to us: How can our psychic power be expressed and thus be made effective in the best and purest way? Indeed, the soul becomes the real content of life, and life itself becomes truly human only as these treasures of the soul take shape. The word, speech, and conversation seem to him to be the great means of sharing, the means by which life becomes human. The word liberates us; it is a divine force which is imparted to man. To be sure, this indicates at the same time that we face a crisis from moment to moment: Psychic power must, as it were, go through the narrow gate of the word; only then does it become forceful and truly alive. But does the soul allow itself to be restricted to this gate? Does it submit to the power and control of the word? Of what use is the greatest depth of the soul if it remains confused and locked up in itself? Only the word, only speech, converts the vague psychic fluctuations into mental life in which others can also participate. Once again: Only the fact that man can speak and does speak makes him man.

We do not deny that this view comes very close to the biblical testimony. Man's articulateness points back to his responsibility before God, which from the viewpoint of Holy Scripture is also its basis. Man can speak since he is summoned to answer God as the one addressed by God. In the last analysis, the mystery of speech is identical with the mystery of personality, with the image of God in man. Furthermore, Adam Müller's insistence that speech breaks our isolation because its power of communication brings us into fellowship with our neighbor is in line with biblical anthropology. The latter sees man as God's image appointed to fellowship not only with God, but also with his neighbor, who stands with him before God. This fellowship is again founded in the Word which God speaks to us and which he awakes in us. This is how we must understand what Müller has to say about articulateness as the decisive sign of our humanity.

We must, however, immediately remember that this is a romanticist speaking. He ascribes this articulateness to man, so to speak, without presupposition. For him, man possesses it as the sign of a divinity granted him by nature. But we have learned to understand that even if man possessed personality and therefore articulateness—if he were by nature an orator and poet—he would in no way have proved his existence as a "living soul" before God. The whole man, even the articulate man, is subject to sin. In spite of his articulateness, he can no longer speak with God on his own or hear God's Word. Hence, speaking as such is by no means the "creative" act in which his destiny as man is fulfilled. Speech by itself does not yet signify that man has become man in the full sense, man before God, and thus has attained the deliverance and redemption of his soul.

To be sure, there is a theological doctrine which, following the path of Romanticism like Adam Müller, would understand the spiritual discourse in preaching and pastoral care as the redeeming act to be accomplished in the church. This doctrine starts with the idea that man is endowed with a natural articulateness which unites him with God simply because he is a creature. Although muted by sin, this articulateness can be restored by an appropriate step of man's own initiative. What is this step? The linking of his speech to the treasure of faith within the church and the corresponding life of faith. Insofar as man lives in the Christian community and allows his soul and his conscience to be awakened, his natural articulateness which has been corrupted by sin is restored. Awakened by the divine words that go back and forth in the church, he can discover and awaken the divine Word in himself. In and with his act of speaking, he becomes a true man, born again to his own divinity.

We think of Schleiermacher. This is the meaning of the preacher's discourse within the church in Scheiermacher's famous passage in the fourth of his discourses *On Religion* (secs. 181ff., 224, 228). The preacher is the virtuoso who can bring the spiritual life of the church into focus in his words and, powerfully filled with it and driven by it, he "inoculates" his listeners.

We also think of Alexander Vinet, a younger contemporary congenial to Schleiermacher. In his homiletic doctrine and practice, man's natural religious sensitivity and articulateness likewise plays a significant role. With the founders of our church, the preacher's discourse is strictly bound to the Word of God in the Holy Scripture, which is really alive only if there is added the work of the Holy Spirit, who as a free Spirit blows when and where he pleases.

At the most decisive places in his speeches Schleiermacher omits any reference to the Word as the Spirit of God. Everything rests with the preacher's innate articulateness. Not unreasonably, Schleiermacher has even been considered a mystic (cf. Emil Brunner, *Die Mystik und das Wort*). With Vinet, the concept of personal conviction and of conscience is decisively set forth as a divine impulse present in man by which he who speaks in the church is to be led. It is certainly no accident that Vinet called his own sermons not sermons but "religious discourses." These discourses as a rule are not meant to be exegetical interpretations, but thematic expositions. A romanticist element is quite unmistakably manifest in this important theologian.

Within the church, therefore, man's discourse once again becomes a special problem. It undergoes a crisis which does not affect the speech of the secular poet or philosopher. It becomes evident that preaching—but also pastoral conversation, insofar as it deals with the communication of the Word of God—is a special discourse distinguished from profane and natural speech. The question which arises is this: How is it at all possible for sinful man to hear and communicate God's Word? He is not able to do it by virtue of his natural articulateness alone, for it is also subject to sin.

One more control comes into force to which human speech must submit in order to gain—if it does occur—the authority it needs to communicate the Word of God legitimately and vitally. It is a control and authentication of which the romanticist philosopher Adam Müller understandably knows nothing, and perhaps does not need to know anything for his purposes. Unfortunately, the romanticist theologians do not seem to know anything about it either, and their ignorance is certainly important enough. *God's Word in Holy Scripture* is the name of this control or this limitation. On it depends the authentication or nonauthentication of our spiritual discourse; the human word must unconditionally submit and account to God's Word.

The romanticist theologians (I refer again to Schleiermacher) also know about a binding of the preacher and pastor to the Word of God; for them, the Word of God is the prototype of a potential articulateness residing in every man. Again according to Schleiermacher, an eternal movement is initiated within man himself at the prompting of the Word of God in Holy Scripture. The Scriptures are used to activate this impulse. But according to the inherent self-explanation of the Scriptures, as well as according to the teaching of the church fathers, God's Word is strictly a *verbum alienum*. It is a Word entirely of its own order, and it is never in our power to speak it. It is a Word which in its own power and majesty stands against all our words. It retains this power and majesty and does not abandon it even when it is clothed in human garb and is pronounced as the human words of prophets and apostles and through them in the words of a preacher or pastoral counselor. This is the great proviso of the Holy Spirit, moving as the Spirit who spoke to prophets and apostles and makes his spoken word newly alive when and where he pleases. Where he blows, and only there, man can and man may legitimately and vitally speak and hear, hear and speak, God's Word.

This proviso is the crisis which makes our speaking in the church so very special. When we are called to speak in the church—and as pastors we have a very definite vocation here—we cannot rely on natural articulateness. God's Word does not lie somewhere in the depths of the human soul, waiting to be awakened, perhaps with the help of the Bible. We must certainly be prepared and shall be authorized to speak. Our own articulateness will be used, yet wholly in the service of that other, alien Word and its own divine power. Our speaking, insofar as it concerns divine things, must be considered merely as an instrument at the disposal and in the service of God's Word.

When it is so used, our speech certainly is a splendid, an admirable instrument. Adam Müller is right; one cannot think highly enough of this instrument. But with all its power, it is an instrument subject to the Spirit and the Word of God as an alien authority which uses it as it pleases. Even if it is the speech of a born philosopher or poet, it is now made captive. It must let itself be usurped; it must let itself be governed by this alien Spirit and Word. It must be a repetition; it must repeat only this alien Word which is never engendered by our spirit and its natural articulation. It must speak this alien Word and not its own words. It is a speaking within the church! Church means and is nothing else than the spiritual realm in which this speaking is manifest and practiced. It is certainly man who speaks even here, and his own human depth with all its powers shares in his speaking. However, he does not speak out of his own depths, but he speaks with all the power given him by that alien Word now conferred upon him; he speaks the Word of God.

All of this concerns first of all the church's *preaching*. But it also concerns *pastoral counseling*, the conversation which is based on preaching and leads back to it. We may say that all of man's speaking is properly the prototype to conversation. This is simply to say it is never a mere monologue. Human speaking makes sense only when it is intended to awaken response. It wants to be heard. And the sign of its being heard is the answer, the response following our talk. This is the meaning of the concept of conversation. Even the church's preaching is but such a speech which awakens response. But in the church, the speaker is no longer just man, but God himself. To be sure, he lays claim to human speech as an instrument, but so as to pronounce his own Word. It is not simply a conversation in which man remains by himself. Rather, it is the conversation which God conducts and into which he draws men. Therefore, the answer solicited by the church's preaching is not just whatever one man addressed by the preacher now repeats to some other man. Rather, since it is a conversation between God and man, man's response is directed to God himself. And this means it is expressed in hymns and prayer. Martin Luther understood it in this way when he called hymns and prayer in worship the proper answer returned by man to the Word that God has directed to him in the preaching of the Word.

We have a definite name for this response awakened by God's Word; we call it *liturgy*. In fact, this is the whole basis and justification of what we call liturgy. Preaching can and must under no circumstances remain an isolated discourse; it anticipates a quite definite answer; it intends to be surrounded and borne by this answer. Indeed, the purpose of the Word of God in preaching is our entering into conversation with God. For conversation is fellowship, and fellowship with God is at hand wherever his Word is pronounced. But because it is *God* who becomes the partner in conversation here, man's answer, as it is directed to God, can be nothing else but praying or singing, inasmuch as our singing also intends to be prayer. This means once again that our answer will be a liturgical answer, which is to say, an answer in the service of the Word of God.

Alongside this liturgical answer there exists *pastoral conversation*. This also deals with the Word of God pronounced in a specific way among men. However, it proceeds not in the liturgical form of man's response to God, but rather in the profane form of two men talking *about* God. One man now tells the Word of God to another, from "man to man." The one addressed accepts it and answers; however, he answers not with prayer or hymns but responds conversationally. What now occurs is properly human conversation. But this conversation, too, takes place within the church. It is placed under the proviso of the Word and Spirit of God as purely human conversation is not.

Of course, this conversation does not always occur on church premises. The place is perhaps the living room, the park, the street, or—why not?—even the restaurant. It is nevertheless the church, the Christian community within which, spiritually speaking, this conversation takes place. For what is at stake is not simply the fact that two men speak to each other about God in their own articulateness and out of their own inner depth. True, inner depth and human articulateness are presupposed, but as they speak with one another, both men endeavor to hear and utter God's Word. This alone makes their conversation concerned with the soul and its salvation.

I say both men! But is it actually both? This is certainly a valid question. From the very outset, the criterion of pastoral conversation may be stated as follows: Content and character of pastoral conversation depend on the fact that *both* men who speak and answer here are or are becoming men confronting the Word of God. If this is not true at first, it must become true in the course of the conversation. If this does not happen, if one man evades the Word of God or at least evades seeking and questioning, if he locks himself up or even repudiates it, then the conversation has failed. It may have been an attempt to speak with one another about God not only about profane things, not only intellectually or philosophically or poetically, but on the basis of God's Word or with reference to God's Word. Yet the attempt has failed since one partner in the conversation could not or would not go along, but remained stuck in merely sophisticated, philosophical, or poetic talk. But when this dialogue between two men, started perhaps entirely on the profane level, succeeds in submitting the partners to the authority of the Word of God, then a true pastoral conversation has been achieved. Then the conversation becomes quite unintentionally, yet necessarily, liturgical conversation in the proper sense. In such pastoral conversation, the Bible is opened, the Word of God is read and interpreted, there is prayer; God is praised and thanked.

We summarize: Pastoral counseling happens in the form of a conversation—listening to the Word of God and responding to the Word of God. The partners in the conversation become servants of this Word for one another. Even in pastoral conversation, God intends to speak through human words, and he may get the proper response when both partners in the conversation confront him and do not simply remain by themselves. Pastoral conversation is therefore never that characterized as "romantic," confined to that in which one person bares his soul to the other. On the contrary, it must be conversation within the context of the church in which God's Word interpenetrates and determines all the inner forces of man.

We must point out that with this characterization of pastoral conversation we do not abandon, but rather accept, the concern of the philosophy of Romanticism. The romanticist is right when he thinks of human speech as highly important. We also agree with him when he declares that human speech is the point at which the encounter with God takes place, and therefore celebrates man's articulateness as the event which really makes him man, man before God. We can also say this, but with the difference that it is valid only for that conversation which recognizes its own weakness and accepts the control of the Word and Spirit of God. It must remain clear that it is not in our power to encounter, to hear, and to understand God by our own eloquence; he grants us this privilege according to his good pleasure. Apart from this fundamental obligation to the Word and Spirit of God, all exalted affirmations about human eloquence are vain.

This means that we can indeed express our individuality apart from the action of the Spirit of God in our speaking; yet we remain by ourselves; we do not reach God, and we do not even reach one another. We do not remove the mutual loneliness so long as there is nothing but reciprocal self-expression. We lack that overarching continuum of the Spirit, surrounding both of us before God and hence uniting us with one another. Only in the presence of the Spirit is true encounter in fellowship possible. However, if our speaking is accepted in the service of the Word of God; if we not only say our own words but also let our words become instruments for perceiving God; if there is genuine conversation with God, then the loneliness of our self-expression is shattered. Then we are drawn out of our self-sufficiency and are for the first time placed in true fellowship with one another before God. Man's self is no longer left alone; God's "I" says "thou" to us and gives us the neighbor for a brother as he addresses him together with us and redeems us from that loneliness which we cannot pierce by our own power. Seen in this way, pastoral conversation is the prototype of true conversation, actually bringing us together and redeeming us. And so understood, the romanticist is right: Such a conversation is one of the greatest events we may experience.

One final question: Should not *every* conversation reflect the splendor and the magnitude of this pastoral speech which makes us encounter God and one another as long as it is conducted within the church, by two people who both are sustained by the preaching and the sacrament of the church? Should not the basic form of all valid conversation in the church, as it is revealed in pastoral conversation, also furnish the basic form of everyday, profane conversation? How could the members of the Christian community encountering one another in conversation ever forget that they are addressed by God's Word? In so-called profane conversation, how could they suddenly deny and renounce their common experience of being addressed by the Word of God? How could this fail to become effective and significant, determining and penetrating all their conversations? It is actually intended to be this way. This is the promise and command over all our speaking with one another. Therefore our speaking, even when it concerns the most common things of life, can be done on the basis of the Word of God and with reference to the Word of God. Every conversation can show this care for man before God, therefore for his soul, as is proper in pastoral conversation.

The above is intended to be an exposition of what two passages from Ephesians say about our speaking with one another; they deal with the spiritual nature and life of the Christian community. First, Ephesians 4:29, "Let no evil talk come out of your mouths, but only such as is good for edifying, as fits the occasion, that it may impart grace to those who hear." The Apostle speaks here of the everyday dealings of Christians with one another, of the daily and hourly conversations. He envisions a twofold possibility: Either we speak "evil" with one another, or we speak "good" even if we converse on quite ordinary matters. He characterizes this good as something which imparts grace. A lofty declaration! It can only signify that one person advances another's spiritual life in speaking with him. This may well mean pastoral conversation. The counterpart to this is "evil talk," that is, speech which is of no use. For "evil" signifies something out of which nothing can grow, something which is therefore never worth the effort of speaking, however sublime it may sound. Speaking with one another would thus be the great occasion for advancing together. The Apostle speaks to people who have been summoned by the Word of God and awakened to life. Such people should also help each other along in common, everyday speech. They can no longer enjoy idle chattering. Every valid conversation must be a step forward together. Such people truly have something to say to one another. Their speech is to reflect the serious, the peculiar, the joyful experience of the Word of God in their lives. Conversing, they are not to stir up only the joyless, useless, common things which fill our lives to such an extent that God's Word does not stand behind us. Or it remains just "evil talk."

Therefore—and this is the second passage to be quoted—the Apostle adds the quite positive admonition, Ephesians 5:19, "Addressing one another in psalms and hymns and spiritual songs, singing and making melody to the Lord with all your heart!" This is again a lofty thought; this is already liturgical conversation, conversation that is transformed into prayer and song. But are not the boundaries fluid even here? As there is a way from the worship of God to pastoral conversation, which in its proper way—like preaching—is a speaking before God and can lead to speaking with God, so there is a way from this pastoral conversation back into common conversation. Even this common conversation then becomes substantial. It concerns nothing less than the salvation and life of the soul before God. Where a man makes room in himself for the Word and Spirit of God, there is something of the joy in the presence of God about him even when he does not sing. It echoes even in his common speech and lights up even in the midst of everyday conversation in a word that he says, perhaps unintended and unsought, perhaps in table conversation or in a discussion of secular matters from the newspaper.

We conclude our exposition with three observations: *First*, with all that has been said, the boundaries which separate pastoral conversation proper from common everyday conversation must in no way be obliterated. Not every conversation should be intended to be pastoral care toward another person. That would be a dreadful constriction of our speaking and would lead to impossible and intolerable situations. It is certainly significant that a special pastoral conversation exists. It stands as a particular sign amid our common conversation and apart from it. This does not exclude the fact that this proper pastoral conversation discloses the meaning of all human speech. It is valid at any rate to say that we have not yet recognized and experienced what it means to speak properly with another person so long as we know nothing about this explicit and definite pastoral conversation, so long as we ourselves have never yet conversed within the church in this proper and explicit sense on the basis of the Word of God.

Second, it will have to remain clear that preaching, which is essentially different from pastoral conversation, must continue. Under no circumstances may all spiritual discourse be dissolved into pastoral conversations. This must not happen because true pastoral conversation is impossible on the basis of human articulateness even when one person speaks to another about God and divine things. It becomes possible only through the sovereign Word of God itself, first to be established in its freedom and power by the proclamation of the words of the prophets and apostles in Holy Scripture. Only in the shadow, or better in the light, of such preaching does true pastoral conversation exist.

Finally, the resulting pastoral conversation will always be distinguished from all merely profane speech, although it itself stands almost unprotected in the midst of profane speech. Contrary to preaching, it is garbed in profane, everyday speech. The separation will be manifest as a breach which appears in pastoral conversation and characterizes it. Precisely because we cannot engage in spiritual conversation on purely human grounds, because we need to be summoned by the Word of God which sanctifies our conversation, this breach exists as a sign which runs throughout profane speech if it is to be more than ordinary talk and become pastoral conversation. This breach is the consequence of that authority to which we submit our pastoral speech and by which we allow it to be measured.

This is perhaps the simplest formulation in which we can summarize all that is involved here: Our speech must be measured by the question of whether it can exist before the Word of God or not. Either it is useless, unfruitful, and evil talk which gives nothing to him who hears it—talk which leads no further, out of which nothing grows and develops—or it is that talk which imparts grace to him who hears it, grace in which we ourselves may share. But here we have arrived at the point where we must reflect in detail upon the character of spiritual conversation as such.

The form of pastoral conversation is determined by its claim to see even the remotest human concern in its relationship to God and his Word as established by the incarnation of Jesus Christ. Accordingly, it is a conversation within the church. It is a constant listening to the Word of God and constant listening to man who only in the light of this Word can come to a true understanding of his life.

6 The Form of Pastoral Conversation

Pastoral care is a conversation resting on a very definite assumption. It intends to be a conversation that proceeds from the Word of God and leads to the Word of God. The conversation is integrated by the fact that the two partners in conversation are already engaged or at least about to be engaged in a confrontation with the Word of God. They are already or soon will be addressed by the Word of God. For this reason and purpose they now talk to each other. Being initially and continually addressed by the Word of God is the one great assumption each of the two partners makes for the other. It permeates and determines their whole conversation. At first, they perhaps do not mention this Word of God and its content at all; instead they speak of certain very concrete problems and concerns of their lives. Even so they proceed on the assumption that the Word of God whereby they are addressed or are to be addressed is important for these very problems and concerns.

What does this mean? It means first and foremost that the two partners in conversation, whoever they are and wherever they come from—and perhaps they come from widely differing streams of life and thought—nevertheless experience deep fellowship with one another. It springs from the Word of God which is valid for both of them, affecting and determining their relationship.

We might ask whether or not they share a common concern

even apart from the impact of God's Word. Do they not share the realm of human speech in which encounter is possible by mere human conversing, without the Word of God? We have already established the narrow boundaries of this natural realm of speech and of man's natural articulateness. We indeed meet one another through conversation; yet this encounter in no way establishes true fellowship. It leads up to a confrontation; yet mutual understanding is not thereby assured. Human conversation only furthers and confirms the discovery that we do not really understand each other. Is it not true that in speaking and being spoken to we realize how alien our partner is, and how different we are from him? Where else can we discover the other as a dissimilar person from ourselves than in a conversation which discloses his otherness to us? In this perspective, conversation reveals our human loneliness. Speaking, we mutually delimit ourselves; we set ourselves apart from one another.* We are up against the wall of partition between persons. We become aware of all that is veiled, opaque, even hostile in our fellow man. The realm of human speech, therefore, instead of uniting us intensifies our opposing views and our drifting apart. I recall Genesis 11:1-9, the story of the Tower of Babel, with its provocative truth about human language and communication. Human language is the very place where fellowship breaks down.

But now the Word of God is addressed to us, divided and isolated as we are in our human outreach. Addressing us, it brings about the conditions—again in the realm of speech—under which true encounter and true fellowship become finally possible among those who were driven into opposition and isolation by their human conversation. Much as they drift apart or confront each other as aliens, even enemies, the Word of God nevertheless speaks to them. Enemies as they are and perhaps remain, they are addressed by one and the same Word. They cannot destroy this "togetherness" which binds them to one another. The Word of God—and not their own—becomes the

* The German expression, *sich auseinander setzen*, is very striking in this context.

ground on which they meet each other and understand each other. The Word of God says to both that their failure to understand each other is rooted in their sin, in their estrangement from God. It says to both that by themselves they will never find the reuniting word. Lastly, it says to them that their sin is forgiven in Jesus Christ; in the power of this forgiveness a new conversation becomes possible in which those far apart draw near to each other, and enemies become brothers. I recall Acts 2, the story of Pentecost. Pentecost is indeed the manifestation, by the power of the Spirit and the Word of God, of this new speaking and hearing of the Word of God, and thereby of the new fellowship in the realm of speech. It is a fellowship of the sinners and the dying, of those totally estranged from one another, who are now sanctified together through the Word of God in Jesus Christ. So strong, so deep, so genuine and fundamental is this fellowship that there are no oppositions and differences between men, powerful as they may be, that cannot be overcome and eliminated in the fellowship of the Word.

Pastoral conversation rests entirely on the real encounter of people who are alien to one another and are now brought together by the Word of God. This Pentecostal reality is the one firm foundation of pastoral conversation which is thereby essentially characterized as a conversation *within the church*. It is distinguished from other, profane conversation by the fact that it must be sustained by Christian fellowship. Only within the Christian community can it be realized; only here is it conceivable at all. The realm of this community, however, is constituted and staked out by baptism, preaching, and the Lord's Supper. However difficult it may seem to impose an external criterion whereby the churchly character of such a conversation can be recognized, this much can be affirmed: Pastoral conversation within the church is carried out within the province of the signs of Word and sacrament. Their strength and their protection stand behind it; their nearness or distance is of decisive importance.

This is not to say that this conversation cannot deeply penetrate the realm of profane things, but rather that even out of bounds it has to remain the fundamentally churchly conversation which it essentially is. It must not be forgotten for a moment in this conversation that there is a Word of God incumbent upon both partners and intending to address and to challenge both of them. Pastoral conversation, in fact, serves to validate this presupposition about men even where they are far removed from one another. To speak pastorally with another certainly does not preclude getting involved in every conceivable profane subject. But it must be done in such a way as to bring God's Word into force as the great proviso over this talk. The conversation must quite concretely move in the direction of revealing the relation in which all things stand to the Word of God.

The christological statement of the *assumptio carnis* delineates the proper and ultimate background of the form and effectiveness of pastoral conversation. All things stand in relation to the Word of God and can be lifted up and sanctified by it not by nature nor by virtue of an indwelling analogy to the divine, but because God's Word in its *incarnation* has accepted all things. Because Jesus Christ has become flesh, there is now nothing fleshly and human, however sinful and corrupt it may be, that cannot be reached and grasped by the Word of God and translated into God's own. Since Jesus Christ was born, died, and rose again, the name of God is set over everything that is on earth. There is no problem, no sorrow, no sin, no pain, and no death over which a word of judgment and of grace cannot and must not be pronounced in the power of this name. All valid pastoral care refers to and claims this prerogative when it engages in conversation about any worldly subject. To practice pastoral care indeed means to take nothing seriously except the sovereignty of Christ in the midst of the distant and dark realms of human problems, into which the pastoral conversation inevitably leads us. Pastoral care claims to see even the remotest human concerns in their relationship to God, established by Jesus Christ. Pastoral care realizes ever anew that which the Confession of Faith describes as communion of saints initiated by the forgiveness of sins.

Therefore, if we enter this conversation, we will not be greatly concerned about its *subject matter*. For is there any subject which does not need to be brought into the light of God? Is there any subject so remote that the power of his Word cannot reach and affect it? Is there any problem to which an answer cannot and must not be given by the Word of God? Pastoral conversation is characterized by the fact that its subject does not need to be of a spiritual nature in the proper sense; everything can become its subject, provided the presupposition is validated and everything is drawn into the realm of the divine Word. Such conversation does not primarily deal with the presentation of the content of this Word. It is not proclamation in the usual sense; nor is it the liturgical communication of the message. These are presupposed. Preaching of the Word has occurred and will continue to occur; and because it has occurred and will occur again, the whole realm of human life is claimed by the Word of God. This becomes manifest through certain questions and problems which remain open or are newly raised. It is above all expressed by the fact that the partner in conversation has so far been scarcely, if at all, touched by the Word and must now be challenged as to the why and wherefore of his being untouched.

Pastoral conversation is concerned with the raising and answering of such questions. This defines its form. Life, so to speak, bursts open in these conversations—life in all its dimensions, yet life in confrontation with the proclaimed Word. The subject of the conversation can therefore be all of life in its open, or secret and still to be disclosed, relatedness to the Word of God. And insofar as man—in his heights and depths, but especially in his hearing or not-hearing of the Word and thus as "living soul"—is both the subject of all things human and the object of the divine Word, these conversations are concerned with this living soul of man and nothing else. Man's soul is the one subject which is at stake in all the many subjects of this conversation. The more fully this comes to light as the specific intention of the dialogue, the more meaningful and helpful the conversation will be. This is what pastoral conversation within the church means. This is the openmindedness precisely of this churchly conversation, to draw even the most worldly matters into its sphere of concern. And this is the wisdom and love whereby it brings all these things under the light of the divine Word and sanctifies them.

The particular character of pastoral conversation will be evidenced by *fearlessness* and *openmindedness:* The scarcely accessible concreteness of the stark facts of earthly, human existence is not evaded, but tackled and dealt with. Even difficult human problems are no longer difficult if those sharing in them as of one mind view them in the light of the Word of God. Admittedly, the reverse is also true; even the simplest matter becomes immediately complex and questionable, occasionally even prompts the eruption of far-reaching dissension and resistance if those sharing in it think they can do without this common view. As soon as they engage in conversation with one another, their inner estrangement will immediately be brought into the open even if their subject is perhaps very harmless in itself. And their conversation ends then in fierce anger and mutual rejection.

We cite, for example, discussions about some event on the political scene. What can make them so unbearable is not their subject, but the variety of opposing points of view which fully emerges. Or we recall certain theological conversations in which the same thing can occur in a demonic way. But if such a conversation happens to be conducted within the realm and reach of the Word of God; if both partners, in and with all their prejudice for their own opposing views, recognize and make operative in their conversation their being addressed by the Word of God, or simply their baptism in the Christian community—then a common bond would become visible. Their opposing views would perhaps not be fully reconciled, but at least relativized. To relativize, however, means to set in relationship. And the valid point of contact is the Word of God, which judges both and possesses alone the power graciously to include even the most opposed human standpoints. To judge, and at the same time graciously to include, is the function of the Word of God in general and therefore also of pastoral conversation. Law and gospel are here revealed in their indissoluble togetherness as the whole content of every Word of God.

As we emphasize judgment and inclusion of the Word of God as the distinctive form of the pastoral conversation, we recall the great *biblical* paradigms of such conversations. Let us consider from the Old Testament Nathan's conversation with David, II Samuel 11 (cf. the indispensable book by Wilhelm Vischer, *The Witness of the Old Testament to Christ*). David the adulterer is placed under the judgment of the Word of God by the words of Nathan. But is it only judgment? Is not this judgment at the same time the narrow gate to life which, in the conversation with the prophet, opens to the king who is entangled in the inextricable problem of his sin? Would his life not have been irremediably lost, meaningless, and dark if the pastoral conversation had not taken place and set before his eyes what he already basically knew, but only now got to know concretely—that everything depends on forgiveness?

Consider further from the New Testament Jesus' conversation at Jacob's well, John 4:1-42. The Samaritan woman, likewise confused and ravaged by adultery, becomes a messenger of the gospel to her whole city, thanks to her conversation with the Messiah of Israel. But now, we must be clear about the fact that it is fundamentally incorrect, or correct only in a quite figurative sense, to speak here of paradigms as if these biblical conversations were to be regarded as examples for some conversation which we were to conduct ourselves. Far from it! The Word of God itself accomplishes its own sovereign work here. David as the king of God's people pointing to the Messiah is summoned out of his sin and set under forgiveness to make it evident that such judgment and such mercy are everywhere and essentially the work of the divine Word. And with the Samaritan woman, the essential thing is not her fate and her restoration, but again the revelation of the incarnate Word of God, Jesus Christ, as the Saviour of the world, disclosing and forgiving sin.

The primary event in these biblical conversations is the Word of God itself, which, in and with these conversations, emerges and shows its might over all obscure human affairs. It is the *assumptio carnis* itself, the acceptance of human life by the Word as it occurred then and there in the biblical testimony, as it spread and will occur again and again. Because in the Christian community we are confronted with this biblical testimony, conversations proceeding from these biblical examples and leading to them may and will happen among us also. The same Word of God is here and now shown in like power to be mighty over our darkness and sin. There will now be in the church a pastoral conversation which, conducted in the sphere of the Word of God, effects this judgment and inclusion, thereby establishing the forgiveness of sins in the midst of the dark provinces of the world.

The personal reminiscence of such conversations as I myself witnessed them as pupil and student in the circle of the younger Christoph Blumhardt (cf. my paper *Christoph Blumhardt*, Munich, 1926) may serve here as an example in the proper sense. When in 1904 I first went to Bad Boll where he worked, I had great mental reservations. I had resolved to examine very closely and to ponder carefully what was going on before I joined in it; I was in no way inclined to submit without questioning to the spiritual authority of Blumhardt. What won me for Blumhardt and his cause almost at first hearing was not so much his meditations and his sermons as his *conversations*. I think first of the pastoral interview in the narrower sense which he readily granted; it radiated a remarkably liberating, judging, and comforting power. When I left his room after such a conversation, I knew again where I belonged spiritually, as if fetched home out of all lostness. Often it was as if in the conversation with him invisible bonds in which a man was chained were cut through as with a sharp sword.

I think also of the broader conversations which Blumhardt conducted with all his guests and in which the secret of his conversational practice can be most easily grasped. Sitting together after supper we used to get involved in one of those conversations which by no means were confined to spiritual matters, but were prompted by the events of the day, for example, by social and political questions. Or we discussed problems of research in nature and history or even problems as they arise out of the personal experience and suffering of men. Blumhardt took all the questioners and their questions utterly seriously. But he then led the conversation in quite unsought ways, masterfully and openmindedly, *sub specie aeternitatis,* and this always meant for him, *sub specie verbum divini.* Human life, the life of the time in which we lived, was unfolded, yet it basked in a light which had fallen on it through Blumhardt's direction of the conversation. This way of considering all questions, this discourse in which the presupposition was never abandoned that all things are really well taken care of under the gracious reign of Jesus Christ, had a liberating effect on the listeners. Much more forcefully than could have happened through preaching alone, these conversations opened our ears to the two Blumhardts' message of the coming of the Kingdom of God as it was primarily proclaimed in their sermons. At any rate, Blumhardt's conversational practice convinced me most strongly of the significance of true pastoral conversation as a means for confirming the good news within the Christian community. What Blumhardt's conversation demonstrated was nothing else than the vigor, the openmindedness, and the sympathy whereby he accepted the human situation, presented by the partner in conversation, and disentangled it in the light of his perception of Christ and his Word.

The famous table talks of Martin Luther may provide a further example of such conversation in the church and of the pastoral care practiced through it. To be sure, we can also discern in them the dangers and limitations inherent in a discourse that is all too loose and not always entirely responsible. Nevertheless, the overestimation of Luther's growing fame does not sufficiently account for the overly exact transcription of these table talks. They must have had a deeply significant, edifying, and helpful effect on his contemporaries. If it sometimes happened that Blumhardt referred his partner to the sermon he had just delivered or was about to deliver, it happened even more frequently that Luther's conversation turned into preaching. This is additional proof for the fact that this extraordinary means of conversation cannot be applied independently. However, it powerfully accompanies the ordinary means of proclamation, which are thereby underlined and clarified.

Finally, we recall that Holy Scripture itself practices conversing about this and that, about things of a thousand kinds. We think of the Wisdom literature, in particular of the Proverbs and Ecclesiastes. Of Solomon it is said, "He also uttered three thousand proverbs; and his songs were a thousand and five. He spoke of trees, from the cedar that is in Lebanon to the hyssop that grows out of the wall. . . . And men came from all peoples to hear the wisdom of Solomon" (I Kings 4:32-34). And we think of Matthew 12:42, where it is said that Solomon is far surpassed and his wisdom only fulfilled by the wisdom of Jesus himself. This biblical Wisdom literature broadens thought and speech so that they become spiritual in all their dimensions. That is, they become pastoral, worth hearing in the deepest sense, since everything that is said proceeds from the Word of God and leads to the Word of God, thereby ministering to the awakening and edification of the soul of man. (Cf. on the biblical Wisdom sayings again Wilhelm Vischer in his *The Witness of the Old Testament to Christ;* and also his *Der Prediger Salomo,* translated with comments and notes, and "Der Prediger Salomo im Spiegel de Montaignes," *Jahrbuch der Theologischen Schule Bethel,* 1933.)

Two specific remarks need to be made as to the practice of pastoral conversation. *First:* We have seen that it is mainly acceptance of the human life situation as it happens to be presented to us by the partner in conversation, yet acceptance which proceeds from the Word of God and leads to the Word of God. This signifies that such conversation involves a *risk* and a *danger.* Figuratively speaking, we may feel that in such conversations we are sent on a patrol far into unknown, even into enemy territory, far away from the familiar home base. Everything depends on our standing the test out there; we are not to abandon the task given us by the Word of God, nor to allow ourselves to be cut off and to get lost. We may, indeed we must, wholly engage in conversation; but we shall not forget for a moment that we are commissioned servants pledged to remain true at all costs to the cause of God. God must obtain his rightful place with this Word in all realms of human life. He must be their signpost, or else there is no help for them. This must be before our eyes in all such conversations. Then they may bear fruit.

We think, say, of a table conversation that arises between us and an expert on Goethe's thought and world view. Perhaps we are not even asked whether or not we want to carry on such a conversation. We are suddenly thrust upon an educated, cultivated, well-born man of the world who has drawn us into this conversation. We are members of the Christian community, perhaps even theologians; how can we lose sight of the fact that we have something to preserve and to protect in this conversation? How can it not be clear in our minds that we are now claimed and summoned by the Word of God that we can betray, but perhaps may also represent and communicate something? We have to be clear that this is a conversation, and not an opportunity to preach. For, who knows, the betrayal could also consist in our "casting pearls before swine." Let us understand the words rightly; this is a parable. It is not meant to say anything contemptible about our partners in conversation; it serves as a reminder that we shall not communicate God's Word all too directly in a situation in which it would only be misunderstood, exposed to a shrug or to derision. The wisdom of our conversation will consist in that neither the one nor the other happens, that we betray nothing, but also conceal nothing. We shall neither preach nor remain silent; we shall simply carry on a conversation and bear our witness in the form of this conversation.

We may also think of the pastoral conversation in the narrower sense. How often must we venture far into the territories of the world where we could perish, where we could lose and forget ourselves! This is shown, for example, in a difficult marriage conflict. The man or woman addressing us comes directly from the psychiatrist. The whole, perhaps very complicated, psychiatric view of the case is first laid before us. We hear how the patient suffered from insomnia; how headaches and other neurotic symptoms appeared. Quite correctly and appropriately, the psychiatrist discovered unsatisfied libido as the root of these disturbances. The patient is married to a man who no longer understands her and whom she no longer understands. Deep frustration prevails. And under the circumstances, the psychiatrist advises that something must be altered in this innermost conflict of marriage, or else the marriage, seen from the psychiatric standpoint, is bound to break up. When all this is laid before us, we must not refuse to accept and to take seriously this whole problem, even if it is at first purely biological and psychological. But at the same time we must be clear that we are only at the beginning of the conversation; it has properly not begun at all. We have received only the facts seen in a worldly perspective. We know from the Word of God that the human situation in all its often incomprehensible and fleeting dimensions must come into a new light. To this end, we have first accepted this situation. But now the danger exists that we stop at this worldly aspect and lose sight of our proper task. The danger exists that we, perhaps enticed by our own psychological knowledge (which is necessary for accepting such things), engage in a psychological and philosophical conversation; in turn, perhaps quite awkwardly, we play the psychiatrist and continue the conversation on the level on which it was first offered.

Our real task is very different. We should bring the whole problem into the light of the Word of God, should lay bare the roots of the problem as it is raised by the Word in this difficult human situation. Why did this patient come to us? Why did perhaps the psychiatrist himself send her to us? There are indeed psychiatrists who know about the necessary practice of pastoral care alongside psychiatric treatment, not as a substitute, but because of its inherent force and importance! Aware of our task, we must stay on our path and cultivate our own fields; we must remain true to the message to be communicated by the Word of God in this special situation on the basis of the special insights and words demanded by this situation and hour. The Word wants to become flesh, or rather the incarnate Word wants to speak here and now to men who, in the entanglements of their lives, no longer expect to hear additional psychological advice and human counsel, worthwhile as this may be; they long to receive light and truth from the Word of God in such a way that they understand it, that their sins are disclosed to them and their forgiveness made known. In the light of this forgiveness they can begin a new day of life. This end is to be served by our conversation with them.

Second: Because it concerns this concrete working out of the human situation in the light of the Word of God, the act of accepting the situation becomes of decisive importance in pastoral conversation along with the Word which is to be spoken to this situation. But what is the nature of this act of accepting? How is it accomplished? The answer will have to be: It consists of and is accomplished in *hearing.*

This hearing actually defines the form of pastoral conversation. It first implies *listening* in the usual sense of the word, a listening to the person who turns to us for counsel and help. But how can this listening take place without first and at the same time becoming the hearing of the Word of God, which alone teaches us to understand man and his concerns? We cannot separate one from the other. Such listening to man and attention to the Word of God is the true characteristic of the hearing which is at the heart of pastoral conversation. It will be difficult to give detailed and what might be called technical advice about this act of hearing. As over the whole pastoral conversation, the proviso of the Holy Spirit extends particularly over this central act of hearing. God himself must open our ears both for the voice of man and for the voice of his Word, and therefore any technique in this matter is ruled out.

If any instruction at all is valid in this area, it would be that one must be prepared in the pastoral conversation as nowhere else to be a listener—a patient, concentrated, attentive, alert, and understanding listener and nothing else. Everything depends on our ability to listen, our desire to listen, and our urge to listen, totally involved, for the sake of the Word that now intends to go forth to the man unfolding his situation to us. Without exaggeration, it can well happen that outwardly one scarcely does anything else for a whole hour or more than simply listen, listen again, and continue to listen. Of course, this hearing which is to serve the acceptance of the other's situation is interrupted by questions which we direct to him, but they in turn will be questions that serve this hearing. We want to see certain things more plainly; we want to help the other to open and to present himself more clearly. In this listening, we shall attend not only to what is said, but also to how it is said. For instance, the way a person describes a situation in which he is caught clearly indicates whether this situation is normal, or whether it perhaps shows demonic traits.

In the process of listening, our whole attention will be directed to seeing the situation presented to us in the light of the Word of God; listening to our neighbor, we shall at the same time listen to the Word of God and seek to perceive its answer to our neighbor's problem. In the process of hearing, we shall form an opinion of the other's situation and problem, an opinion which is already shaped by hearing the Word of God, for the communication of this Word is ultimately at stake. This hearing must never be arbitrary. No merely psychological interests, arising out of pleasure in the richness and diversity of human experience, must interfere. It must be controlled, obedient hearing, and this means a hearing which already includes the partner in the realm of the Word. It will be a hearing that comes very close to *prayer*, that indeed becomes prayer. We think of a passage like Philippians 1:3-6, where the Apostle says: Whenever I think of you, I offer to God my prayer and thanksgiving for you. It will be a very full listening, a listening that in itself, without a single word passing our lips, is an *act*, proceeding from the Word of God and leading to the Word of God. This act already accepts him to whom we listen, grasps and includes him.

We cannot simply acquire this ability to hear. It must be given to us. It springs from the love of Christ, for whom no man is too little and whose Word seeks the way to every man. Still, there is a way for him who wants to attain this art of hearing: more diligent *association with the Word of God*. The Word of God possesses the power to open our eyes to man. If we want to understand man, we must become students of Holy Scripture, since it unlocks the innermost secrets of man. There is further the possibility of being willing to get to know and to consider things human as comprehensively as it is in our power.

As pastoral counselor, one cannot know enough about man, cannot be educated enough in the broad field of human concerns. But even such consideration, such desire to understand, such education must occur under the guidance of Holy Scripture, or it is of no help to us. For example, our *reading* has to serve such understanding of human life. We cannot study enough the description of life as given by great portrayers of mankind like Balzac, Dostoievski, and Jeremias Gotthelf. Even a good film or modern play makes a significant contribution in penetrating the human situation today. Does not the question urgently arise in us as to what might be said from the Word of God to elucidate the problem of human life as shown in drama, novel, or film? Should we not encourage such practice in spiritual judgment concerning human life situations? Finally—and this is the last advice that can be given in this matter—we do well to study the writings and, as far as possible, the *conversations of true pastoral counselors*. Many a way will be shortened if we let our own deliberations and conversations be guided by their perceptions, their immediate understanding of the Word of God, as well as their understanding of things human.

A true storehouse of such knowledge is the writing of the elder Blumhardt and his biography by Friedrich Zündel. Among his writings there is a volume entitled *Glaubensfragen*, reproducing pastoral answers which he gave to questions directed to him. Other names would deserve mentioning; the number of such biographies and collections of letters which offer valuable insights into pastoral care is indeed not small. But the general reference to them must suffice here. And not to be omitted, in closing, is the reference to our *own experience*, in the sense that we shall be able to practice true pastoral care, true acceptance and understanding of the other person only to the extent that we have experienced such pastoral care in our own lives. Because we felt ourselves understood and were met by the Word of God in such conversation, we now know what being understood means to another. But this really belongs to the chapter on the personal qualifications of the pastoral counselor himself.

Pastoral conversation places under the judgment of the Word of God the whole field of human life with all the psychological, philosophical, sociological, and ethical explanations and critical interpretations pertaining to it. Therefore, a breach runs through the whole conversation which indicates that although human judgment and evaluation and the corresponding behavior are not invalidated here they are recognized as provisional. Since man does not submit to this relativization and its attendant restriction of his natural judgment, but resists it, pastoral conversation becomes a struggle for the priority of the judgment of God in man's salvation.

7 The Breach in the Pastoral Conversation

We have dealt with the *form* of the pastoral conversation and have now to deal with its *content*, which consists in the communication of the forgiveness of sins. But before doing so, we must consider a characteristic of pastoral conversation which still partially concerns its form and already has partially to do with its content. We are speaking of the *breach* which runs through pastoral conversation.

Pastoral conversation proceeds, so to speak, on two levels. Its subject matter is derived from the general human situation. The conversation takes it up just as it takes up any fact, problem, or concern and analyzes it with the help of psychological and philosophical insights. But at one point in the course of the conversation these preliminary viewpoints are definitively surpassed by the inclusive consideration of all things as imposed on us by the Word of God.

In pastoral conversation, the subject under discussion is removed from its own level and exposed to the light of the Word of God. The whole process of pastoral conversation is therefore characterized by a movement of accepting and taking away, of comprehending and apprehending and analyzing the human facts, and of simultaneously submitting these facts to a wholly new judgment surpassing any human judgment. This removal, transference, and submittal is not a second act that completes a first; it is rather the whole meaning of the conversation, its true intention and goal. The discourse from the beginning aims at this transition. In pastoral conversation, we accept the facts in the secure knowledge that the forgiveness of sins through the Word of God must become effective in these facts. We evaluate everything not from the vantage point of some human prejudice but of the divine prejudice in favor of all things human. To this prejudice we unabashedly cling; from it we live. This enforcement of the divine judgment which rules over everything human as a *pre*-judice in the true sense and the exposure of all human concerns to the new light of this judgment—this is meant when we speak of the breach in the pastoral conversation as a formal, and more than formal, characteristic of decisive importance. We have already encountered this breach in our previous considerations about the form of pastoral conversation. We now attempt to define it more clearly.

We must keep in mind that pastoral conversation is concerned with *a real understanding* of the human situation. We have characterized this understanding as listening, but a highly active listening, which proceeds from the Word of God and is willing to communicate its message and make relevant its truth in man's life. Understanding, so conceived, means coming toward our fellow man and standing by him, where he is; yet coming from a quite different perspective, we desire and are enabled to help him in his situation. We help our neighbor in pastoral conversation when we totally accept him in his own situation, but also totally expose him to the light and strength of that other perspective from which we come. Because this understanding determines the meaning and content of the whole conversation, we will have exhausted this understanding only at the end of the conversation, if ever. In other words, this dual movement of acceptance and exposure, and thus the breach which runs through this conversation, must permeate the whole conversation from beginning to end. Indeed, to the dual movement of acceptance and exposure there is a corresponding duality in the external function of the conversation—in the form of a *listening*, in the simple sense of the word, and an *exhorting*. Distinct as these two external functions may be, they nevertheless serve the *one* purpose of understanding and are therefore not to be separated. The one never exists without the other. The procedure is comparable to that of the physician: He has first to take the case history, to listen to the client, to examine him, and to make the diagnosis; only then does he prescribe a remedy. In order to prescribe the right remedy, he must constantly keep in mind the sick person's total situation. In the same manner, accepting the neighbor's situation and exposing him to the Word of God are inseparable acts.

Acceptance occurs in the form of investigating and comprehending the situation with the help of all available means. The means of *psychology* is the first of these. Hardly any pastoral conversation can be conducted without psychology being applied, perhaps in a very simple or even primitive manner, if we interpret psychology as the attempt to penetrate the psychic situation in which our neighbor finds himself. Perhaps—and this can occur every day with the pastor or teacher—a student calls attention to himself by some kind of rebellion, reserve, or impertinence and needs a talk in private. Such a talk is doomed to failure if we do not take cognizance of the inherent psychological implications.

As an example, I cite the conversations between the priest in Bernanos' important novel, *The Diary of a Country Priest*, and the aggressive, yet shy girl. In a very complicated way she responds erotically to him and he, without realizing it, reciprocates with a secret erotic response. The result is a very complicated relationship of alternate attraction and repulsion, which leads humanly and pastorally to an almost insoluble situation. How lost we are when, naive and psychologically ignorant, we get involved in a situation like this! How necessary it is to be thoroughly conversant with psychological matters! The pastoral counselor cannot be spared the study of psychology. He needs it even to measure up to conversation with a child, let alone to counsel about the marriage problems as they are increasingly brought before the pastor in town and country.

Nevertheless, important as psychology is for accepting and listening, it must under no circumstances have the last word. Exposure to the Word of God must immediately and from the beginning accompany acceptance. The observed facts must immediately be challenged by definite questions directed by the Word of God to everything human. Indeed, even the observation of the facts is undertaken for the sake of the message of the Word of God to be communicated to the person before us in distress. This is the breach which runs through the conversation. Again and again we must leave behind us everything merely factual and psychological, or rather, we must move it, as best we can, into the light which will fall upon it from the Word of God.

Furthermore, we believe that on occasion our knowledge of psychology needs to be supplemented by a knowledge of *law*. For example, there is scarcely a pastor who will not be called upon to explain legal implications to a woman in a case of marital conflict and even to refer her directly to a lawyer. He may, in fact, become involved in a trial quite unintentionally by his own (perhaps imprudent) utterances in counseling, or at least fall in danger of being called to testify in divorce proceedings of a third party. It can also happen that the question which is laid before him as a pastor is essentially a legal one. Once more, we must not refuse to take up such a question in a given case, since this is a part of accepting the specific human situation which we as pastors have been called to clarify. But again, we must beware of losing ourselves in the realm of jurisprudence and be cut off from our proper task. As does psychology, legal matters become the occasion for us to consider and communicate the very different message for which we exist as pastors. We recall the *word of Jesus* in the conflict over the inheritance (Luke 12:13-15): "Who made me a judge or divider over you?" The transition from the merely legal advice to the Word of God may be radical. Woe to the pastor who, perhaps seduced by a juridical inclination and gift of his own, sinks to the level of a mere legal counselor!

Further, no pastoral conversation lacks occasion and invitation to *moral judgments,* or at least to moral considerations and evaluations, which are suggested to us and even urged upon us. The knowledge of good and evil is indeed (according to Genesis 3:5) the first form in which human sinfulness is clothed. And pastoral care has to do with this sinfulness. Indeed, everything, positively every human concern brought to our attention, is robed in a definite moral value judgment. This is expressed with more or less reticence, with more or less emotional overtones; it manifests itself in the form of complaint and frustration about inflicted injustice; it increases to the point of accusation and condemnation of another person's or even one's own guilt; but it also comes to light in the never-failing self-exonerations and whitewashings of one's own self.

If he really accepts the situation laid out before him, the pastor cannot avoid thinking and joining in the conversation, perhaps very reluctantly, in terms of these moral categories. But here again the warning sounds: no side-tracking at this point! At no time in the conversation can we be content with morals. The field of moral value-judgment must be entered only to be left behind again immediately. For this field is full of its own peculiar pitfalls, and their detection is indispensable for him who has to proclaim the forgiveness of sins as his sole message. Does not the forgiveness of sins in itself mean that there is a Word which sovereignly stands over against all human evil and all human good, a Word which reduces the contradiction of good and evil, as seriously as it is to be taken in its place, to a relative contradiction, since the forgiving Word includes the evil and the good, the unrighteous and the righteous, and transfers them to a new ground beyond good and evil? Does not forgiveness in itself mean that our good cannot redeem us, but our evil not condemn us either? What saves us is the mercy of Christ alone, and what condemns us is our overlooking and forgetting this mercy. Therefore, more clearly than anywhere else, the breach must appear in regard to the moral value-judgments for the sake of the judgment of God, who in Jesus Christ "makes his sun rise on the evil and on the good, and sends rain on the just and on the unjust." The whole mystery of the new righteousness of the Kingdom of God is at stake here! (Cf. Matthew 5:43-48 and 6:33.)

The related province of the *social and cultural judgment* of human things borders closely on this field of moral value-judgments. When a man opens his mouth, he speaks not simply for himself; he speaks at the same time for the whole class to which he belongs. The judgments and opinions of his social class color quite unintentionally, yet quite self-evidently, the picture which he draws of his situation. He speaks as a farmer, or as a worker, or as a small businessman, or as a representative of the so-called upper class. He speaks, above all, as one who owns some kind of property, or as a "have-not," the poor man that he is. And this perspective will characteristically influence the question which the conversation poses. We must make his outlook our own if we are to accept his situation. Moreover, we ourselves belong to a specific class and have specific social and class prejudices which play upon our understanding of the other person.

How can we get to the point of actually caring for and counseling our neighbor if we do not succeed in shaking off these foggy social and class evaluations? However, how can we shake them off unless, from the beginning to the end of the conversation, we know our fellow man and ourselves to be accepted into the sphere of the Word of God? It is the only Word that speaks not for a specific rank or class, but rather reaches across all classes since it seeks and addresses man as "a living soul" before God. This is the one crucial act to be accomplished in pastoral counseling: that we step into the free air of the Word together with our partner in conversation and thus leave behind us all prejudices in which we are caught at first. The relentless danger at this point is very great that we avoid the breach in the conversation by accident or misplaced good will. Given the circumstances, we seemingly can meet each other quite amicably through pastoral conversation on the ground of a bourgeois or otherwise class-defined human "understanding," and entirely forget that far from leading to a genuine encounter such a meeting of minds actually avoids and betrays our real task.

This escape is so dangerous because it can take place under religious and even explicitly Christian disguise. Unfortunately, the church has been eminently successful in portraying even Jesus himself as a figure who was only too well adjusted and adapted to the bourgeois way of life to which the church has committed itself, especially in the last two centuries. The pastoral care corresponding to this picture of Jesus then serves to confirm and strengthen the spiritual and religious traditions and ideals of this bourgeois class, instead of leading to repentance and to the knowledge of the Word of the true and living Jesus Christ. For instance, look at the pastors in Theodor Fontane's novels and at the nurture of souls they practiced. These pastors reflect the generation of theologians and pastors of the era of Kaiser Wilhelm, and their form one recognizes all too clearly in the numerous biographies and autobiographies of theologians before and after the turn of the century. They are almost without exception very educated, not unappealing personalities; at baptisms, confirmations, and weddings of the families of the bourgeois social class to whom they minister, they know how to turn out well-pondered "Christian" discourses, both in the chancel and at the subsequent family celebrations; their speeches serve to deepen and adorn the festive occasion spiritually; but no breach appears, and they never lead beyond the bourgeois framework into the realm of the message of the gospel proper.

If we have hitherto advocated the necessity of a clear breach in the pastoral conversation, we must also now add a warning: Our well-founded fear and concern—that we lose sight of the Word of God and its communication when we agree to listen and talk to the person seeking counsel—must not lead to the consequence that for the sake of avoiding the breach we go so far as to avoid properly developing the conversation and do not sincerely listen to and encounter our neighbor. The breach and the decision to which we must lead our conversation must not become for us a doctrinaire intention which we, scarcely having begun the conversation, abruptly and suddenly communicate.

No genuine conversation develops in this way, but only a staged conversation in which we do not truly listen to our neighbor but ambush him immediately with the supposedly straightforward and radically delivered "message." He does not at all become our neighbor in whom we take an interest, into whose place we step, in order to come together with him under God's Word; he is for us the object of an "evangelizing" effort which can in no way be successful since it does not grow out of a sincere encounter. This must not happen. We must not engage in one of those spiritual manipulations of our partner in conversation, which a certain pastoral care, falsely claiming to be especially "evangelistic," praises as highest wisdom.

Renunciation of all merely human opinions and judgments and submission to the divine judgment alone must cut through the whole pastoral conversation, comparable to the mountain cleft that menacingly separates the precipice of the peak from the level glacier field. The conversation is actually characterized as pastoral by this breach. But as this "broken" conversation, it must really unfold. That is, the human apprehending and evaluating of the concrete situation, the visualizing and the understanding of it must fully take place. But it now happens that this process of unfolding, from the very outset and throughout, is cut through, disturbed, outdone, and broken by the fact that the sign of the Word of God was erected and remains erect over the whole human conversation.

The judgment already spoken over us by the Word of God hangs over us like a precipice which is both threatening and protecting. In its shadow our thinking, speaking, judging, and understanding continues, but our consideration and discussion of the situation only prepares the field for receiving the quite different judgment of God. The conversation is conducted so as to lead to the great pastoral turning point, the disturbing and breaking of the conversation by the hearing of the Word of God.

THE BREACH IN THE PASTORAL CONVERSATION

Once in a while this turning point is reached very abruptly. But as a rule it will happen in this way: A few words of human understanding are said to the other person, but in each of these words and considerations the breach becomes visible to which the quite different judgment of God reveals and leads.

For example, we begin to converse with a modern individualist, a stranger to the church. He bares his spirituality before us; he leaves no doubt about the fact that he is interested in religion. We even talk together about Jesus Christ. He finds high and deeply felt words for the Sermon on the Mount and the cross. The conversation at first moves entirely on the philosophical level. The breach in the conversation which must be present from the beginning appears, however, in the fact that in everything he says, our partner consciously keeps to this level of philosophical consideration and appreciation of Jesus Christ, whereas we just as consciously depart from it. We know that something quite different is to be said of Jesus Christ and would like to make this other dimension accessible and perceptible to our partner in conversation. This will be expressed in the critical reservation which we must make to everything our partner says. We shall make him understand, sentence by sentence, that in our innermost presuppositions we come from a different origin and move to a different destination. We still take him seriously, walk beside him, and attempt to accept everything he brings to us, but from the beginning we show him the new direction that is commanded us.

Probably the conversation will reach its climax when the problem of revelation and faith is set in opposition to mere reason and its corresponding world view. It can come to an open breach when our partner turns out to be closed to the knowledge that the truth of God can only be comprehended on the basis of the Word of God in faith. He will decry our understanding as dogmatically narrow and dependent, and contrast it to his own as the free, intrinsic, and vital understanding. And we shall have to show him in subsequent conversations how falsely he sees and judges in this respect in order to open his ears if possible to the hearing of the Word, to faith and prayer. But we cannot get this message across if we do not allow our conversation with him to be broadened and enriched through the discussion of his idealistic and religious opinions.

The same may be said of conversations about the practical problems of life. Take the failures in the course of human life as they are repeatedly presented to us in pastoral care. Here again, the conversation at first does not move within the realm of thought determined by the Word of God and faith, but on the level of psychological considerations and interpretations on human behavior. We shall not shun this behavioral analysis of the problem. For example, we establish in the scheme of Individual Psychology that each man is destined to follow his own, unique inner way, and that it is imperative for each individual to find this inner way. But now, this unique way has been missed. The result is the present concrete conflict. Our partner in conversation, perhaps by a false choice of his vocation or by undertaking a task to which he was not equal, has been hopelessly caught in an inner dead-end street. He is dangerously close to a breakdown. In such a situation, everything depends on the next step which must be in the right direction if still greater bewilderment is to be avoided.

The heart of the matter will be the definite advice to be given about what is to be done, so that the way into freedom opens up. This advice can again not be given on the basis of merely psychological fact-finding. Quite a different, new territory must be entered. Once more there must be a breach which leads the conversation over into this other, new territory. This breach will occur when we remember that in the eyes of faith the unique way which each individual has to go, and of which Individual Psychology has much to say according to its own insights, is the way on which we are placed before God and which is traced by his guidance of our lives. We must search for this guidance of our lives by God and the will of God for us contained therein, if we are to keep a sense of direction amid the perplexities of the course of our lives. This signifies, however, that the step to be taken and the solution to be reached cannot be found by purely psychological means. God's hand must extend over us and give us what we cannot take for ourselves.

The advice to be given, therefore, cannot consist in specific counsel about human behavior, but, if we succeed in rightly conducting the conversation, in guidance about *prayer*. For it is the secret of right prayer that we seek out in it God's will and open our hearts to it. And the secret of the right way is that we follow in obedience to this will. The step which then turns out to be necessary and correct will certainly be manifest on the level of psychological knowledge in the form of a definite decision which we have to carry out. An inner clarity will be given us enabling us now to do or not to do something we were formerly not in a position to do or to leave undone. Our prayer thus makes the psychological considerations and decisions on behavior not at all superfluous, but it forms and informs them. They are, as it were, the material that must be prepared, so that we may arrive at a definite and plain knowledge of the will and way of God. Again and again, we shall very seriously endeavor to evaluate as clearly as possible the inner and outer life situation; yet any such judgment gained on the ground of psychological insight of human behavior is to be understood in the strictest sense as only a preliminary judgment, through which and beyond which we must advance to the final judgment, that of God. This reservation toward all human considerations and interpretations will appear in the pastoral conversation only by our provisional acceptance of psychological knowledge and by the intensity of our looking beyond, from the start, toward that other and greater knowledge which must be revealed to man by the Word of God and by prayer. This again makes visible the breach which must run through such a conversation.

Finally, we consider once again that in all our conversations unequivocally *ethical* facts and problems appear. Questions are raised about ethical behavior, our own and that of others toward us, and our partner in conversation must justify or condemn it. What shall I do to be relieved from my own and other people's guilt? How can I be morally justified before myself and before others in a given situation? How can I straighten out my relationship with someone who does not understand me or whom I do not understand and yet with whom I must live? Such questions will repeatedly be asked in the pastoral conversation.

When these questions are serious and inescapable they can shake the whole structure of a person's life, can cause torments of conscience or outbursts of hatred and bitterness. To be sure, the contrary can also happen: One may attempt some kind of escape from the difficulty of the conflict, because the question cannot be squarely faced. In psychological terms, the whole conflict is *"repressed."* The inner perplexity and degradation is hidden under an external front of defensiveness which is unavoidably accompanied within by feelings of inadequacy and failure, perhaps even by despair of oneself and others. Frequently the result is severe neurotic disturbances. The pastoral conversation must under no circumstances follow this tendency of repression. It must accept and work out the ethical conflict, and not "counsel it away." It must lead to utter frankness. But it will only hold forth a solution when it does not seek this solution on the same ground on which the conflict arose and exists, namely, on the moral ground. The pastoral counselor, directed by the Word of God, must know and remember throughout the whole conversation that moral conflicts cannot be worked out morally.

It is simply not true that ethical matters are "self-explanatory." These matters cannot be understood and solved in themselves. The conflict which arises when one intends to do the good and does it not, but mysteriously does the evil which one does not intend to do, points far beyond itself to quite another dimension and depth. It needs for its solution a Word that comes from elsewhere and that itself is not simply a moral word. It may well happen that one can dispel guilt according to some law, either by taking it upon oneself or by blaming it on someone else. Yet a peculiar fogginess hangs over just such a situation which has been so interpreted on moral grounds. Or is a man helped when the place of guilt is established, perhaps even rightfully? Does not the whole situation in which we find ourselves after the establishment of guilt, whether it is imputed to us or to someone else, rightly wait for a light to fall on it and finally illumine it from elsewhere, from outside, from above, if we are not to be abandoned to ultimate distress and despair?

The redemptive Word for any merely moral interpretation and judgment, accusation and guilt, in a given situation is again inevitably the divine Word, the Word of the forgiveness of sins. Matthew 18:12-35, Romans 7 and 8, and Psalm 51 must be before our eyes whenever we face such a situation. And this will happen again and again, for not a single real pastoral conversation can be carried on without the moral question cropping up in some way. The fifth petition of the Lord's Prayer will be the final word which must come into our heart and upon our lips. Here again, the breach is visible that separates the pastoral conversation from the realm of mere psychology, of social ideology, and of moral judgment, although we cannot avoid entering and penetrating these realms in the course of the conversation and must do so in complete seriousness.

A final word must yet be said: The pastoral conversation, through the breach it advocates, challenges both the pastor and his partner to make a concrete *decision*. While all previous interpretations and judgments are granted only provisional value, they are found to conceal the real truth and must be left behind. But man clings to these provisional judgments. He defends them as long as he can. If we want to take them from him—and in the pastoral conversation we must take them from him—he fights for them. It appears to him that the whole edifice of his life stands or falls with these psychological or moral or philosophical interpretations. And indeed, it not only appears so; it actually is so!

The forgiveness of sins shakes the whole ideological edifice of life that man constructs for himself so long as he has not yet heard the Word of God. And therefore, he fights it as one fights an enemy who threatens one's life. The reference to God's guidance of our lives, the reference to the judgment and the grace of Jesus Christ, the reference to prayer and faith, is for natural man and his way of thinking such an unprecedented demand that if it is actually set before him—and this happens in true pastoral care—it seems to him like a leap into the dark. It is a leap into the dark, in the case of a guilt that burdens our life, to be willing to give up all our own attempts at interpretation and justification, but also to lay aside all unfruitful self-accusations and all despair and to surrender entirely to the forgiveness of sins. It is a leap into the dark, in the face of an obscure and insoluble riddle of life, to abandon all evasions and attempts to help oneself and instead to trust the guidance of God and live from it, as we gradually come under his power and do his will. It is a leap into the dark for someone wrestling with philosophical problems to renounce his own perhaps well-developed and profound reasoning and simply to believe and pray; he is of course not forbidden to think, but accepts faith and prayer as the beginning and end of all thought. It is hardest of all, however, in the actual possession of faith and piety and a secure, perhaps even seriously Christian, world view and way of life, to admit that even these in no way assure the firm foundation and ground on which we can rest our own life. Even he who holds such positive values is declared by the judgment of God to be a sinner and mortal, in need of forgiveness which can only be found in the cross and in the resurrection of Jesus Christ from the dead.

The pastoral conversation that proceeds on the basis of such presuppositions will not be easy; it will meet the strongest opposition. Holy Scripture speaks plainly of this. It calls this opposition *struggle against grace;* it sees man, without exception, in the grip of this conflict and recognizes in this the prototype of sin. We recall what we have said about man's wholeness before God. The conversation that proceeds from and leads to the forgiveness of sins and thus understands the whole man in the light of such recognition will have to reckon with this struggle in a very real way. It will burst open in the course of the conversation itself and must be settled and brought to an end. Something happens in such a conversation; a real breach occurs; it is no purely intellectual conversation resulting in merely psychological, philosophical, or moral interpretation, as surely as this will also happen. It is a truly *existential conversation;* if this term from the spiritual psychology of Kierkegaard is at all appropriate, it is appropriate here. Things do not go on in the same old way; a transition is accomplished in man's life from an old pattern to a new one. Once again, the old and past is unforgiven sin but forgiven sin is the new; unsanctified life is the past, life passed over into God's hand, and this means sanctified, in the present. This is what the breach in the conversation means, a mighty act, a revolution, relief, and deliverance.

We mentioned Søren Kierkegaard. We may say that this truly Christian thinker was exclusively concerned with this existential character of Christian speaking. Throughout his work, he battled against the emptied Christian word and for the Christian Word refilled with its true content. According to Kierkegaard, it is emptied because it has become the mere aesthetic word of a spectator. It is mere meditation, meditation on the Cross, meditation on the Resurrection, but no longer testimony in the spirit of the God of the Cross and the Resurrection. Were it this testimony, the word would initiate anew the breach in the life of him who hears and expresses it. This breach as the sign whereby the reality of Christian speaking can be recognized was in the center of Kierkegaard's thinking. Perhaps it carried so much weight for him that he tended to forget the signal character of even this breach and let the sign become the fact itself. The fact is the Word of God. We cannot challenge men to accomplish the breach as such; we can only call them back to the Word of God and return there ourselves; then this breach will appear again as a sign in our lives. In his way, Kierkegaard absolutized the concern for this breach, and thus for sanctification, as Pietism had done before. But he saw before him a church which certainly needed to hear the urgent question about the sign of the breach to which he was totally committed. Everyone who has to practice pastoral care should therefore let the pastoral care of Kierkegaard become operative in his own life before he goes out and begins to speak to others. (Cf. concerning Kierkegaard the worthwhile study by Heinrich Barth: "Kierkegaard der Denker" in *Zwischen den Zeiten*, Vol. 4, 1926, pp. 194ff.)

Since pastoral conversation deals with this breach and conflict, the pastor will be on a lonely outpost. Like "the man from Judah" in I Kings 13, he must repeatedly lay his hand to the altar on which sacrifice is offered to false gods. Like this man he must not be afraid to step into the field of the various and rich interpretations, considerations, and judgments whereby man provisionally seeks to help himself; he must be the stony guest who upsets this whole field with a strange new message. To be sure, he must accept all these interpretations, considerations, and judgments, but as he accepts them, he must question them and disturb the peace of mind they seem to give. But he will also experience the magnitude of the deliverance when man as a "poor in spirit" submits to this disturbance and listens to the proclamation of the new righteousness of the Kingdom of heaven.

This is like a reflection of the great disturbance challenging and questioning the whole of human life in its roots as it is manifest in the prophetic and apostolic preaching. But this is also the light of the great promise of which this disturbance is but the shadow. The breach in the pastoral conversation thus becomes the door that leads to a new life.

Like the proclamation of the church generally, pastoral conversation has as its only content the communication of the forgiveness of sins in Jesus Christ. For it is the conversation in which man in his totality is addressed with full authority as a sinner under grace. What makes this conversation pastoral is that it proceeds on this presupposition. Its power of consolation depends entirely on the unconditional communication of forgiveness, which means that it is free of all legalism and thus obedient to the Word of God.

8 The Content of Pastoral Conversation

Pastoral care is a broadening and extension, by means of conversation, of the church's proclamation through Word and sacrament. This conversation is fundamentally concerned with the same content as contained in Word and sacrament. That is to say, the pastoral conversation is also concerned with the *forgiveness of sins*. For this is indeed the sole and sovereign content of sermon, baptism, and holy communion, the content of that gracious judgment which God himself in Jesus Christ has passed on human life in its totality and charged his prophets and apostles to proclaim. There was and there is, therefore, no other content of pastoral speaking within the church than forgiveness of sins.

The forgiveness of sins as *content and goal of all pastoral care* is generally acknowledged within the Protestant churches. This was already given with the fact that Protestant pastoral care must be distinguished from Catholic pastoral direction. The demarkation can only be achieved through reflection on the Reformers' doctrine of justification, which is based on the forgiveness of sins in Jesus Christ alone.

This doctrine found its classical expression in the first manual on pastoral care within the framework of the churches of the

Reformation, Martin Bucer's *Von der wahren Seelsorge und dem rechten Hirtendienst,* published in 1538. "True" pastoral care, according to Bucer, centers in Jesus Christ who is present and effective as the proper Shepherd and Counselor of the souls in his fold: "as a King in his kingdom, a Master with his disciples, a true Shepherd with his flock, a Bridegroom with his bride, a Physician to the sick, a Chastiser to those who need chastisement." This "Lord Jesus in his blessed pastures" is to be served by pastoral care, "so that all the chosen ones of God turn away from all sin toward all righteousness through true faith in him."

In contrast to this "true" pastoral care, the false pastoral direction of the Catholic Church replaces the one true Shepherd by human substitutes and binds the souls to these. Zwingli's *Der Hirt* should also be mentioned here. It calls no less urgently than Bucer's book for the true pastoral guidance of the congregation through the Word of Christ, and for the repudiation of the corrupted pastoral direction of the Roman Church. Lastly, reference is made to the *Berner Synodus* of 1532, written by Bucer's friend Capito. It is a confession characterized by the concentration on the message of Christ as the one true Shepherd and by the truly pastoral way in which it usefully interprets this message for the leading and feeding of the congregation.

In later times, this centrality of the forgiveness of sins in Jesus Christ as content and focus of all pastoral care is lost. To be sure, it is still recognized that this, and this alone, should be the proper concern of all true pastoral care, but other goals and motives interfere and obscure this center. According to the more anthropological than christological orientation of Schleiermacher and his followers, the determinative elements in pastoral care are first the stilling of the disquieted religious feeling in man, and second the concern for the individuation of the Christian within the church (cf. his *Praktische Theologie* as well as the *Kurze Darstellung des theologischen Studiums,* where he defends the thesis that pastoral care has mainly to stimulate the lagging, sections 290, 292).

With the Lutherans Von Zezschwitz and Theodosius Harnack,

THE CONTENT OF PASTORAL CONVERSATION

a specific definition of the purpose of pastoral care in terms of content is missing because their doctrine of pastoral care is built into the system of their practical theology, which has as its goal the preservation of the Christian community in the Word and sacrament of the church. Within this framework, pastoral care has of course a definite function, but one which needs no new definition contentwise. This function points to a rather defensive and protective activity, corresponding to the apologetic character of the theology of this whole period of the second half of the 19th century. The emphasis falls on protecting the purity of cult and sermon; pastoral care contributes to "the preservation and nurture of the existing life of the Christian and of the church, or the restoration of it when it is vanishing" (Theodosius Harnack in *Praktische Theologie*, II, p. 291). Nowhere is there any consideration of the significance and nature of the pastoral conversation and its content. But at least the close relationship of pastoral care to the administration of the Lord's Supper and the confession preceding it, assures the direction of pastoral care toward the forgiveness of sins. But the nearer we get to the present, the more indefinite, uncertain, and thin become the definitions of the content and purpose of pastoral care.

As its relationship to the sacraments and the preaching of the church becomes ever less visible, the presentation of pastoral care increasingly resembles a casuistry of corporate and individual pastoral care, although very broadly and in its detail very carefully and interestingly conceived. This is true for H. A. Köstlin in his *Lehre von der Seelsorge;* for Martin Schian in his *Lehrbuch der Praktischen Theologie;* for Leonhard Fendt in his *Grundriss der Praktischen Theologie.* To be sure, we find in Fendt the recognition that pastoral care must deal with the redemptive work of Jesus Christ as it is operative in the community. But in practice, this purpose disappears behind far-fetched statements about "knowing the Christian community." The weight does not lie on the knowledge of grace, sin, and repentance as already present in the community or to be planted there through pastoral care, but on folklore, on a "new experience of the people," on "love for the German nation." (As especially useful for the theologian are recommended—hear this!—the works of Alfred Rosenberg and Himmler and also the research on human races and types in *Lehre von der Praktischen Menschenkenntnis*, pp. 305ff., published by the psychological laboratory of the Reichskriegsministerium!!)

In contrast to the above, J. D. Benoît in his *Direction Spirituelle et Protestantisme*, a lengthy and critical appraisal of the Reformers on one side and of the Catholic doctrine of pastoral direction on the other, unearths much that is essential. But unfortunately, the christological and soteriological center is also lacking in his work; he rejects it bluntly and instead elaborates a doctrine of pastoral guidance on the basis of the moral, intellectual, and religious problems of the man of today. Hans Asmussen's handbook, *Die Seelsorge* offers a welcome change among these presentations. Here the connection with the Reformers' doctrine of justification is fully re-established. Asmussen starts from the affirmation, "Pastoral care always has to do with the pardoning of the sinner," and he develops it further: "Therefore, pastoral care deals with the wrath of God and its application. The result is a battle with God and with himself, in which the sinner attempts to bring himself or God around. It is essentially concerned with grace and pardon, but brings conversion with it" (pp. 26-42). As intimated earlier, we do not agree with Asmussen's definition of the relationship between gospel and law and see the problem of his book at that point. But in distinction to Fendt, pastoral care is here again set wholly on a clear basis and ground. A similar appraisal can be made of the more aphoristic book by Walter Hoch, *Evangelische Seelsorge,* dealing in the chapter "Das Ziel der Seelsorge" (The Goal of Pastoral Care) with edification, comfort, regeneration, justification, redemption, and sanctification.

If we postulate the forgiveness of sins as the content of pastoral care, we must indeed see this forgiveness in the powerful and complete way it was seen and understood in the 16th century. In Luther's Shorter Catechism, in the interpretation of the second article, the work of Christ is described, as is well known, with the words: "I believe that Jesus Christ, very God, born of the Father in eternity, and also very man, born of the Virgin Mary, is my Lord, who has redeemed me, a lost and damned man, and has won and delivered me from all sins, from death, and from the power of the devil." Here man in his totality is seen as lost and condemned on account of his sin. He no longer belongs to the Father in heaven, but to death and the devil. In fact, it is God himself who has delivered him to these powers. Indeed, "to damn" means that God as the Judge has sentenced him and has called the executioner to carry out the sentence. To this man thus condemned and therefore lost, it is affirmed, "redeemed, delivered, won!" How is this possible? Answer: Christ has taken the place of this man, has wrenched him from the province of sin and death, and put him into his own Kingdom "so that I may be His own." Now man can and must no longer regard himself as subject to the alien power of death and the devil; he now knows about the establishment of the reign of Christ over his life. The whole work of redemption is thereby described as the work of the *forgiveness of sins*. We read the same in the explanation of baptism: "What does baptism give us and of what benefit is it? It effects the remission of sins, frees us from death and the devil." And again in the interpretation of the communion: "That is to say, that in the Sacrament forgiveness of sins, life, and salvation are bestowed on us by these words."

Calvin describes redemption in the same way in the Geneva Catechism. He deals in the interpretation of the third article with the fact that in the church we partake of the deliverance and redemption wrought by Jesus Christ. This deliverance and redemption consists in the purification of our conscience through the blood of Christ. Because we are sprinkled with and washed by this blood in the power of the Holy Spirit, a real change takes place in our lives. Our hearts are renewed and transformed; a knowledge and feeling (*cognoscere et sentire*) of the power and benefits of Christ are born in us. In short, a new man is created —through what? Through the blood, and this again means through the *forgiveness,* of Jesus Christ. This is reiterated in the interpretation of the sentence: "I believe in the forgiveness of sins." The forgiveness of sins is there unmistakably presented as the great promise of salvation in store for believers within the church. To live in the church means precisely to participate in the forgiveness of sins. The forgiveness of sins thus becomes the one and only content of the Christian faith as it lives in the church.

Following Luther and Calvin, we find the same teaching in the Heidelberg Catechism. In the first question, the power of comfort in life and death is found in the fact that I am no longer my own, but belong to the faithful Saviour Jesus Christ, "who with His precious blood has fully satisfied for all my sins, and redeemed me from all the power of the Devil." Question 56 states with particular force: "*What dost thou believe concerning the* FORGIVENESS OF SINS? That God, for the sake of Christ's satisfaction, will no more remember my sins, neither the sinful nature with which I have to struggle all my life long; but graciously imparts to me the righteousness of Christ, that I may nevermore come into condemnation." That is to say, God should properly regard my whole life as a perverse and lost life. But he regards it quite differently. He regards me as one who has been absolved before his tribunal. However, this is not my work and achievement, but the work and achievement of Christ. And this means again that the whole content of the faith is gathered up in the forgiveness of sins through the blood of Christ.

That this is its meaning is also shown by the fact that both Luther and Calvin retained the confession of sins in their pastoral care. Although they rejected, as we have seen, the confession as a sacrament, the voluntary, private, and corporate confession of guilt remained for them the most important piece of pastoral care that could not be abandoned and was inseparable from the partaking of the Lord's Supper. The communion is indeed concerned with the forgiveness of sins, and how can our sins be forgiven without recognition and confession of guilt? Therefore, the Apology of the Augsburg Confession says in Article XI: "*Nam et nos confessionem retinemus praecipue propter absolutionem*" ("for we also retain confession chiefly for the sake of absolution"). And Calvin requires the confession of sins in prayer as an essential part of the Sunday worship of God. He remarks that such a confession is something like a key that opens the door to true prayer, corporate as well as personal (Institutes III, 4).

Bucer had already recommended the personal and private confession of sins in his *Kurtze Schriftliche Erklärung*, the catechism which was used in Strassburg. This once again testifies to the central position which the forgiveness of sins occupied in the proclamation and pastoral care of the Reformers. Measured against their teaching, it is absurd to postulate beside and beyond the forgiveness of sins another content of the faith, such as sanctification or the new life, as happened in Pietism, as if sanctification and the new life were something additional to forgiveness and not already given in and with forgiveness. It is equally absurd to see in the centering of the faith on the forgiveness of sins a narrowing down that does not respect the breadth and richness of the Christian life of faith, as it happened in Liberalism as if the forgiveness of sins did not concern the whole of life, as if there could be something that would be wider, freer, more alive than the life of the Christian in the forgiveness of sins. Only because they lacked the perceptive power of the Reformers were the spokesmen of Pietism and even more of Liberalism compelled to set up new purposes for preaching and pastoral care which were to reach beyond the forgiveness of sins, yet were only seemingly more serious and more substantial.

In order to understand rightly the forgiveness of sins in its significance for pastoral care, we begin again from the biblical view of the wholeness of man. Our whole life in all its parts, in body and soul, inside and outside, is in the grip of sin and death. And our whole life is rescued from these powers by Jesus Christ. This rescue was accomplished on the cross at Golgotha; it is the work of Christ as described in the second article of the Apostles' Creed and set before our eyes as an objective, true fact. This fact becomes our reality through our subjective participation in faith.

Such faith, however, is engendered "neither in our own reason nor strength" (Luther), but it is the work of the Holy Spirit, as described in the third article, and as explained by Luther and Calvin in their catechetical interpretations of the third article. It is especially Calvin who lays strongest emphasis on this subjective appropriation, perception, and experience of the objective fact by man. He speaks of a *"conceptio in mente,"* a mental conception of forgiveness which shall take place in us through the illumination of the Holy Spirit.

Contentwise, the actual forgiveness of sins signifies the coming into force of the *peace treaty* which God has concluded in Christ with us men. *Sin* is described in the entire Holy Scripture as a conflict which man wages with God, in which God, therefore, becomes man's enemy; *forgiveness,* as peace whereby God terminates this conflict. It is therefore no accident, but it is the core of the biblical message itself when in the pastoral care of the church the crucial matter to be solved in a person's life appears in the form of the question: Are you at peace with God? But this question is rightly asked and rightly heard only when it coincides with the question: Do you know that all your sins are forgiven you in Jesus Christ? So asked and so heard, it is indeed *the* question with which pastoral care is concerned.

Sin is already seen as conflict and dissension in the decisive passage, Genesis 3:1ff.; the passages in Holy Scripture are plentiful where forgiveness is described as the end of this conflict, as the peace sent from God. For examples of the numerous passages in the Psalms and in the Prophets, see Psalms 4:9; 37:11; 46:9ff.; 119:165; Isaiah 9:6; 32:17; 52:7; 53:5; 54:10; 66:12; Jeremiah 29:11. In the New Testament, Jesus Christ is plainly proclaimed and believed to be the author of peace, Luke 1:79; 2:14; 19:42; 24:36; John 14:27; 16:33. In the proclamation of Paul the word "peace" is the word that comprises the whole promise of salvation; cf. the formula of the Pauline greeting and passages like Romans 5:1; 8:6; 14:17; Ephesians 2:14.

Everything depends now on the appropriation of this forgiveness offered to us and the peace with God it guarantees as a peace which encompasses our whole life. Peace is not only an inward reality; as surely as it is this too, it is also the spiritual realm surrounding the whole man, and in which the whole man is well taken care of and may breathe and live. This rules out the idea that the peace of God in the forgiveness of sins is exclusively a matter of the soul. We are not divided; we are again "in body and soul" entangled in sin before God, and the peace of God in the forgiveness of sins wants to reign undivided over our whole life in body and soul. The tragedy of so many pietistic penitential battles lies in man's attempt inwardly to grasp the peace of God by his striving for piety and sanctification. And he believes he has already grasped it in his mind. But in the next moment the old Adam breaks forth unvanquished from the depths of his sensuality. Where now is his peace of mind? The whole person must have peace. But does this exist, this peace for the whole person, peace according to the flesh and to the spirit, according to body and soul? What is offered to us in the forgiveness of sins is this total peace, not only a peace of mind, but actual peace. That is, it is not a peace which is ours only so long as we overlook or forget the lower, the vulgar, and the animal instincts in us alongside the spiritual and good aspirations. It is a peace for man as he is, marked by the word "sin," the words "lost and condemned." But wherein consists this peace? It consists in the fact that God addresses us just as we are, and this means as sinners. He addresses *you*, your total being, and this means not only you in your mental capacity, but you as lapsed into sin in body and soul and spirit. Addressed by God, we belong no longer to ourselves and to the sin reigning over us, but are people under his Word, and this means under his command and promise. To this person addressed in his totality by God we have already previously ascribed the word "soul." This "soul," addressed by God and so declared his property, has peace. And pastoral care is concerned with the distribution of the treasure of this peace given through the Word of God. Pastoral care means and primarily functions as *care about such peace*. Its practice consists in man's being regarded and addressed in the pastoral conversation as one on whom God in Jesus Christ has laid his mighty and merciful hand.

To view and address man as God's property is essentially different from sizing him up in terms of psychology or of human reason and experience. It is a pure act of *faith;* it is positively *the* act of faith. To believe means to see ourselves—we refer to the great negation in the first question of the Heidelberg Catechism —*not* as our own, but as Jesus Christ's, as lying completely in his hand. Only now do we rightly understand the importance of asserting that pastoral care is concerned with a conversation proceeding from the Word of God and leading to the Word of God, and this always means proceeding from Jesus Christ and leading to Jesus Christ. This is significant because the Word of God is always concerned with the forgiveness of sins and because forgiveness of sins consists in a new way of viewing man that is possible only on the basis of the Word of God. And only now do we rightly understand why that *breach* in the pastoral conversation occurs. This breach is nothing but the visible sign that the forgiveness of sins and its appropriation are fundamentally distinct from any other human understanding.

Forgiveness of sins and belief in it are in themselves something so very different from all other human perception and understanding of life that, where they are demonstrated, a breach occurs; the rest of this knowledge is left behind and surpassed by the truth of the Word of God sovereignly imposing itself. And we understand, finally, what must be meant by the designation of the pastoral conversation as a conversation *within the church*, carried out within the framework of the Christian community. Church, Christian community, denotes that new, other province and realm, that province and realm of peace in which man, however things stand for him elsewhere, is regarded as a pardoned sinner. Both words, "pardoned" and "sinner," are important. Man is a *sinner*. Much may be said to explain and excuse the difficult situation of the man before us—for example, a deprived youth, faulty education or lack of education altogether, severe hereditary defects; yet within the church, the key to the understanding of the whole situation, despite the knowledge about the above factors, is not sought primarily in the circumstances, but deep within the human soul where even this man is exposed as a sinner separated from God and therefore in need of his forgiveness. Certainly his life is burdened at all the indicated points; he is insecure, perhaps even psychopathic; nevertheless, the real threat to his life comes not from these symptoms; the disintegration of his life lies in the fact that his life, like all life, is not in order before God. But now this man is at the same time *pardoned*. He lives under the promise of forgiveness, as surely as Jesus Christ has died and risen again also for him. "The works of God should be made manifest in him" (John 9:3). His whole life waits for this revelation, and so far as his life is lived in the light of this expectation he is already accepted and redeemed, he is already saved.

No situation exists, however difficult, into which God cannot open a door and find a way. This is what forgiveness means. It is the work of God (John 9:3) by virtue of which sin, in all its seriousness and with all its consequences, is canceled out in Jesus Christ; it is a settled matter, neither to be rehashed nor to be feared again. Sin is no longer to be taken seriously now, but only the work of God; it means that man, now really accepted by God and no longer left to himself, may and must go on living; it means that with the forgiveness of sins a new day has dawned for him. He is placed under the governance and guidance of God. Jesus Christ has taken over his life; he has made it his own life so completely that he now bears all responsibility for it. Such is Jesus Christ's acceptance of the responsibility for my truly sinful life that the Catechism can say: "He preserves me so that without the will of my Father in heaven not a hair of my head can fall; yes, everything must also serve me to my salvation." Thus we speak, and not only speak, but think and live within the Christian community by the forgiveness of sins.

If this is the implication of the forgiveness of sins, then we must affirm that every attempt to straighten out our human situation, even at a single little point, must miscarry insofar as it undertakes to bypass the knowledge of our sin and its forgiveness. There is no available means to help oneself or others *without* the forgiveness of sins, not even the profoundest psychological or moral advice. It is not lack of compassion or understanding when in the pastoral conversation we point out sin, expose it, and challenge him to come to terms with it. Instead, this is true compassion. For how shall he otherwise obtain forgiveness? In order to reorient his life by the forgiveness of sins, we must talk seriously of his sin; merely psychological, moral, or any other deliberations will not do. To be sure, the moral or psychological or even pathological facts of the case shall in no way be invalidated or trifled with. On the contrary, they are to be accepted and acknowledged in their place. The pastoral counselor will never be able to know enough about them. But such an understanding of the situation serves only to empower him rightly to communicate the quite different Word of the forgiveness of sins.

The recognition of sin and grace occurs directly out of the background of the thoroughly established psychological and ethical facts of the case; and the more soberly and plainly this whole background is seen, the more really this recognition occurs. It must remain clear that this recognition comes from faith and thus from a realm sovereignly superior to all other realms. This makes pastoral speech the special speech it is: that it proceeds from the knowledge of this other realm. Indeed, we must even say: Pastoral care happens exclusively where this other realm is known, where it is created ever anew, comes into force, and gains ground. No psychological or other form of worldly conversation from man to man, however thoughtful and well-meant, can ultimately help—or helps only in a quite preliminary way—if it is not focused on the recognition of forgiveness. Wherever man actually finds help, it happens because and only because he benefited from such pastoral conversation, even if perhaps in a very hidden way.

This can certainly be verified by numerous examples from one's own experience or from the testimonies of others, as they abound in biographies. For a more recent example consult the confession of Alfred Birsthaler, entitled *Mea Culpa* (Verlag Francke, Bern). It is an almost worldly and objective account of a man's road from deep depravity to the heights of Christian recognition of sin and grace. The perception of his own guilt already expressed in the title of the book leads in his life through the encounter with the Bible to conversion and regeneration. Detours are inevitable; the author spends long years in jail and there engages in much unnecessary psychological and philosophical thinking, but he also reads the New Testament with complete devotion and finds the way to the good news and to faith.

No detailed rules may be established for the concrete practice of pastoral conversation since the course of the conversation depends on the human predicament which differs in each case. One thing, however, can be said: We must have a clear vision of the great, divine proviso which unconditionally covers the whole encounter in conversation. It implies that our sins will be forgiven us—more still, that they *are* forgiven us—and that our only concern must be with perceiving and appropriating this fact. As the descent of the riverbed determines the whole course of the river, so this presupposition permeates the whole pastoral conversation from beginning to end and gives power, color, and fullness to everything that is said. Whether a factual situation is to be clarified or a definite decision to be made, whether we admonish or comfort, encourage or seriously reprimand—our whole talk should flow from the heights of forgiveness; its whole content should explicitly or implicitly be the proclamation of the mercy of God in Jesus Christ.

This downward movement is evident in all the calls that go out to men in their concrete situations in the Holy Scripture of both Testaments. What else characterizes them as biblical if not that there are words delivered by prophets or apostles on behalf of God? As these words of God they are without exception words of grace addressed to sinners. There is no other Word of God. That God speaks to us is in itself, regardless of the content, the act of his grace, the event of his condescension, the manifestation of his care for us. This is incomparably expressed for the Old

Testament witness in the 176 verses of the 119th Psalm. For the New Testament witness, no particular proof is needed in this matter. All its admonitions, reprimands, and even threats are filled to the brim with mercy. We point in particular to the Pauline counsels. What is their distinctive mark? What sets them apart, say, from the contemporary discourses of the Stoics? As to its form, an admonition of the Apostle Paul may resemble a rational-moral admonition of a Stoic as one egg resembles another. Yet it is quite unmistakable: When the Apostle admonishes, he intends only one thing—to comfort through admonition, and only to comfort. Even when he chastises and judges, he keeps in mind that God's light has risen in the forgiveness of sins; as he speaks, he translates this thought into reality. He sees the people to whom he speaks, be it very earnestly and even harshly, from the outset as those who have long ago been met and seized by this light and whose eyes must now be opened to it. This is what is meant when he issues his admonitions in conformity with the call of Jesus to repentance "by the mercies of God" (Romans 12:1). He knows and reckons with the fact that the people to whom he speaks are in many respects still entirely caught in the various thought- and life-patterns of this world; however, he sees the cross of Christ, erected between himself and them, and now he speaks to them from that perspective; dark as the shadows of sin and death may extend over their lives, he calls out to them through the cross of Christ. He does not want to know anything else of them except that they do not belong to sin and death, but to God. Because he starts with this presupposition, he exhorts them severely and earnestly no longer to place themselves on a par with the world. In the form of such admonition, he assures them of the forgiveness of thir sins. Calling them out of the world that still surrounds them on all sides, he calls them into the province of grace which has already enclosed them and their sin. (Cf. the discussion in Karl Barth's *The Basis of Ethics* on the "Content, Form, and Goodness of the Divine Command," *Church Dogmatics* II, 2, 37.)

It makes an immense difference whether we encounter our

The Content of Pastoral Conversation

partner in the conversation on the basis of some kind of human assumption, or whether we encounter him on the basis of this divine assumption of forgiveness. If we meet him on purely human grounds, we judge him according to some perhaps psychological, perhaps moral, perhaps sociological presupposition which is thoroughly correct under the circumstances. The man with whom we begin to talk actually is the fickle babbler, the moral weakling, the gloomy introvert, the unstable and indecisive neurotic we have discovered him to be. But if we address him in these terms, we shall be left with only a very narrow margin for our conversation with him. We then can only, so to speak, lock up ourselves with him in the prison of his introversion, his neurotic weakness and instability, and wait and see what kind of advice to give him, in order to help him cut down the most extreme excrescences of his bondage and instability. However, what we properly owe him then remains unexpressed. But if we encounter him on the ground of the divine assumption, we shall still be confronted with the serious reality of his instability, his moral irresolution, and his bondage, but at the same time we shall see the whole man with all his problems set within the light of a great hope. We may then comfort him in one way or another with this hope; we may talk with him on the basis of it. We shall certainly discuss his problems with him very earnestly and exhaustively, yet in doing so we shall never forget that Jesus Christ died and rose also for this man. Also for him, a new beginning is made and given in the forgiveness of sins, whoever he may be. Our conversation will take a joyful turn which is perhaps very hidden, but yet very real; that "forbearance" will shine through which we are to make known unconditionally to all men, as the Apostle says (Philippians 4:5).

We must keep this joy, friendliness, confidence, and reassurance, even if our partner in conversation wants to know little or nothing of it, as far out as he is on the edge of despair and self-resignation. This joy and confidence is not some sort of contrived confidence in life, an artificial optimism, a thing compelled by strenuous effort, since we promised ourselves a result from our conversation. Rather, it is the strong hope of the biblical testimony, the hope of the resurrection which the Apostle in the beginning of the Letter to the Ephesians counts together with election and forgiveness as the foundation of the faith of the Christian community (Ephesians 1:3-14).

It is that *"fiducia in desperatione,"* that *"confident despair,"* of which Luther wrote in his letter to Georg Spenlein in 1516:

> Also, I would like to know what is the state of your soul. Are you finally weary of your own righteousness and are you learning to trust in Christ's righteousness and to be revived by it? Even as a sudden fever, the temptation to presumption attacks very many in our day, especially those who zealously strive for righteousness and peace. But they know nothing of God's righteousness, which is richly and mercifully sent to us in Christ: They seek to do good by themselves until they have attained the joyful confidence of existing before God adorned with virtue and merit. But this is impossible to attain. When you were with us, you lived in this belief—rather, in this delusion; I thought so, too. Now, however, I fight against such error; admittedly, I have not yet won. Therefore, my dear brother, learn Christ and him crucified. Learn to praise him and to despair of yourself. Then say to him: "Dear Lord Jesus, thou art my righteousness, but I am thy sin; thou hast accepted what is mine and given me what is thine. What thou wast not, thou didst receive and gavest me what I was not." Always beware of aspiring to such purity that you no longer wish to appear before yourself as sinner or even to be one anymore. Christ dwells only with sinners. He came to them from heaven where he dwelt among the righteous, so that even he may reside among sinners. Meditate upon such love as his continually, and you will behold his sweetest comfort. If we, by our own pain and toil, were meant to find peace of conscience—why would he have died? No, only in him, through confident despair in yourself and in your works will you find peace. To this end, learn from him that he has made his righteousness yours, as he has accepted you and has made your sin his.

This is one of the most powerful pastoral letters that has ever been written. It is truly pastoral in that it rests entirely on the presupposition of the forgiveness of sins. Everything here turns on the fact that our "own righteousness," that is, what moral or psychological reasoning we may demonstrate and advance in our favor, is regarded as of quite doubtful value. But the righteousness of Christ and the forgiveness of sins stand over against our reasoning as the clear and firm foundation on which we can stand in spite of and with our sin.

Once again, we name here the two Blumhardts. It is the secret of their pastoral care that they dared to rely unconditionally on the mercy of God in their dealings with people. The breaking forth of this mercy in the face of all the sin and all the evil of man is the core of the message of the Kingdom of God they proclaimed.

This message early had taken possession of the elder Blumhardt with the power of a new discovery in his initial struggles at Möttlingen. It brought him into opposition to the sanctification of the Pietism of his time. This discovery signifies the decisive blow to Pietism in that generation. It occurred precisely in the field of pastoral care, where already the elder Blumhardt had won the victory, carried the day, and secured the acceptance and establishment of his new understanding. He no doubt also made a significant contribution as an interpreter of the Bible; he even did a considerable piece of work in dogmatics—we think of the new light he shed on eschatology in his preaching. Yet we cannot say that he was primarily an interpreter or systematic theologian. There are critics who for this reason would deny him any significance for theology. This will not do, for the elder Blumhardt was a theologian, but a theologian almost exclusively in the field of pastoral care. He was a true shepherd to his congregation, a shepherd later also for many souls entrusted to him outside his congregation. As a shepherd, he was given the knowledge of forgiveness *as a power,* which also had a far-reaching theological significance and effect. It is a power that enters the life of man as a reality.

Both Blumhardts admittedly abandoned to a great extent the current theological formulations in their mode of expression and tried to communicate their knowledge in the language of their time. But again, this is related to the pastoral character of their work. They speak to the man of their time in a way that he can understand and that really hits him.

I am reminded here of the sentence coined by the younger Blumhardt: "Man is God's!" In pastoral care, we cannot avoid seeking ever anew a mode of expression which reaches the man far removed from the language of the Bible and the church. In so doing we run the risk of altering the content with the language; we may think we speak very plainly and strongly, when our meaning actually is inarticulate and weak. This could be the case even with Blumhardt's apparently powerful "Man is God's!" This exclamation is good, true, and appropriate only if it is said and understood in terms of Jesus Christ. But how easily can someone who hears it without knowing its origin or its goal interpret it in the sense of a common declaration, a declaration which claims to be true and valid even apart from Jesus Christ. As such, this word is empty and void. This deviation was not to be feared in the thinking and speaking of the two Blumhardts. Therefore, this sentence can still impress us as a summary of their message of the forgiveness of sins in pastoral care.

This much is certain: If in Bad Boll, the place where both Blumhardts labored, men were freed from the oppression of tormenting problems, if they were enabled to shake off inner bondage, if even cases of severe psychic illness were decisively cleared up, indeed healed, then it did not happen because an especially genial psychologist and therapist had performed the duties of his office here; it happened because and only because, with an unprecedented onesidedness, certainty, and childlikeness, the one declaration, "Man is God's!" was presented and lived on the basis of Jesus Christ, presented and lived in relationship and conversation with countless weary and heavy-laden men who gathered here. Both Blumhardts could also be eminently relevant on purely psychological ground, in the diagnosis as well as in the ensuing conversation, but this was again due to their absolute certainty of their cause, the forgiveness of sins in Jesus Christ. Bad Boll has occasionally been called a "place of evangelical grace." This is in order as long as we remember that the only

The Content of Pastoral Conversation

real place of grace is the cross on Golgotha and that "places of evangelical grace" are everywhere the forgiveness obtained by the suffering on the cross is purely and clearly proclaimed and believed.

Finally, it must be remembered that the forgiveness of sins can come into force only when it is communicated *unconditionally*. The reason that the church as a whole is perennially so weak and helpless in its pastoral care, indeed shows a widespread lack of true pastoral care, lies in the fact that even though the church knows and stands for the affirmation of the forgiveness of sins, it knows and stands for it only with limitations or reservations, and under provisos. It does not dare to relate men to God unconditionally. It fears that a too generous and too openminded declaration of forgiveness would induce men to frivolity. It does not really believe in the inexhaustibility of the forgiveness of sins. It does not believe in the unconditional validity of the fifth petition of the Lord's Prayer (Matthew 6:12), of the seventy times seven of Matthew 18 (vss. 21-35). It does not acknowledge that frivolity comes not out of forgiveness, but out of the withholding of forgiveness.

The withholding of forgiveness always signifies some sort of *legalism* forced on man, whether in the form of an ideology to which man is invited and pledged, or simply in the form of moral or religious exhortations which are imposed upon him. But where legalism rules, man is placed before the insurmountable wall of commandments which he cannot fulfill, and against which he will only be knocked to pieces. Then despondency enters; man renounces further efforts, he gives up the battle, and the end is, if not despair, then frivolity and freedom from restraint. Morality, insofar as it is only morality, corrupts man; it simply makes him wicked. While on the contrary, grace and only grace awakens the ethical decision and will power of man. Admittedly, only when it has a free run!

Grace must be able to flow unhindered in order to be effective and healing. But where legalism governs, grace is no longer unhindered. To be sure, one continues to take account of it, but one does not reckon with it fully; one does not reckon with it alone, but in addition to grace one takes into account man's own will and ability as independent elements. The forgiveness of sins is also concerned with the coming into force of man's own free decision, man's own free will and ability, for it is concerned with the totality of man, who is to love God as his Lord with all his heart, with all his soul, and with all his mind (Matthew 22:37), but it is grace and only grace that makes this love operative. For it is God who "is at work in you, both to will and to work for his good pleasure" (Philippians 2:13, R.S.V.; cf. also James 2:14-27). But how shall grace, limited and hindered by law, become that power which so totally grasps and moves the life of man? Legalism and forgiveness are mutually exclusive. Therefore, where there is legalism, there is no forgiveness however much we talk about it; neither does the correct willing and doing of man come about.

The *law,* insofar as it is rightly understood and executed, has certainly its good place in the communication of faith. It even gives the actual form and shape to the message. The gospel is never proclaimed otherwise than in the form of a call of God to man, and this means always in the form of God's commandment. The law therefore belongs to pastoral care as we shall argue later on. But—and this is the decisive matter here—the law has its place wholly within the declaration of the forgiveness of sins. It must under no circumstances appear apart from forgiveness, thus limiting and conditioning it.

We must never let the law somehow precede the communication of forgiveness, so that man would first have to know rejection by moral law, and only then to understand forgiveness as a second thing which will cover and heal his rejection. But on the other hand, the moral law must not simply follow the forgiveness of sins, so that only by fulfilling the law following his forgiveness would forgiveness become valid. In both cases, the law decisively limits the validity of the plainly sovereign, all-inclusive, unconditional forgiveness. In both cases, it presents a prior or subsequent condition to be fulfilled by man in order for forgiveness to come into force at all. But then it is no longer the great divine assumption on which everything depends. It has become a first element to be followed by a second, or a second element preceded by a first. Whenever this relativization is made, the law separated from forgiveness will necessarily get the upper hand and will smother and extinguish the forgiveness of sins. The consequences in the form of discouragement, frivolity, or despair are bound to appear where the law limits forgiveness, where sanctification occupies an independent position alongside justification.

We may look, for example, at pastoral care with children and young people. Here, the dangerous effect of pastoral care corrupted by a false communication of the law is particularly visible. We often hear that youth needs the establishment of the law even more than the forgiveness of sins: that youth lacks a proper consciousness of sin. Therefore, we can approach him only by way of the law. This is understood to be the moral appeal, the idealistic challenge, the summons to steer one's life by the strength of the self, as seems to please and befit young people according to a very superficial psychology. Reference is usually made to the ideology of the Boy Scout movement and its law. On the basis of the biblical understanding of man, however, the idea that the young person is less needy of and accessible to the forgiveness of sins at his age than the adult is fully and firmly to be contested. The biological fact of his youth cannot mean that he is not already man in the fullest sense of the word and as such is not to be taken seriously. He already lives in the totality of his existence under the "law of sin and death" (Romans 8:2) and therefore needs forgiveness, which "in Jesus Christ" will do its work also in him.

The forgiveness of sins must of course be communicated to young people in a form in which he can receive and understand it. This is of greatest importance, and the insights of the psychology of youth are to be fully used for this purpose. How this is to be done would have to be discussed in a separate presentation dealing with special cases of pastoral care. We only assert here that there is such a special communication of the message of the forgiveness of sins by the church to young people and that it must happen in full power and awareness in the realm of pastoral care.

Young people suffer, admittedly in a way corresponding to their age and therefore quite differently from adults, but they really suffer, deeply and markedly, from their unforgiven sin. The time of youth is actually characterized by such suffering, since the power of feeling is much less subdued than later and since the young person as a rule has fewer ways available to avoid his problem than the sophisticated adult. The latter knows manifold means of diversion and takes refuge in some kind of ideology or simply in hysteria or neurosis when he no longer can stand the gloomy realities of his existence. This signifies, however, that the young person is in special need of forgiveness if he is to survive the crises of adolescence. If he is offered only morals and law instead of forgiveness, he is driven into the above-mentioned frivolity or obstinacy and despair. The truth that mere morality does not help man, that, on the contrary, it only leads him still deeper into the entanglements of his sin, since sin is awakened by the law, comes nowhere more shockingly to light than in young people; on the other hand, once young people have understood what alone can help, they tend to live by forgiveness more purely than adults.

I know of young people who suffered hopelessly from the sexual problem of their adolescent years. A false upbringing had subjected them to the law in this matter. They fought with all the strength of their will for the ideal of purity, only to experience defeat after defeat. They saw nothing else before them than a deep depression which left no further possibilities of life open. At last they grasped the forgiveness of sins as the only way leading out of the struggle and despair into freedom. I observed in my own life and in others how from the moment we were awarded the forgiveness of sins through the conversation and preaching of the younger Blumhardt, a confidence came over us that liberated and gladdened our youth. This confidence nourished us and bore us through the critical years like nothing else did. It made us immune to the legalistic idealism of modern thinking as it was impressed on us almost exclusively in school and church, indeed through the whole education of our time. We came out of certain discussions with Christoph Blumhardt with the exuberant feeling of deliverance. The crucial fact was the unconditional forgiveness as Blumhardt expressed it without in the least inviting the danger of frivolity or of lawlessness. Law and obedience were in no way the losers with Blumhardt, but it was the obedience of faith to which we were submitted; what was proclaimed to us was the law bedded down in forgiveness, that "law of liberty" of which the Letter of James speaks (James 1:25).

Not only the pastoral care of young people, however, but pastoral care in general suffers from the fact that the forgiveness of sins is not believed and proclaimed with that straightforwardness which is entirely indispensable here. This is the deepest reason why so many people turn away from the church, its proclamation, and its pastoral care, or at any rate no longer expect very much from them, and turn to all sorts of sects and other religious groups. There they expect to get something stronger. And perhaps they are not always entirely wrong; for these circles, keeping more or less apart from the church, speak more unequivocally and straightforwardly than the official church of the blood of Jesus Christ, of the power of the cross, of the Saviour of the soul, and also of the forgiveness of sins, even though they often enough do it naively and inappropriately. To be sure, something else happens still more frequently: People are alienated from the Christian proclamation in general and settle in the churchless realm of a modern secular piety or world view so as to satiate themselves with the husks of some kind of substitute religion.

There is no shortage of such substitute religions today, or, as they have also been called, of "crypto-religions." We cite again the Anthroposophy of Rudolf Steiner and now add the teaching and practice of the Christian Science of Mary Baker Eddy. Whatever the founders of these movements may have intended and envisioned, their work signifies for a countless number of their supporters nothing but such a substitute religion. This is proven for our purposes by the fact that he who seeks membership and spiritual nurture here is lost to the Christian community. Seen as a whole, everything in this depends constantly on one thing: Men seek to escape the distress of their inner life. They recognize more or less strongly and plainly that at one of the deepest points of their being they have run into disorder and confusion, and they yearn to be rescued. But is there another distress, another disorder and confusion than that designated by the word "sin"? Is there another rescue, another way out than forgiveness? Whether they know it or not, men need the forgiveness of sins. Since the church's proclamation does not offer this forgiveness clearly and unequivocally in the power of redemption they seek help elsewhere; Jesus' saying about the flock which lacks proper direction is fulfilled anew.

The crisis we face here extends to almost all the traditional theological positions and their corresponding pastoral care. It is clear that theological Liberalism, with its proclamation adjusted to man and his religious needs, readily inclines to change the cause of faith into a humanly idealistic morality and thus to invalidate the forgiveness of sins as the sole content of the faith. We no longer understand Jesus as the Son of God who died for sinners and in the resurrection from the dead brought to light forgiveness as a power. He vanishes behind the vision of the exemplary Leader, the Friend of man, the Hero and Helper, who creates and pours out a new mind, enabling man ultimately to help himself by way of an idealistically conceived imitation of Jesus. Consequently, pastoral care becomes spiritual instruction in such self-help. Grace is proclaimed as a power in man to fulfill the ethical law by himself and thus to grow into a mature member of the "Kingdom of God," a Kingdom that seems to be emptied of its eschatological meaning and only designates the goal of evolution within history.

Things are somewhat different, though only relatively so, in the so-called "theology of mediation" and the corresponding trend within the church. Sin and grace are recognized for what they are with much deeper seriousness; as a result, the Word of the cross and the resurrection of Jesus is proclaimed much more forcefully than in Liberalism. But fundamentally, this emphasis rests on a fortunate inconsistency. For the theology broadly representative of this trend is that of Albrecht Ritschl, whose final orientation is again purely anthropological. In dependence on Kant, whom he understood moralistically, Ritschl conceived the Christian faith as man's great possibility for the realization of the ethical law. What natural man cannot attain is conferred upon him, according to Ritschl, through faith in Jesus Christ: the power to fulfill the ethical imperative. Man then goes to work and manifests his faith in the sphere of the vocation into which Providence has placed him. Thus the evil rift of sin is closed; the Christian recognizes himself as reconciled with God in the ethical act, and reaches maturity in "Christian perfection." Within this theology, the forgiveness of sins is once more robbed of its majestic independence and unconditionality. It is simply the means and the vehicle to ethical perfection. It is no longer the sovereign work of Christ Jesus alone; it is no longer the one and only content of the Christian faith. Therefore, in the corresponding proclamation, the person and work of Jesus Christ, grace and the reconciliation of man with God are indeed communicated, but are considered only as a step and path to the ethical action by which man proves his membership in the Kingdom of God. Ethics as the doctrine of the work of man in imitation of Christ gets the upper hand over justification as the doctrine of the work of God in Jesus Christ. This explains the rational tendency to a certain legalistic trend; moralism repeatedly appears even in the "orthodox" proclamation associated with Ritschl's theology.

Things are different still in Pietism. Although its teaching rests on the proclamation of grace in the cross of Christ, a decidedly legalistic piety is the outcome. I have in mind here the conversion and revival preaching as it is practiced during the evangelistic campaigns and attempts at mass pastoral care made by pietistic circles. This kind of preaching and pastoral care is actually characterized by an often very massive imposition of the law and judgment preceding and accompanying the promise of grace. People are to be exposed to terror and insecurity, supposedly to make them all the more willing and ready to grasp forgiveness. But what really happens here is that repentance is made the condition of grace, instead of grace furnishing the sole ground for the change of mind growing out of gratitude as the fruit of grace. The essential element of grace, the freedom of God in which alone grace can proceed, is limited and thus eliminated by the prior condition of contrition and repentance required of man. When one has had to counsel people coming to him from such evangelistic campaigns and the accompanying pastoral care, frightened and shocked by the impossibility of living up to the requirement of repentance, he knows how much confusion and distress can be caused in the soul by such endeavors, even with the seriousness of their proclamation, indeed by just such false seriousness.

But has not the Moral Re-Armament founded by Frank Buchman struck a new note and brought a change into this picture? For the forgiveness of sins is the center of its proclamation, and it intends only to be a genuine movement of pastoral care with a new message for sinners and "only for sinners." This is even the title of one of Moral Re-Armament's distinctive books (*For Sinners Only* by A. J. Russell). What kind of message can this be if not that of the free grace of Christ? The pastoral care of the movement indeed did and still does achieve genuine deliverance for some persons in the bondage of sin; it did and does occur here that one man encounters another with the message of grace in a conversation under the Word of God and is able to bring to the light of forgiveness the evil secrets weighing upon the fellow man. But something else must also be seen and said of Moral Re-Armament from the very beginning: The message of grace is unfortunately narrowed down by an explicit new legalism hindering the proclamation of true forgiveness flowing out of free grace.

The strong emphasis on the so-called "four absolutes" (absolute purity, absolute honesty, absolute unselfishness, absolute love) in the pastoral care of Moral Re-Armament must be mentioned in this context. They impose themselves as the great imperatives confronting man to make him recognize his sin, but also as the great life goals he must keep before his eyes as wholly realizable. Furthermore, note the abstract way (i.e., separate from the concrete Word of the Bible) in which these imperatives are imposed and the new life depicted, with the testimonies and examples of those who have already acceded to the new way of life playing an important role of encouraging imitation. These testimonies can be truly inspiring; they can even express true belief in the overcoming of all sin by forgiveness. But they can also be the mere sign of an idealism which all too self-evidently presupposes an ability of man to free himself from sin and to undertake the transformation of his own life. This idealism, even when it invokes the gospel, does not reckon seriously enough with the demonic power of sin, which is not to be conquered by any appeal, however strong and reasonable, to man and his will power.

The testimonies and appeals of Moral Re-Armament have on occasion an exciting and invigorating ring. There are those for whom the movement has for the first time revealed that faith can be a power grasping and liberating man's life. Quite possibly these people have never been really touched by the ordinary Christian preaching and pastoral care in the church. But to awaken and shake up is one thing; really and truly to set on the way of the grace of Jesus Christ is another. There are also those who do not succeed in accomplishing the required transformation of life in spite of all their being awakened and trying hard. What about them? They are left doubly disappointed. Their idealism has collapsed after a passionate upsurge and they feel cheated. But of the fact that one could also succumb and fail in his "attempts at Christian life" both as pastor and as one in need of pastoral care, and that only then the properly decisive question can be put concerning the grace of God, there is strikingly little evidence in the testimonies and accounts of Moral Re-Armament. They seem to know only of victory and conquest.

"Defeated Christians" scarcely seem to exist. In Holy Scripture, we read differently. The testimony it gives of the transformation of life that happened on Golgotha may not simply be applied to a change of life to be wrought by ourselves, as it happens in part in Moral Re-Armament.

Here a third reservation must be made. True, Moral Re-Armament strongly focuses on the surrender to Christ the crucified and resurrected. And again, this is certainly its good fortune and must not be minimized. But the surrender is understood and described as a nonrecurring act, required of and to be accomplished by man, whereby one is able to press through to forgiveness and to the new, victorious life of the reborn. Here we are again up against a legalism which cannot be reconciled with the message of grace. The "surrender" becomes the prerequisite of grace which then cannot flow freely. To this corresponds the building up of pastoral counseling into a method by virtue of which the act of surrender is to be solicited, instead of only the effective Word of free and liberating grace being offered and received free of all concern for methods. We repeat that, in spite of this concern, people continue to be helped by the pastoral care of Moral Re-Armament, as by all related movements of awakening; they are for the most part people who could not find access to the gospel in the more scrupulous and more rigid atmosphere of the average churchly proclamation with its frequently narrow morality. But it also appears that such people then must part company with this movement, or other penitential movement, in order to come completely into the church, which alone is gathered around the Word and sacrament.

Moral Re-Armament, which intends to be thoroughly rooted in the church, often performs pastoral service through its call and the impulse it gives toward bringing people to the church of Jesus Christ and what Vilmar calls its "ordinary means." (Cf. Emil Brunner's positive presentation and critique of Moral Re-Armament in *Die Kirchen, die Gruppenbewegung und die Kirche Jesu Christi* and his paper: "*Meine Begegnung mit der Oxforder Gruppenbewegung*" in *Kirchenblatt für die Reformierte Schweiz*,

1932; but cf. also the *"Kritische Thesen zur Gruppenbewegung"* by Karl Barth in *Evangelische Theologie,* 1936, pp. 205ff.)

At any rate, the church has every reason to be shaken up. It must no longer neglect and set aside the central position given it in the forgiveness of sins. It must concentrate on winning it back, setting the light of free grace again on the candlestick, and gathering its members in new faith and new obedience around it. This new awakening must not and will not be the exclusive affair of its theologians and pastors. But it must and will—in this the church has to learn from Moral Re-Armament—shake and penetrate the local congregations and their members in the form of a pastoral care occurring among them from person to person. Everywhere in the everyday encounter of men with one another, even in common discussion and conversation, the light of forgiveness must begin to shine in a new attitude of understanding, openmindedness, and mutual forbearance. Everywhere the good works of joyous, compassionate living as promised in the Sermon on the Mount must become visible. Everywhere the spirit of a new life together must blow among men. It must be seen and felt even in the social, economic, and political spheres that a church exists which lives by the fact that God in his Son has had mercy on all men, really *all* men, *unconditionally.* Barriers that otherwise separate us insurmountably from one another must and will fall—we mention only the gulf between the so-called *bourgeois* world and the *proletariat* with its *Communism*—if the grace of Christ becomes visible and operative in a church that believes in this grace and lives by its faith. That mutual consolation and reproof, of which Luther and Bucer and Calvin already knew and spoke, must be newly strengthened, enlarged, and given a significance that was hardly imagined before. The universal priesthood must be freely and joyously exercised even in the midst of the profane territory of human action and behavior as one, not only by words but in the realities of life, regards and treats his fellow man as his brother who belongs with him under the power of the God of Jesus Christ who lets the sun of his goodness and help shine over all differences.

This is especially relevant for the preacher and pastor. One cannot proclaim the forgiveness of sins from the pulpit without immediately practicing and confirming it from moment to moment in discussion and conversation with his people. If there is anything from which the pastor and minister must be aloof, from which he must protect himself, and before which he ought to flee as before the Devil, it is any kind of refined and disguised Pharisaism. Pharisaism and grace, Pharisaism and forgiveness, are as incompatible as fire and water. To be a minister, to practice pastoral care, and to proclaim forgiveness, really to live from forgiveness, are one and the same. No special "movement" within the church, no new "founding of an order" of some kind, is needed in order to represent the work of free grace and the forgiveness flowing from it as a special "concern." If the matter of forgiveness becomes a special concern alongside others, it is no longer the overarching concern which it should be and is. Special movements and organizations as they appear from time to time within the church in order to give new emphasis to a neglected cause are always symptoms of sickness which should disappear as swiftly as possible in the course of progressing convalescence. The church must be moved and filled to the brim in the totality of its life by the one thing that matters, the "great mercy."

In conclusion, it is appropriate to refer to a man who in his way discovered and proclaimed this mercy, but who also, on account of his radical position, turned into a strong opponent of the official church although he was one of its theologians and ministers. I am thinking of the late Hermann Kutter, pastor in Zurich. Kutter presented the forgiveness of sins in its unconditional validity and power and tested it in the attitude of the Christianity of his time toward the estranged and godless proletariat. Coming to his position through the message of the two Blumhardts, he applied the truth they newly proclaimed—that man, not only the pious, the honest, the good, but man as he is, is God's for the sake of Christ—to the *social question*, to the Socialists and Communists. (Cf. among his numerous writings

Sie Müssen!, *Gerechtigkeit,* and *Wir Pfarrer.*) But also in his sermons and in his pastoral care with numerous individuals the message of free grace was a penetrating and liberating force. He thus became a true comforter and helper in difficult situations (cf. his devotional book, *Aus der Werkstatt,* and *Das Bilderbuch Gottes*). He addressed himself mainly to ministers, trying to show them the way out of the legalistic traps—into which the official spokesmen of the church so easily fall—onto the new ground of the mercy of Christ, which alone makes the understanding of man and the lively communication of the gospel possible.

Kutter saw that the pastor in his congregation is at first easily looked upon as the representative of ordinary Christian-bourgeois morality, whose charge it is to subject men to the law of a specific social viewpoint and to chastise them if they deviate from it. If he lives up to this expectation, he is considered a good pastor. It is repeatedly overlooked in the church that in so doing, the pastor irreparably robs the message of God's mercy upon sinners, which he is commissioned to deliver, of its priority and force. As a result, all the well-intentioned and the intellectually and spiritually elite congregate around him, whereas the sinners, the wayward, and those disgraced under the law will avoid him; they are afraid of the moralistic reproach to be expected of him as a good pastor, although it does not help them at all, let alone rescue them from their abyss. What alone helps and saves is the proclamation of the fact that "while we were yet sinners Christ died for us."

Kutter did not grow tired of reiterating and applying this central affirmation of the Letter to the Romans (5:8), in which the whole message of the gospel is contained as in a nutshell, recommending it to the pastors as a guide. He has taught us anew to see man as a child of God in and with and in spite of his sin. His teaching cannot be understood plainly enough today, in exactly the social and political application he gave to it. How can we advance even a step further in our time of deep dissensions if this perception is not revived in the Christian community? How can we survive as pastors in our confrontation with the uprooted and straying and estranged men of today, with the bourgeois or proletarian, caught in the prejudices of his class, if we lack this attitude of unprejudiced openness and concern and real readiness to forgive? How can we find the true Word actually reaching him if from the first we cannot proceed from the fact that the other facing us in his otherness is our brother before God in Christ, and despite all his sinful obduracy and perversity, is called back to the community and must give ear to this call?

Once again: We cannot be surprised that the church fails in its pastoral care as long as it is so uncertain at the central point of its task. It will immediately recover when the forgiveness of sins, in complete unconditionality and freedom, becomes the only ground upon which it stands.

Pastoral conversation proceeds on the assumption that man is able to receive the Word of forgiveness. However, this ability is not innate; it is given through a new, special act of God. By his Holy Spirit he calls us and opens our ears, so that we hear his gracious Word and live in the power of such hearing. That it is God himself and only God who brings about both forgiveness and faith does not exclude, but rather includes, our doing everything in our power to cause his Word to flow among men, so that many may be saved. It implies at the same time that prayer for the gift of the Holy Spirit is central to all pastoral care as the decisive action in which we are to be engaged.

9 Man's Responsiveness to the Forgiveness of Sins

We are faced with the fact that the church does not dare approach man unconditionally with the message of forgiveness. Why is this so? Because it assumes that man is not prepared to accept this message immediately and without something more, or if he does accept it, he misunderstands it and is hurt by it. This hesitation of the church to come forward with forgiveness emphasizes the continual risk involved in entering into pastoral conversation. We abandon safe ground, step into the void, indeed we begin a quite new and strange work when we communicate the forgiveness of sins unreservedly to someone.

From the standpoint of psychology, pedagogy, or simply of law and morals, such an undertaking is totally unwarranted and unjustified. For forgiveness of sins in fact means that I see man in a wholly new perspective which is beyond any other available human criterion. Nothing, really nothing at all, entitles me to assure a sinner in a concrete case that his undeniable transgressions, his perhaps dreadful demoralization and depravity, are really annulled, so that I may regard him and he may regard himself as justified and cleansed from all the filth oppressing him. As I see him, he is bound, he is ensnared, he has gone astray and climbed too high—am I simply to ignore all this? Am I to take the risk of pronouncing judgment and, as I pronounce it, of executing it? Can I say it so powerfully, can he accept its validity to the degree that it actually becomes the determinative force for him? Where do I get the right and authority to speak, where does he get the freedom to listen? Does not everything in him and in me rebel against it? But now it happens: I pronounce forgiveness, and my neighbor receives it—what makes this possible?

As we raise this question, it once again becomes evident that the forgiveness of sins is actually the Word from afar, from beyond, from above, the radically other, new Word which approaches us in Holy Scripture. It is the deed of God himself and of God alone, not to be approximated from any human presupposition, approaching man only in the power of its own, new presupposition, and radically reversing his life.

The forgiveness of sins is proclaimed in the whole Bible as this new, free Word. It is not made more accessible by any preliminary understanding or any predisposition on the part of man. Even with the prophets, the announcement of God's gracious bending down to the sinful people is completely unexpected. God's love for them is groundless and entirely self-sustaining. Nothing is present in the people that would approach or correspond to this love of God. Here is God's faithfulness to his promise, there the obstinacy of the people struggling against this faithfulness. But this faithfulness proves its divine character, in that it remains faithfulness in the face of this obstinacy. We see this in the introduction to the book of Isaiah (1:1-20), which begins with the announcement of the great judgment over the faithless people for whom there is no rescue. And then quite abruptly, God's wonderful art of dyeing is pictured as he transforms the scarlet of sin into the snow white of the new righteousness.

It is no different in the New Testament witness: On the one hand, the complete inextricability of sinful man, but on the other, the Word of forgiveness descending into it, unprecedented and met by no human readiness for it. So in the encounter of Jesus with the paralytic (Mark 2:1-12). He lay helpless in front of Jesus. Of course, he expects and gets help, but he gets it in the form of the new Word of forgiveness he does not expect, and as it hits him, it cuts through the chains in which he lies imprisoned in soul and body. So in the parable of the royal forgiveness (Matthew 18:21-27). The great debtor stands before his judge. He is sentenced. Whining, he promises to repay everything. But how could he? Again with total abruptness the king's word comes to him as something wholly new and radically changes the situation: "And out of pity for him the lord of that servant released him and forgave him the debt" (Matthew 18:27). This is the heart of the parable. Here the decisive turn occurs. But it cannot be explained. It is the free deed of the king. There is no reason whatsoever on the part of the debtor for this unconditional remission of all his debt. On the contrary, every reason speaks against it. Nevertheless, he is now forgiven. Why? Just because! Because it is the king's will and in his power. An entirely new law is given here, the law of mercy, and with it a new possibility of life for the man overwhelmed by his guilt. This is forgiveness as the act of God in Jesus Christ. To communicate such forgiveness in obedience to the testimony of Holy Scripture is the hazardous enterprise of true pastoral care.

But does not a condition and prerequisite remain which man must fulfill if forgiveness is to become effective: namely, that man reaches out toward the Word of forgiveness and, when it approaches him, accepts it? If man were to prepare himself for forgiveness, he would have to show forth a previous knowledge of his sin and the desire to be released from it. Both of these then would constitute the inner change of direction which is designated by the word "repentance." And this contrition would be the one requirement to be satisfied if forgiveness is to be granted. The summons to repentance is then not unreasonably bound up inseparably with the announcement of forgiveness.

There can indeed be no proclamation of the forgiveness of sins without the accompanying *call to repentance*. We have yet to speak of this. So closely is the call to repentance tied to forgiveness that it is like the dress or the form in which the message of the grace of God to the sinner is clothed. God remains faithful even to the sinful man; therefore he summons him to turn to him. We find this in the prophets, but so also in the New Testament record; we recall the synoptic summary of the whole preaching of Jesus in the words: "Repent, for the kingdom of heaven is at hand" (Matthew 4:17).

Such summons to repentance, such readiness for contrition on the part of man is conceivable, however, only when man is assumed to be responsive to the call to repentance, responsive to the message of forgiveness addressed to him in the call to repentance. This responsiveness implies man's active participation. Man does not behave in the encounter with forgiveness as a stick or stone, but he possesses and realizes the capacity to hear and to understand what God says to him. Biblically speaking, he has a "heart," an "understanding heart," a heart which listens, which is already regarded in the Old Testament as the decisive mark of a contrite man (cf. I Kings 3:9). We shall have to remember that "listening" appears in the whole Bible as the *one* event, the *one* action required of man. The subjective side of the act of faith consists in nothing but a complete opening of man's ear, in his listening willingly to the Word of God and accepting the promise of the forgiveness of sins. This is what is meant by man's responsiveness to forgiveness.

The extent and the scope of this responsiveness to forgiveness may be broadly or narrowly conceived; it may be drastically scaled down to an almost passive receptivity, or it may be built up into the all-consuming act of man's wholehearted and exuberant self-opening to God. Both extremes are possible. But it is certainly not possible to contest and deny this responsiveness. It exists as surely as the reception of forgiveness summons man in the totality of his existence. If there were no responsiveness, if man could not be counted upon to be this participant hearer of the Word, how could proclamation and pastoral care be possible at all? Any further discussion of the manner and method whereby man accepts the Word of forgiveness would be cut off, as would any reflection on the events of repentance and conversion. Everything that needs to be said from the subjective side about the transformation of man would be in vain. Pastoral care thus stands or falls with this responsiveness of man to the Word being communicated to him. One could compare this responsiveness with a door through which the Word of forgiveness enters into man's life, gains ground there, and takes possession of him. By virtue of this responsiveness, those changes and transformations in man's soul and spirit are effected which are made visible and tangible by the Word of forgiveness and are the indispensable sign of repentance. Forgiveness enters the "flesh"; it becomes what it certainly is not originally, a humanly comprehensible fact. The whole reality of forgiveness depends on its impetus to such psychic changes and decisions, which no doubt are not forgiveness itself, but which appear as man's response to forgiveness and in a way represent the human exterior of forgiveness.

But does not man's responsiveness to forgiveness so conceived contradict the transcendence and self-sufficiency of the divine Word? Can the power and freedom of the Word of forgiveness be fully maintained if it is countered by this listening and accepting and becoming effective of the Word in man, even if only as the necessary psychic response? Must we not then assume at least an interplay between the spiritual-heavenly fact of forgiveness and the natural-earthly fact of the human ability to receive? Must not God and man work together as a team, if forgiveness is to become effective, although the divine contribution would undoubtedly outweigh the human? Does not this co-operation signify an irreparable limitation of the self-sufficiency and self-validation of the Word of forgiveness? Man's contribution need consist in nothing but a humble opening of the door through which forgiveness enters; yet this would represent a prerequisite and condition which must be fulfilled by man if sins are to be forgiven. But what then happens to the freedom of the Word, which is evidenced and confirmed by the unconditional and unwarranted release by the power of the Word of the hopelessly captive man?

We answer: It is still true—the freedom of the Word is completely unlimited. God in his act of forgiveness knows no partnership with man, not even in the most subtle form. Jesus Christ as the Son of God alone has carried away the whole burden of sin. Man has not the slightest share in the work of reconciliation, not even in terms of meeting-half-way and door-opening. Here grace is in command, and grace rules; it rules alone, or it does not rule at all. But *at the same time,* everything we have said of man and his responsiveness remains valid. Yes, grace is present and rules alone when forgiveness goes forth; but man is also present and not only as an object—but as truly as he is the object of whom forgiveness takes possession, he is also the subject who accepts forgiveness. However, this happens in such a way that even this "also" of man, even his hearing and accepting, his door-opening, his unlocking of himself (or remaining shut!) to forgiveness is wholly effected by the power of grace alone. This means that man's responsiveness remains uncontested. Man remains uncontested as a partner to whom the Word of forgiveness can and ought to be communicated, who can and ought to hear and understand it, and who is led by it to repentance and deliverance. But however natural and real this communication, acceptance, and repentance is, it remains an event which cannot be traced back to the natural faculty of man's hearing and understanding. The hearing of the Word of God is quite certainly a hearing like any other, but where it occurs as the hearing of this particular Word, it is a hearing which has entered into the nature of man, entered from above like no other hearing. It takes place in the natural province of man, perhaps in a sermon, perhaps in pastoral conversation. But when it takes place, it also takes possession. A door opens in man, but man does not open it by himself; indeed, this door is not even present until the Word of forgiveness simultaneously creates and opens it when it reaches man. Forgiveness is not only the speaking mouth of God; it is *at the same time* also the hearing ear of man.

But what does this mean except that *included* in forgiveness is *man's responsiveness* to forgiveness? Here again, forgiveness emerges as the entirely free, sovereign act of God, who is bound by nothing, whose Word is not dependent on any *natural prerequisite* or *response* since he and he alone creates every prerequisite and response. What man may know of sin and grace by himself and apart from the grace of Christ may signify this or that, but it certainly does not reach the heights and depths of actual forgiveness. Man by himself knows nothing of actual sin; he knows nothing of his real, deep, and final separation from God. He will know it only when his sin is disclosed to him in forgiveness, and already is taken away from him. This is why there does not exist any kind of "pre-knowledge" upon which the message of forgiveness could build. But the power of forgiveness is such that as it comes upon man, it creates in him a real perception and understanding of the actuality of sin and grace. As an alien, new Word, the message of forgiveness enters man's life and places him under the great divine proviso of grace.

This is additional evidence for the total lack of presuppositions and protection to which the pastoral counselor is exposed when he must communicate this message of the forgiveness of sins. He has to conduct the conversation in full recognition of the natural sinfulness of the man before him, in recognition of his bondage and helplessness; yet he may and he shall really count on a change and transformation in the life of the person he addresses. It consists in man's acknowledgment of his sin, but at one and the same time also his acknowledgment of the hand of God rescuing him and granting him a new life in the light of grace. Neither the recognition of sin nor the certainty of forgiveness comes from us, but they are, in the counselor as well as the counselee, awakened from above by the Word of God, powerfully at work in their lives.

When forgiveness thus takes effect in man to whom it is addressed, we must understand it in its final expression as our *election*, as wrought, however, by the Holy Spirit. The Holy Spirit is indeed no other than God himself approaching us and grasping us; he is *our* God, the God acting *with* us and in us through his Word and choosing us to be his children. God is the Creator and Father *over* us; in his Son he is also *with* us, and in the Holy Spirit he is *in* us, in order to open our eyes and ears so that we learn to recognize, love, and fear him as our Father in his being with us in the Son. Here we are back to what we called man's responsiveness to God. Ability to respond to God through God —this now summarizes everything which is to be said about our human existence before God in and with our sin. Ability to respond to God means that we may and can truly hear and accept God's Word as his Word directed to us, calling us sinners and mortals to him, to the holy, eternal God. It means and is one and the same as to be open to grace. We are open to grace, but not by nature, not by virtue of some given talent, nor because of a psychic faculty however secret. We are open to grace because and insofar as God stretches out his hand to us, calls and summons us in the incomprehensible, groundless freedom of his (gracious!) election, and we live before him in the power of this election and calling. Our responsiveness to God thus means and is first and last our being elected by God; it is the exclusive work of the Holy Spirit, who speaks and makes acceptable the electing Word.

We have already said that the Holy Spirit is the great proviso under which the *speaking* of the pastor proceeds. Here we must emphasize that this great proviso covers also man's *hearing*. God is free to give his Word as he opens our ears for it where and when he pleases, but he is equally free to take away his Word as he closes our ears to it where and when he pleases. We hear God's Word (or do not hear it!), thereby becoming his elect (or rejected!), but in election as in rejection God in his Word and Spirit becomes mighty over us. It is the power of his grace that is at work in us, for even where God rejects, he rejects primarily in order to rightfully elect. Both hearing and not hearing are real, tangible psychic events determining human life in its totality. They entail certain tangible and psychologically recognizable developments, as truly as it is man who is here addressed or not addressed. But they are still events which are wholly initiated by the Spirit of God from above.

The problem, so important for the practice of pastoral care, of the point of *contact* in the pastoral conversation is here raised with full urgency. It can be summed up in the question: How shall I formulate the message of forgiveness that it may fall on a willing ear with my neighbor? According to what has just been said, the fundamental answer to be given must be: It is the Holy Spirit alone who predisposes man for right hearing. He brings about the right condition and situation in man so that he may be accessible to God's Word.

The forgiveness of sins needs no natural and human predisposition and mediation at all. For man as receiver inescapably confronts grace as did the paralytic in the Gospel, as helpless, perplexed, dead in sin. Psychological and pedagogical efforts are of no use at this point. But does this recognition not hopelessly frustrate any human endeavor, even any endeavor of pastoral care? If the Word and Spirit of God do the whole job, what is there left for us to do so as to lead man through pastoral conversation to the right hearing, to repentance, and to faith? The truth is just the reverse. The certainty of the power and self-sufficiency of the Holy Spirit, if anything, awakes in us that total confidence in the Word of God which sustains and permeates all true pastoral care. *Because* we are certain of the assistance of the Holy Spirit, we shall as his instruments set out to use everything to the winning of man for the Word of God. We no longer need to ask ourselves even in apparently quite hopeless cases: Shall I, can I, address the Word to this human wreck before me? Will he be able to hear it?

Such questions and doubts are now invalid. There is not one person who does not need the Word of forgiveness, not one with whom it could not find acceptance. Indeed, the more deeply a person lies imprisoned, the more we are required to communicate the liberating Word to him. The more all psychological and pedagogical prerequisites are lacking, the more valid is the proviso of the Holy Spirit as the one and victorious prerequisite of all our talking. The more firmly the door is closed on which we knock, the more must the man inside be regarded as being ripe and ready for the Word which God intends to speak to him and which he must hear as spoken to him by God himself. There is not a man for whom Christ did not die and rise and in whom this could not become alive and effective through God's Spirit. Therefore, precisely therefore, we must abandon no attempt in pastoral care that might serve to make the Word of forgiveness accessible to him. Paradoxical as it may seem, it still corresponds to the fact that as servants of the Spirit and Word of God we summon and apply every psychological and pedagogical means to further that contact and meditation which the Word and Spirit of God still effect and accomplish alone. He who trusts in God and in the work of his Spirit, he who in pastoral care expects from God everything, will not become weary in seeking ways that lead into the closed heart of man; rather, he will get busy genuinely struggling and caring for the souls of men.

As a sign that we do not rely in vain on the victorious power of the Word and Spirit of God, surprising liberations can take place; the Word of God may break through, and people thought least accessible open up to this Word. Did not Jesus himself marvel that he found greater faith in a Gentile than in Israel? (Matthew 8:10.) And did not the Canaanite woman understand him better than his disciples? (Matthew 15:28.) Should we not be a great deal more audacious in our pastoral care than we are, on account of man's responsiveness through the Holy Spirit? Why so fainthearted? Why so reticent? Why so hesitant? Why so inert, so unimaginative, so lacking in patience, tenacity, and perseverance in our laboring with man? Yes, it is God who elects in the power of his Spirit. We do not possess the power to win men. And this will always imply that it is he who closes and rejects. But there is certainly no balance between election and rejection! God closes only in order to open. He rejects in order to elect overwhelmingly. Therefore, we have no excuse if, while waiting for him, we do not hasten, run, and labor to communicate his electing Word where and in whatever way we can.

The history of the church, especially the history of missions, gives us example after example of the electing power of true pastoral care. I cite an incident from the biography of Josephine Butler. Once upon entering a cell in a women's prison, she met an especially depraved woman. The chaplain had just tried to help her and had been thanked with wildly abusive speech; he had turned from her bed with a shudder. Even Josephine Butler shrank back for a moment as she witnessed this scene. But then she got hold of herself and stepped up to this woman's cot. At first without speaking, she did her the small favor of straightening her pillow and then without reproach said a few kind words to her. She herself confessed afterward: I do not know what I said to all this vulgarity and brutality, but I thought of Christ and of the fact he shed his blood even for this woman. In this moment, Josephine Butler by her faith in the forgiveness of sins through Christ saw this woman as a child of God. This was true contact in the power of the Spirit, contact from above. As a result the woman calmed down. A few days later, she died, believing in the forgiveness of her sins through the care of Josephine Butler.

We were bound to refer here to the doctrines of the Holy Spirit and of election in their application to pastoral care. They are closely related to and answer the problem raised by the question of man's ability to respond to the Word of God and of the possibility of a contact. For they make room for the recognition that man's encounter with God is brought about by God himself, who in the power of his Spirit blazes a trail for his Word into man's heart. God himself furthers his cause within us. We come to believe in him. He effects this faith, but he so effects it that it becomes *my* faith, *my* being grasped by God in the totality of my existence. I share in it with all my strength. Both affirmations are true: Faith is entirely transcendent since it is the work of the Spirit of God whereby I participate in the benefits of Christ; it is at the same time entirely immanent since it wholly becomes a work which I am called to do. That is, the doctrine of the Holy Spirit affirms and confirms man's responsiveness to the forgiveness of sins, but it affirms and confirms them by the action of God. Man's ability to respond to the forgiveness of sins is to be understood solely in a spiritual way—on account of its object! For its object, forgiveness, is indeed no "object" at all; it is the holy and merciful God himself who gives us a share in himself in his free act of forgiveness.*

From this understanding of man's responsiveness to forgiveness, the first inevitable lesson to be learned in regard to pastoral care is the imperative to pray. The relationship between pastoral care and prayer has proved to be a recurring issue in our discussion so far. Here we are at the root of this relationship. Because there is responsiveness to God's Word only in the Holy Spirit, each and every act of pastoral counseling has to arise out of the attitude of prayer. No wisdom, no psychological knowledge, no psychic power we may be able to demonstrate in our pastoral talk, and no action accompanying our talk, hence no practical technique for the benefit of man, however effective, can replace the decisive act of prayer. To be sure, none of these ingredients should be absent; pastoral care will never be able to do without practical wisdom and help, but in the center and at the heart of pastoral care, prayer must stand out as its principal activity. Praying is truly the one decisive action in which the pastoral counselor must be engaged ever anew and without intermission. The practice of pastoral care and prayer are actually one and the same. Pastoral care *is* prayer.

The biblical testimony is unequivocal here. John 17 must be mentioned first. There the work of Christ is interpreted as work of "pastoral care," i.e., as the deliverance and preservation, through his *high priestly prayer*, of "his own" who are in the world. That it is prayer through which "the anointed" does his work for his people is attested throughout the Old Testament. It is announced in advance as well as confirmed subsequently. This

---

* On the whole doctrine of the Holy Spirit, cf. Karl Barth in *Church Dogmatics* I, 1, 6: "The Knowability of the Word of God," and I, 2, 16: "The Holy Spirit as the Subjective Reality of the Revelation." On the doctrine of election: *Church Dogmatics*, II, 2, ch. 7, especially 35: "The Election of the Individual."

is how we must understand the calls to prayer that are sounded in Israel by all those who represent the people as forerunners of Jesus Christ. As especially characteristic of this pastoral praying the prayer of Moses in the battle with Amalek (Exodus 17:8-16) and the prayers in the Psalms need mentioning.

The "high priestly prayer" in John 17 is to be understood as the fulfillment of the whole Old Testament promise of prayer. Jesus Christ, however, by letting his followers share in the benefit of his prayer, also gives them the task of praying. His prayer continues in their prayer. Now his own also call upon the Father "in his name." It is Jesus' commandment that they do so: "Pray then like this: Our Father who art in heaven . . ." (Matthew 6:9). Praying, we are what we are not by nature, but by grace, God's children whose sins are forgiven in the Holy Spirit (Romans 8:2, 14ff.). According to the testimony of the Gospel, all those words whereby men bring before Jesus the needs of the body and the soul are therefore calls to prayer (cf. Matthew 8:2; 15:22). And praying is the one act in which the Apostle is unceasingly engaged as pastor of his flock (cf. Ephesians 1:15; Philippians 1:3-6); it is also the act to which he summons his people (Ephesians 6:18; I Thessalonians 5:17).

Prayer is thus not simply a means of pastoral care as is often maintained, not even the chief means. It is rather the very center of all pastoral counseling. We know no "means" of pastoral care at all insofar as the term denotes some kind of technique by virtue of which we could attain the goal by ourselves. The goal is indeed man's being addressed by the Word of God. And no way leads from us to this goal. Way and goal coincide here. Like a drawbridge, the way must be lowered from within the goal itself. A force coming from the goal must take hold of us, so that we really cross this bridge and arrive at the goal. In view of the actual event of pastoral care, we are robbed of all means. Neither can we speak God's Word by ourselves; nor can our partner hear it by himself. We control neither mouth nor ear. Therefore, only the prayer remains that God may open our lips and our ears. But even this prayer must be effected by the

Spirit of God. We do not even know what to pray for (Romans 8:26). Prayer is an imposing and sovereign matter, but also a mighty and merciful event. Everything is exclusively entrusted to the one who alone acts in pastoral care. Without him we can do nothing (John 15:5). Thus, prayer is the one indispensable act of pastoral care.

This indicates that there is basically only *one* content of prayer: the petition for the Holy Spirit (cf. Luke 11:13). Although prayer extends to a multitude of concrete concerns, they all converge in the supplication for the intercession of Christ Jesus in our behalf with the Father, in whose presence alone the comfort and counsel we need is imparted. To ask for this presence of the Father in the Son means to ask for the Holy Spirit.

The doctrine of prayer to which we have to refer here is extensively dealt with in Calvin's *Institutes* III, Ch. XX, and in Luther's and Calvin's catechisms in the sections about the Lord's Prayer. It is not our task to develop this doctrine here. But we note how already with Luther and Calvin prayer is closely related to pastoral care, thanks to the point of departure and the foundation they gave to the whole doctrine of prayer. According to Luther's Larger Catechism, prayer follows the teachings about law and faith. Knowing what to do and what to believe, says Luther, is not enough, for a new problem emerges as to the *doing* of faith and obedience in the life of the Christian. Three enemies are ready to attack: the Devil, the world, and the flesh. I must do battle with them, and only my steadfastness in the trial decides whether my obedience and my faith are alive. The "temptation" so frequently mentioned by Luther arises and calls into question the faith and obedience I presumably possess. What is to be done in the face of temptation? The simplest answer is: to listen to God's Word and to do God's Word. But this answer is not enough. What is at stake is the reality and the effectiveness of this hearing and doing, the real entering of the Word into my life. But this means my actually being addressed in the power of the Holy Spirit, who effects the entrance of the Word into my heart. At this point, says Luther, only one thing is left: *prayer*. In order to believe and keep God's Word I must pray. Luther describes this praying with the words: "To prevail upon God's ears." He envisions the Christian in the predicament of a man who is brutally attacked and exposed to mortal danger. He is beaten down by the enemy, and only one thing can help him: neither thinking nor willing, but crying out. In *crying out to God*, which in itself is a helpless gesture, lies a great promise. The whole faith is packed into it. For this outcry in fact presupposes God as the mighty Lord who helps and gives where no other helper and giver exists anymore. It presupposes Christ, through whom I stand before God as his child toward whom he is like a father. Therefore, I cry out to him. I am already accepted by him. But my being accepted must now be validated, must be realized. This happens in prayer. There are powers that cut me off from God, but there is also a way out—crying out to him. Deeply concerned about the soul of man, Luther assigns such a central place to prayer. His doctrine of prayer necessarily joins his dogmatics and ethics.

From this point of departure he further develops the doctrine of individual prayer. Prayer is a *commandment* of God; it is *necessary to salvation*; it has the *promise of fulfillment*. Luther also insists that it is revealed to us *how* we shall pray, and how prayer has its concrete *occasion* and possesses strong *power*. But he always understands it as this outcry in the grip of temptation, as this crucial return of weak man to God his helper.

Though in other ways, Calvin teaches the same thing in the Institutes and in the Geneva Catechism. Everything that is taught about prayer falls within the subject of the *glorification of God*. How is it achieved? Answer: In faith and in obedience. Faith and obedience are therefore dealt with first. Here again, the doctrine of prayer follows. Prayer is described as a "flying away" to God alone and not anywhere else. God is the only Helper, and he is so in Jesus Christ. He who admits this in the Holy Spirit will pray. It is characteristic for Calvin that he presents praying as a work of the church and that he quite explicitly bases prayer on the work of Christ. As implanted in Christ we pray in the church. Both Luther and Calvin add the explanation of the Lord's Prayer as a special teaching of prayer to this first part dealing with prayer in general. All that is to be said about prayer in pastoral care has to rest upon such a teaching of prayer.

The current presentations of a theology of pastoral care unfortunately fail to disclose this connection between prayer in pastoral care and the whole doctrine of prayer. True, the importance of prayer for pastoral care is referred to in Nitzsch, Harnack, Köstlin, Benoît, Asmussen, and Hoch. But since prayer is envisaged within the framework of individual pastoral care, the fundamental doctrine of prayer is only lightly touched, and prayer appears simply as a means of pastoral care. The understanding of what prayer really is is presupposed. But with the general confusion in matters of faith, can such a presupposition be made? It is one of the urgent tasks of the dogmatic endeavor to rethink and redevelop the doctrine of prayer.

For the practice of pastoral care this implies in particular that when we ponder, consider, and discuss the concrete concerns, we must intently listen to God's Word, so that this pondering, considering, and discussing leads to the calling upon God himself. There is nothing so great, but also nothing so small, that it cannot or should not be taken up in prayer. In the church's doctrine of prayer we always find the reference to the "windows . . . opened toward Jerusalem" of the praying Daniel (mentioned in Daniel 6). In fact, we can never even rightly admonish a child or write a pastoral letter without such an open window.

One of the values of the pastoral care of Moral Re-Armament is the great stress on pastoral prayer. So we must understand the summons to "become quiet," which continually appears in this movement, insofar as it intends to be not simply a technical help to one's own composure to the suppression of emotions or other inner disturbances, but genuine quietness before God and his Word. Compare to this what the Geneva physician Tournier writes about this quietness in the treatment of his patients. But compare also what was said about the preservation of inner composure in the church's doctrine of pastoral care long before Moral Re-Armament. We recall here again chiefly the older, classical pastoral theology of Wilhelm Löhe and Claus Harms.

Prayer in pastoral care has a threefold form. It is *first* a prayer for myself as pastor, for purification and illumination of my spirit, a prayer that I may become the true instrument of the Spirit of God. In terms of content, it is a petition for the forgiveness of sins. My spirit, my self is filled with the spirit of this world; I lack discipline; that is to say, I am driven about by my emotions and desires; I am reluctant and unfree to serve my neighbor; I am closed to the Word of God (and all the more open to the news and gossip of the day!); I live for myself and my inclinations (perhaps they are even pious inclinations). All this hangs about me like a thick fog in the morning of my working day. This fog must be lifted, for how else shall I help my neighbor? In a word: My sin must be taken away from me. For this I have to pray.

What the pastoral counselor needs for himself and must pray for may be best described by the biblical concept of *"wisdom."* Wisdom denotes the gift of true understanding; it teaches us to see the other correctly, to penetrate his situation, and enables us immediately to accept the neighbor's predicament in all its dimensions and to make it our own concern. Wisdom also denotes the gift of right treatment; wisdom is practical knowledge of life leading to correct decisions from case to case. It is the gift of proving "what is the will of God, what is good and acceptable and perfect" (Romans 12:2). Each act of pastoral care must flow out of such "wisdom." However, it is effected by the Spirit of God, for we are here concerned not simply with some kind of psychological or moral counsel—as surely as this is included—but we are concerned with the communication of forgiveness, and this is greater and different. So understood, "wisdom" stands for the most important qualification we need in pastoral care and for which we pray (cf. James 1:5).

Prayer in pastoral care is *secondly* a prayer for my neighbor; it is intercession. Again, intercession cannot here be treated as such. There is intercession that reaches beyond the narrower province of pastoral care proper. For instance, the intercession offered, according to Genesis 18:22ff., by Abraham for Sodom, and even the intercession of the high priestly prayer, is not only an act of pure pastoral care, but an act of power whereby God's messenger and anointed one ushers in the reign of forgiveness on earth. Such intercession, however, does play a significant role in pastoral care, too. It proceeds from the recognition of our impotence to help our fellow men by our own natural strength, from the recognition that the only real help flows out of God's free grace, and that prayer is therefore the one act of mutual help. But because God's help consists again in the fact that he reveals himself to man in need of help, as "the true Father" to whom we may turn with complete confidence as "his true children" (Luther), intercession will be a prayer for the purification and illumination of our neighbor through God's Spirit and for God's Word. Our neighbor must also be equipped with "wisdom" in order to stand the "trials" (James 1:12). He too must be enabled to acknowledge God's will for him and to submit to it in concrete decisions of life. But because such recognition of the will of God includes the removal of the hardness and blindness of heart, intercession is also a petition for forgiveness. Its fulfillment consists in our neighbor's clearly hearing: "Thy sins are forgiven thee!" This is the one and inclusive petition we can address to God in his behalf.

This is the content of the apostolic intercession in Ephesians 1:16-23 and 2:14-21. But already in the Old Testament the whole content of the prophetic intercession for the people focused on the question whether God "may forgive their iniquity and their sin" (Jeremiah 36:3). Incidentally, this "may" which prominently appears in more than one place expresses not the uncertainty of the fulfillment of prayer, but rather the freedom of divine grace which leads us into prayer.

This must be uppermost in our minds in all our prayers for others. We pray in the concrete case for this or that definite thing. And we may and we want to do so. But we must pray knowing that not this or that, but the will of God must be done, and this will consist in the sinner's repentance. The physical healing or the protection in distress, which I ask for a neighbor, is never the final goal of my petition; the goal is that God be given glory in the person's life because he forgives him his sins. This is "his will" to be done according to the Lord's Prayer (cf. also the connection between the petition for healing and the forgiveness of sins as it comes to light in James 5:14ff.). If we keep this rule of all prayer, we are protected from the unfitting impatience and insistence whereby intercession is so often corrupted and invalidated.

Holy Scripture is full of admonition to intercession and full of promise that intercession will be heard. Surely the whole Old Testament sacrifice is to be understood as intercessory action of one man for another at the altar.

Pastoral prayer is *thirdly* prayer with the other. The neighbor must come to the knowledge of God if he is to be helped. This knowledge is granted in prayer. In praying, man forsakes the attitude of wait, see, and watch, of barren theoretical knowledge, and ventures into the new dimension of the actual understanding of God himself. He encounters God; God encounters him as his God. Prayer is therefore always a step that leads beyond all boundaries into the realm of eternity. For it is actually talking with God, actually being heard by God and listening to God. Hence prayer is the final destination of every way, the deliverance from every distress, the fulfillment of every petition. Here on earth we cannot advance any further than to this point where, awakened by the Holy Spirit, in the name of Christ Jesus, we meet the Father in prayer. What is the weight of my sin, what is even the weight of my death, if in prayer I am assured that already I stand before God accepted by him as his child? Pastoral care will continually seek to encourage this step as its proper goal. Because my neighbor does not find the courage and the strength for such prayer by himself, I as his pastoral counselor must take him with me. I take him with me when I pray not only *for* him, but *with* him. Therefore, the pastoral conversation necessarily ends in common prayer.

Because such common prayer is the last and greatest event

to take place in pastoral care, that wisdom which informs us whether and when and how this joint prayer is in order must govern the situation. There is no fixed rule about it. The occurrence of this prayer is and remains the free work of grace, and a daring enterprise on our side. The circumstances will decide from case to case whether I may and ought to pray with another person. Probably we should run the risk much more frequently and daringly than we now do. But because of respect for the freedom of grace, which alone may initiate such prayer, we must most urgently warn against the use of prayer as a means which I employ, a manipulation which I undertake in order to get ahead with my neighbor. We have just asserted that praying itself is the goal. It can thus never and in no way become a means. Where it becomes this, where the art of prayer is applied in pastoral care, prayer is corrupted. And this is the most dreadful corruption of pastoral care that can happen. It is the sin against the third commandment and against the first petition of the Lord's Prayer. Let us beware of this sin! Let us consider how the words of Jesus in the Sermon on the Mount (Matthew 6:5ff.) make prayer a secret and private affair. Praying with another is in danger of becoming that "praying before man" which the verdict of the Sermon on the Mount condemns with such unprecedented sharpness. This is also what makes praying in the so-called prayer cells a dangerous affair. In approaching the question of common prayer, we must refer above all to the prayer of the congregation during the worship service. There we are taken along by the prayer of all the others and can join our own weak words without running the risk of becoming the hypocrite.

When we have this warning in mind, however, something else must now be added. There is the promise to the two or three who "are gathered in my name," that they may be certain of the presence of Christ Jesus among them. There is the summons in the Letter of James to prayer for one another and about one another and to the strength that radiates from such prayer. But how shall this promise be fulfilled if in praying together we do not dare call upon him who will be invisibly present in the place of such calling? It is therefore imperative to help the other person by praying with him. It must happen because the other finds the way back to prayer through our praying with him. It does not need to be a lengthy prayer; it can be quite simply the Lord's Prayer which opens before our neighbor like a door we are allowed to open for him. Every pastoral counselor will have the experience of being especially thanked by the other for just this common prayer, since it is decisive for him.

The instruction in prayer which must be given in pastoral care will first consist in our asking our neighbor about his praying or not praying. There will scarcely be a pastoral conversation in the course of which the question is not raised by the pastor: "Do you pray?" The answer in countless cases will be: "No, I cannot pray." The conversation will then focus on this "I cannot" and will be deepened. Indeed, with this question of praying or not praying, the whole message will be communicated.

For the concrete practice of prayer, one may again refer to Martin Luther's interpretation of the Lord's Prayer and to Calvin's Catechism, which likewise contains an interpretation of the Lord's Prayer. Of the abundance of examples of pastoral praying as they are found in good biographies, we single out the biography of Christoph Blumhardt by Friedrich Zündel. With Blumhardt, it can become especially clear what powerful and wholesome prayer in pastoral care is.

To address man in pastoral conversation presupposes knowledge of the human nature. Pastoral care, therefore, needs psychology as an auxiliary science which serves to examine man's inner being and to make this knowledge available. Pastoral care, however, must critically dissociate itself from the essentially alien philosophical presuppositions inherent in psychology which could impair its own understanding of man derived from Holy Scripture.

10 Pastoral Care and Psychology

The communication of the forgiveness of sins in pastoral care is concerned with the concrete addressing of man by a Word which, as we have seen, is wholly transcendent in origin and content, but also with regard to the power whereby it addresses man and man receives it. But it is not sufficient to demonstrate the essential transcendence of this Word. This transcendent Word intends to become and really does become wholly immanent. As the Word from above which it is, it enters the life of the man it addresses. It fills and moves him to the hidden depths of his inner life, conscious and unconscious. It becomes the determining power of man's existence, the source of that "wisdom" which informs all acts of life and the choices and decisions in which life is accomplished from moment to moment.

When we reflect, therefore, on the task of true pastoral care, we must also reflect on this inner life of man as the soil where the guiding Word takes root. But as the pastoral counselor turns to this field, he finds it already occupied, worked over, and penetrated by a science specifically devoted to the investigation of this inner life, the science of *psychology*. This fact immediately challenges us to explore the necessary relationship between pastoral care and psychology as well as *psychotherapy* which accompanies psychology and makes practical use of its findings. Why should pastoral care, with genuine interest arising from its task, not take a careful look at what psychology and psychotherapy have to say about man's inner being? How could it, in communicating its Word, bypass psychological knowledge and the psychotherapeutic application of this knowledge? We have noticed the fact of this relationship all along; its fundamental and practical significance as well as the problems it poses are so great, however, that we must now examine them separately.

Our reflection must start with the self-sufficiency of true pastoral care. Pastoral care is a discipline of its own, unexchangeably distinct and different from psychology and psychotherapy. It is no doubt accomplished in the form of surgery on man's inner life comparable to the treatment of a physician. Thus it moves into the field of the psychologist's or the psychiatrist's activity, but it is essentially amenable neither to psychological inquiry nor to psychotherapeutic application.

It can well happen that the Word of forgiveness brings with it psychic and perhaps even physical healing; understood in a new spiritual sense, it will actually be the proper remedial, healing Word for the man who hears it. But even such a remedy and healing by the Word of God is entirely different from the release and solving of psychic conflicts brought about by psychological, psychiatric methods. As a sign of this the reverse can also happen. The message of the forgiveness of sins may be communicated to and grasped by a man, and although the sting of illness remains, there is healing and deliverance of the soul, and thus comfort and mitigation of pain result.

Pastoral care is and remains proclamation of the Word to the individual and neither can nor should ever be anything else. But—and here begins the relationship between pastoral care and psychology—in order to deliver the Word of forgiveness to man, we must avail ourselves of a knowledge of his inner life in as exact, methodical, and comprehensive a way as is possible. Without such a knowledge, our talk with him cannot possibly lead to deliverance, its goal. We would inexcusably blunder in pastoral care, we would close instead of opening, we would wound instead of healing, were we not to care about the psychic and the concomitant physical state in which our neighbor finds himself. It is the Word of forgiveness itself that comes to man with a truly motherly mercy accepting his whole psycho-physical existence, thereby instructing its messengers to muster the utmost understanding of man. If there were no psychology as the knowledge about man's inner being, and no psychotherapy as the attempt to help him, they would have to be called for and developed by the forgiveness of sins. Thus pastoral care needs psychology as its outstanding auxiliary. True pastoral counselors have always been true psychologists. As messengers of the Word to the individual, we cannot know enough about man and, consequently, not be expert enough in the methods and perceptions which psychology and psychotherapy use in the investigation and treatment of man. Hence the relationship of psychology to pastoral care may be defined as that of an *auxiliary science*.

The true pastoral counselor is always a translator of the Word. The word "translate" reminds me of a stream to be crossed from one shore to the other. He who must perform this transition must find the right place to land with his message. He must know very well the farther shore—man—in order to talk to him in the right way. Or I recall the figure of the physician: He must not only know the remedies; he must above all recognize the illness. He must be a good diagnostician. Of what use is the best therapeutic knowledge if the diagnosis is wrong? Of what use to the counselor are all gifts and powers, of what use is even his knowledge of the Word of God itself, if he does not understand the man and the woman with whom he would like to come into pastoral conversation? Mere sympathy, the mere zeal to help is insufficient. Wisdom is needed, knowledge is needed, and this means knowledge of man. In obtaining such knowledge we can be greatly served by psychology.

The sources from which psychological knowledge is to be gained are of various kinds. *First,* there is the knowledge about man and his situation which flows out of one's own experience. The first source of the knowledge of man is self-knowledge. He who consciously lives his own life and does not shun reflection upon it; who does not hide from himself; who does not disregard difficult experiences with himself, experiences of his own misery and sin, does not repress or suppress them, but faces them and works them through—to him a broad and living comprehension of human life will be possible. Even the study of books about these things will only help him in whom this first source of psychic understanding flows richly. *Second,* there are the living relationships with other people, the encounter with their lives as it takes place in conversation, in the home and on the street, quite apart from pastoral counseling. He who avoids the daily, profane meeting with his neighbors will never advance to a genuine understanding of man. Those who go it alone are not fit to be pastoral counselors. The *third* source from which one gains knowledge of man is the view of life as it is found in descriptions of life, not only in pious ones but also in the quite worldly and secular. Writers and poets are foremost among the portrayers of life. Of the really great, there are all too few: Jeremias Gotthelf above all, and he before Gottfried Keller, although the latter, especially in *Der Grüne Heinrich,* is also significant for us. So are Dostoievski and Tolstoy, the great Russians, with their novels, and finally Balzac, who is a master in the description of the intricate perversities of sinful man. But all kinds of novels and descriptions of life written only for the day have something to say to us insofar as they depict the man of today truly and tellingly. Such reading should never be abandoned. A statesman and leader of men like Masaryk confesses in his memoirs that he gained his whole knowledge of man from the continuous reading of hundreds of contemporary novels. *Fourth* and last, the psychological and psychiatric professional literature needs to be consulted. It has today grown boundless. Each counselor will have to decide for himself how far he wants to extend his studies. Here individual inclination and talent are rightfully determining factors.

We will be well advised not to begin with the numerous popularized presentations that are offered today in almost countless number, not even when these are written with special reference to pastoral care. Neither should we seize at once upon one of the works representative of the teachings of a particular psychological or psychiatric school. Rather, we should concentrate at first on the most objective survey possible of all the manifold currents in this field as it is to be gained from a good modern textbook of psychology or psychiatry.

As a philosophical introduction to the problems of theoretical psychology, we suggest: Paul Häberlin, *Der Geist und die Triebe, eine Elementarpsychologie*. From the theological side there is Emil Brunner's anthropology entitled *Man in Revolt*. From the medical side, the distinguished, circumspect, and, even for the layman, easily readable presentation of the respective problems by Richard Siebeck: "Neurosenlehre" in *Lehrbuch der Innern Medizin*, Vol. 2 (Verlag Julius Springer, Berlin). Later, however, we may get hold of the chief works of the psychological and psychiatric movement: Sigmund Freud, *General Introduction to Psychoanalysis;* Alfred Adler, *Individual Psychology;* and C. G. Jung, *Psychological Types, Über die Psychologie des Unbewussten, Psychology and Religion;* cf. also Jacobi, *The Psychology of C. G. Jung*. Instructive for the pastoral counselor are also the writings of Fritz Künkel, e.g., his *Character, Growth, Education*. Finally, the books dealing with more or less direct guidance and counseling, if not with the application of psychology, are to be recommended. Some are written by physicians, some by theologians; on the whole, the former are even more instructive and rewarding for the pastor than the latter. This judgment is especially true of the writings by the late Zurich minister, Dr. O. Pfister. They lean heavily on Freudian psychology and may be incontestable on that score, but are all the more questionable and inadequate from the standpoint of theology. Pfister followed his psychoanalytic master even philosophically and let the Christian basis shrivel to some merely ethical rudiments. Outstanding among the books written by physicians are Heinrich Meng, *Praxis der Seelischen Hygiene,* and above all the book written out of real understanding of faith by the Zurich psychiatrist Maeder, *Ways to Psychic Healing;* also, Bovet, *Die Person, ihre*

Krankheiten und Wandlungen; and the previously mentioned book by the Geneva physician Tournier, *Médicine de la Personne* and his *Technique et Foi.*

Over against this scientific literature, it must ultimately be asserted that the decisive knowledge of man and his predicament comes to us from Holy Scripture itself. The Word of God opens up a wide and deep view of man and all things human which no psychology can replace let alone surpass. Rather, psychology could gain important insights from it. The Word of God is of its own accord directed to man. It intends to address and touch, to heal and recreate him. He who allows himself to be led by the Word is therefore led into right intercourse with man. He moves man and all his problems into the light of this Word and sees and examines them in this light. Only then does he achieve a real and correct understanding of man and an inner encounter with him that reaches farther and plunges deeper than any merely psychological consideration. It can now be affirmed that in connection with a knowledge of man gained from the Word of God, psychological knowledge can become truly helpful and illuminating for us.

We shall really understand man only when we understand him from the Bible. There is disclosed what man is and what no psychology is able to disclose by itself: Man's misery and man's greatness, to speak with Pascal (who had such a profound understanding of human nature because he endeavored to know himself in the light of the Bible), man's bondage to sin, but also his belonging to the heavenly Father in spite of all sin and in all sin. Only when we understand man on the basis of the double infinity to which he is subject, the evil infinity of sin and the victorious infinity of grace, does our knowledge of human nature reach its true depth. We must not rest until we see each individual with whom we have to deal in this biblical perspective. We must always pentrate to the last depth: to the demonic powers that hold man imprisoned, but also to the divine powers that are stronger than all boundness. Then we shall see concretely and clearly what we have already demonstrated: that the decisive means of all pastoral care is prayer and the communication of the Word. The wisdom of all true pastoral care is not instruction, not interpretation, not even morals and not even psychology, but prayer and joint submission with man to the Word. This is a matter of power: Man is to be liberated from the power of evil by the superior force of Christ. In pastoral conversation, we announce this liberation; in prayer, we grasp and effect it. All this becomes clear from Holy Scripture alone, and for the pastor's understanding of man the most important thing is intimate, daily acquaintance with the Bible.

Thus, in a very fundamental way, we assert the primacy of the Holy Scripture over psychology and its knowledge of human nature. What is generally valid is also valid here: The Word of God is not one source of knowledge among others; it is the basis of all knowledge even in the matter of the understanding of man. This in no way belittles psychology and its research. They are fully recognized, and we shall use them, shall carry their gold with us as once Israel carried the gold of the Egyptians. But if we in pastoral care make use of the findings of psychology, we do not mean by this to replace the understanding of man as it comes to us from the Bible nor to complete the latter only with the former. Our use of psychological findings only serves to elucidate the understanding of man given us in the Word of God. The knowledge of man as provided by psychology furnishes the material in which the understanding of man obtained from Holy Scripture is unfolded and applied and thereby becomes powerful and operative. This is what we mean by our thesis that psychology is an auxiliary science of pastoral care.

But this needs closer investigation. For the service which psychology renders to pastoral care, we have employed the concept of the knowledge of man. We understand by such knowledge of man the knowledge of man's inner life or, as it is currently called, his psychic life in all its dimensions and depths. The terms "soul," and "psyche" so used do not denote the totality of man's existence before God which is our starting point in pastoral care; rather they are applied here in a provisional, technical sense to denote man's inner nature, the subject of psychological research. So conceived, the latter is to be understood as a part of natural science. Man's inner being is distinguished from the outer, physical nature by the fact that, as we have previously shown (cf. ch. 3), it is *personally* structured. That is, it exhibits a mysterious center—man's ego—to which the whole psychic life is related as to an acting subject governing and determining everything. Precisely by this relatedness to the ego as an acting subject, man's inner life is constituted as his internal, psychic life in distinction from his merely external, animal, physical existence. There is thus nothing psychic that is not personal. To have an inner life, to be psychic *and* personal, to be human, to have an ego, are one and the same. This distinction between inward and outward, between psychic and physical life, however, is not absolute but only relative, because man's psycho-personal life is inseparably bound up with his physical existence. The psychic life is not something apart, but it entirely permeates the physical life. The soul exists and is present only as the soul of a body which it governs and fills. The soul is nothing without the body into which it is formed. But the reverse is also true: The body is nothing without the soul. For man at any rate, the body exists only in relationship to the soul which inhabits it as its acting subject. Here again, we are faced with the totality of man who is a unity in body and soul. This is the beginning and the end of all the knowledge of man offered by psychology. This totality of man and the personal existence on which it is based must remain a final mystery as to its origin and nature to any profane anthropology. For psychology, it is a datum which is not to be explained by psychological methodologies but only to be described phenomenologically. An impenetrable veil of mystery ultimately shrouds its proper subject, man's soul. To be sure, it is able to present the psychic facts, and this presentation is the content of that knowledge of human nature which is to be expected from true psychology. But the final interpretation of these facts and the transformation of the knowledge of man into the actual understanding of man is beyond its scope. If it nevertheless attempts to outline such an understanding of man philosophically on the basis of its own presuppositions, it disregards the set boundaries of descriptive phenomenology; thus it becomes speculative and necessarily falls prey to ambiguities, even to fantasies.

Compare here the debate over the body-soul problem in modern anthropology and psychology. See Paul Häberlin in his *Der Leib und die Seele*. Häberlin, however, does not want to see the concept of nature applied to man's inner life and would therefore raise psychology above natural science as a kind of a normative science. In opposition to this C. G. Jung rightly, I believe, places psychology explicitly into the realm of phenomenology. He says concerning his method: "Notwithstanding the fact that I have often been called a philosopher, I am an empiricist and adhere to the phenomenological standpoint. . . . As this statement indicates, I approach psychological matters from a scientific and not from a philosophical standpoint. . . . I restrict myself to the observation of phenomena and I refrain from any application of metaphysical or philosophical considerations." (*Psychology and Religion*, pp. 1-2.)

Here the Holy Scripture becomes powerfully relevant with its declarations about man. It mediates not only knowledge of man; it is also concerned with understanding man. It begins where profane anthropology leaves off and necessarily must leave off: with that totality of man which is grounded in his personal being. It discloses to us its origin and nature as it traces man's whole human existence back to the Word of God, the Creator and Redeemer. Through God's call and summons, man lives as the personal being he is, one in soul and body. Here is the place, the source of that mystery as the center of all the psychic and psycho-physical facts. It is the mystery of man's nature itself in its duality of soul and body, which are yet one since they both belong to the nature of the one man.

We repeat what was already said (in ch. 3) when we reassert: Theological anthropology would do well to abandon the dichotomy of soul and body prevailing in profane anthropology and to return to the ancient biblical view of a trichotomy into spirit, soul, and body. Spirit would then denote the Spirit of God including the breath or Word by which man's nature comes to life in body and soul and is preserved in life, or in short, the lifegiving Word of God, insofar as it dwells in man by virtue of the creation. This "spirit" is of course not conceivable as a psychic or physical fact at all. It can appear in anthropology only as a boundary concept. It signifies, establishes, and guards that mystery which becomes again and again visible in the form of the personal unity of man's nature in the midst of all the psycho-physical facts.

With this distinction between knowledge of man and understanding of man, the field of psychological research is freed for the task befitting it, but at the same time also defined and delimited. Psychology is freed insofar as its object is determined and clearly outlined by the definition of man's inner being we have given. It need no longer waver between empiricism and speculation; it explores and elucidates man's inner being and describes it as precisely as possible. Pastoral care, however, takes over the findings of psychology in order to place them in the service of the required proclamation of the Word.

Even from the viewpoint of Scripture, psychology as this clearly outlined investigation is a completely legitimate and necessary undertaking, a partial fulfillment of the commandment given in the story of creation: "Subdue the earth!" (Genesis 1:28.) We ought not to be disturbed that psychological research is done on the basis of the powers and possibilities of natural perception, with the means and methods of a modern, scientific discipline and by scholars who perhaps count themselves as standing on the fringe of Christian faith. The attempt to establish a "Christian" psychology pursued by Christian scholars is senseless. As there is no Christian zoology or physics, there is no Christian psychology either. Nor is there any need for it. What is needed is a *Christian use* of psychology, an application of its results in the pastoral care of the Christian church. And that is something else.

This is not to say that the territory of natural perception to which psychology properly belongs does not come under the power of the Word of God. Of course it does! As truly as the whole of nature and its knowledge lives from the Word of God. The reign of God and his Word does not coincide with the territory of the church and the faith. God's Kingdom and lordship in Jesus Christ extends even to realms where it is not believed. Precisely this is attested in the creation account of Holy Scripture. And this alone establishes the possibility of any natural knowledge, but also the possibility for the church to make sovereign use of this knowledge, e.g., by availing itself of the results of psychological investigation in the implementation of pastoral care. Furthermore, this also implies that scientific inquiry and belief in the Word of God cannot only coexist, but also very well co-operate. For the benefit of psychology, we suggest, it would be more than good and necessary that we again have psychologists who, more than is the case today, are conversant with the Word of God. It would be of greatest significance even for purely scientific knowledge if we not only made use of psychology as members of the church, but if psychology were also to be fertilized by the knowledge of living faith in the church. The knowledge of man in psychology could immeasurably gain from the understanding of man in the Bible.

The delimitation of the psychological knowledge of man by the biblical understanding of man must be evidenced by the final renunciation of any kind of metaphysics. We mean this quite literally. Psychology should abandon any attempt to make declarations reaching beyond the investigation and description of man's inner being into the realm of philosophy and speculative thinking. Psychology is to stick to its subject. It is to be pursued phenomenologically. It must intend to be nothing but natural science in the broadest sense.

Again, this is not to be taken as a devaluation of psychological research. On the contrary, psychology has been valued most as a science whenever it has abided by this limitation. Does not present-day psychology suffer from its lack of certainty as to its

subject? Instead of persisting in the investigation and description of man's inner being, it constantly undergirds its research by a substructure of some self-styled view of human nature. It raises its subject, the human soul, to a kind of hypostasis which it invests with final, even metaphysical, reality. Instead of being satisfied with the description of psychic phenomena, it develops from them an understanding of man, with the help of which it then interprets and illumines its own data in a particular way. But this changes its statements into philosophical interpretations instead of keeping them on the level of psychological, phenomenological findings. These conceptual, philosophical-speculative interpretations then infect, pervade, and dangerously color the whole presentation of the nature of the human soul.

All these speculative definitions and interpretations carry a philosophical theory of immanence into psychology, the result being a self-understanding of man. The attempt is made to perceive and explain man's inner being on the basis of its own presuppositions. The final substrata and depths of this being are disclosed as resources for the forces and structures of the psychic life, and these depths and substrata are elevated to the level of the transcendent and divine. Yet this transcendence with its asserted divinity is in fact immanent, i.e., it still coincides with man's inner being, even though this being now is conceived as having much deeper roots and as projecting into the transcendent realm. Nothing but the divinization of man's inner being and thus of man himself is accomplished by this procedure. This distinguishes and separates this immanent self-understanding of man from the understanding of man in Holy Scripture. For the actual transcendence of God proclaimed in the Scriptures, the transcendence of faith, is something wholly other than the divine depth of human nature claimed by philosophical psychology. The Word of God brings to light the real transcendence, the true and living God and the relation he sets up with man. God's judgment and grace are at work here as they overwhelm the whole nature and supernature of man, recreating and renewing it; proclamation is the watchword here, and not only interpretation of life; preaching and pastoral care, and not only psychological explanations and counseling.

This critique of the philosophical speculative substructure naturally does not affect the *general concepts* whereby psychology orders its experiential data. Without the application of such general concepts, there is no understanding at all and thus no knowledge. Like every branch of natural science, psychology in turn must set up categories which reach beyond the mere accumulation and classification of observations. The use of the concept of the "soul" already represents such an indispensable substructure. These general concepts serve as working hypotheses for psychological investigation and practice and, so used, exercise a necessary function, though one to be strictly delimited. In the last analysis, the mystery of the ego hidden in all psychic manifestations, the personal itself, compels the use of such substructures. And because this necessitates at least a brush with the supernatural, it may be said that no psychology can properly work without a slight shot of natural theology. But instead of a mere shot, a very potent dose of it is usually injected. For the interpretative and summarizing general concepts by nature are stated absolutely, result in fixed axioms, are condensed into a more or less closed system, and are surrounded with the significance and the splendor of dogmas. This encourages those unhappy border violations which can no longer be tolerated.

This raises a crucial problem for faith and the pastoral care flowing from it. Because of the continually threatening philosophical infringement, true pastoral care, with all the use it makes of psychology, has to be on its guard. It must sharply distinguish between psychological data as such and the concomitant philosophical interpretations. Not that Christian faith should propose its own philosophical thesis about the nature of man. The understanding of man according to faith has nothing to do with philosophical interpretations of human nature. In faith, man is never interpreted and explained on the basis of the depths of his own nature. The opposite is true. He is placed over against nature and all its depths, its roots and substrata. His true nature consists in his standing before God and living by his Word from moment to moment in the totality of his existence in body and soul. The mystery of man's nature is not subject to psychological knowledge, but is accessible only to faith.

This mystery of man's humanity before God is what constitutes the exclusive content of the understanding of man in the Bible in distinction from the knowledge of man in psychology. To this refer all the statements of faith about the sin which clings to man, but also about the grace which masters this sin. To be sure, the inner and outer nature of man participates in both. Man's nature—known and unknown, conscious and unconscious—is very really affected by sin and grace to the depths of its being. But this involvement in sin and grace is not a mark and an attribute of human nature as such and hence cannot be seen in it. Nature in itself knows neither sin nor grace. Therefore, the concepts of sin and grace have no place in a scientific, psychological description of life. If they are employed there, they are improperly, even illegally, employed. They become symbols for data—perhaps for conflicts and forces arising out of the unconscious—which psychology is unable to interpret within its own concepts. A final mistrust toward such use is certainly indicated for pastoral care, which must beware of being confused by this misuse of the concepts of sin and grace. The primacy of its understanding of man obtained from the Bible is never for a moment to be abandoned. Pastoral care knows that it stands or falls with this. If it forsakes the biblical view and tries to understand man otherwise, be it only partially and provisionally—and this means always on the basis of immanent and natural presuppositions—its task is inescapably betrayed and invalidated. Its proper task is and remains the proclamation of the Word of God as the one thing which is necessary. But can proclamation, can the Word of God, can the forgiveness of sins, be the one thing necessary if man's life is secretly or openly, wholly or partially, nourished from other sources, and therefore also interpreted and understood on the basis of them? If this assumption prevails, and the understanding of man in modern psychology suggests it rather insistently, the pastoral counselor will be tempted to turn to these other sources and to expect salvation and help for man from them. He will then no longer use psychology as a necessary auxiliary science; rather, he will begin to practice pastoral care as an auxiliary to the norm of psychology. The Word of God and its proclamation recede. Psychological research and the resulting interpretations become prevalent even in pastoral care. And this means the end of true pastoral care.

Pastoral care then becomes psychological counsel in religious garb. Everything is turned around. Instead of the Word of God, psychological considerations take first place. The words of faith, insofar as they are still used, are stripped of their own content and become mere symbolic concepts which are applied to the investigation of purely psychic facts. "Sin" becomes a symbol for the entanglement of man in neurotic fixation; "forgiveness" another word for the inner release and liberation sought in the psychotherapeutic process of healing; "prayer" a remedy for the recovery of self-confidence applied profitably "to religiously susceptible men." "God" himself becomes the expression for the feeling of "harmony with the infinite," which appears where man regains control of his inner forces. This "psychological pastoral care" no longer recognizes, or sees only quite indistinctly and from afar, that sin is something quite different from psychic disturbance (as certainly as it can appear as such), that man is ultimately helped not by psychotherapeutic healing but by forgiveness, and that forgiveness is once again something other than merely a new orientation of man's inner being.

A pastoral care practicing such a displacement of values from the spiritual to the anthropological may find success and appreciation on purely psychological and psychotherapeutic grounds, but its proper work remains undone. It has sold its birthright. It is to be called pseudomorphic, and the words from the Sermon on the Mount about the salt that has lost its savor apply to it.

Concretely and specifically, the psychology which can be helpful to pastoral care, yet at the same time threatening, as we just indicated, has grown out of the psychological and psychotherapeutic research of Sigmund Freud, Alfred Adler, and C. G. Jung. Its point of departure is psychoanalysis first developed by Freud out of the therapy of neuroses. Starting from this point, psychotherapy with all its related research in psychology has undergone a far-reaching change, a broadening and deepening through the labor of these scholars and their disciples. The result was a revolution in psychology comparable perhaps to the revolution in modern physics. Just as the theory of relativity showed that the description of the external world must rely on a four-dimensional continuum which can no longer be understood in terms of the old Euclidian geometry, so psychoanalysis introduced a whole new dimension in the exploration of man's inner being, the *dimension of the unconscious*. The old view of a world of consciousness as it extends to, and is experienced in, the three realms of thinking, willing, and feeling has been antiquated and surpassed. Experience and the concept of what "soul" is as man's inner being is a problem all over again. Psychic life gains an extent not formerly known and a depth not formerly explored. This puts an end to the quite materialistic thought of a psychic substance however sublimely conceived; it also brings to an end the idea of the psychic as only a function of the physical! What is the soul? This question is asked anew for psychology. The soul is in any case a reality in its own right, might, and majesty in the compass of man's nature, no less actual and significant than the outer, bodily existence, even in fact superior to it and governing it. This brings about a new development of the body-soul problem, which leads finally to maintaining the self-sufficiency of the psychic and its preponderance over all the merely physical. This leads to investigating and describing the psychic life out of new presuppositions commensurate with it. Thus a new depth psychology is developed. Although theoretical textbook psychology has not yet or only partially drawn the consequences of the new situation, everything has come into flux in the territory of psychology as a whole.

Quite obviously this reorientation in psychology heightens the danger we envisioned of an ideological absolutizing of the basic concept and research methods here newly formed and employed. The self-sufficiency, power, and value of everything that belongs to man's inner being emerges most strongly. The principles of the new view of man's psychic life are broadened into a new view of the essence of man generally. They claim a validity which intends to surpass and perhaps even to exclude every other view, the understanding of man according to faith upon which pastoral care rests, not excepted. Only if we keep this development in mind can we be duly impressed by the seriousness of the necessary present-day confrontation between pastoral care and psychology.

In Freud's psychology, the exploration of the psychic life still occurs essentially on the basis of naturalistic, mechanistic thinking. Psychic life takes place in a magnetic field, viewed in analogy to physical events, subject to supposedly rather rigid laws of nature.

The ensuing picture of the psychic life process is that of a machine inexorably operative in all the depths of the unconscious. Man's soul appears as a powerful mechanism that has its greatest extension not in the realm of the conscious, but in the unconscious. Sexuality is its principal motive force. Man's conscious ego works to control its instinctual life governed by sexuality. But this effort is more fruitless than successful. Because of this defectiveness in control, man's inner economy repeatedly falls into deep confusion and disorder. This is shown in the outbreak of neuroses and psychoses, which are to be regarded as symptoms of this disturbance in the depths of man's inner being. In the view of this psychology, man therefore appears as one driven, bound, obsessed, and controlled by the forces of his unconscious. One is tempted to say he appears as a robot of his own psychic mechanism.

Freudian psychology has been frequently and vehemently attacked on this account. Its view of sexuality as almost the only important drive is the special cause for reproach. This view has also been recognized as one sided by Freud's professional colleague Alfred Adler—who basically relies on the same mechanistic presuppositions—in his "Individual Psychology." Yet in spite of this corrective, or better, along with it, Freud's analysis has carried the day. It obviously contains in its fundamental discovery of the unconscious and the forces and powers governing it such irrefutable truth that its opponents cannot prevail against it. No retreat is possible from its essential findings. Its basic perception of the reality and power of the unconscious and its definition of man's instinctual life are not subject to debate for us either; but the mechanistic philosophy operative in Freud's presentation of his psychology is subject to debate. The reality of the secret forces and powers in man's inner being needed to be rediscovered, seen, and brought to light. It is the remarkable achievement of Freud's life work that he did this. But the mechanistic thinking which quite unmistakably forms his philosophical background or superstructure and is repeatedly revealed even in the details of his exposition, adversely influencing and determining his results, is not among the enduring parts of his work. Cannot and must not the inner forces and powers and the incidents and effects they release in man be described simply as such *without* being interpreted philosophically? Or, if interpretation is needed, if a final all-embracing comprehension is indispensable, ought it not issue elsewhere than the place it does with Freud, from a context outside his own vision and categories—a context which he, caught in the web of his own philosophy, dared to call an "illusion"? This is the question which faith and its corresponding pastoral care must direct to Freud's psychoanalysis. (Cf. the book by Freud on *The Future of an Illusion*, where his treatment of the phenomenon of religious faith, which remained unintelligible to him, is not only prejudiced, but regrettably lacks any sound factual knowledge on the part of the writer.)

Freud's mechanistic, naturalistic way of thinking has been surpassed and overcome within his own field of psychology. It is the accomplishment and merit of the Swiss psychiatrist C. G. Jung that he broke through the philosophical orthodoxy of Freud and, maintaining all the psychological insights won by psychoanalysis, set psychology on a new, freer, and broader basis. The method he developed represents the most significant step toward a new foundation of psychology.

Psychology is, according to Jung, pure inquiry into facts without philosophical interpretation. Whether he always succeeds in sticking to this definition and refraining from philosophical interpretations is of course still another question. But at least this is his intention. An important quotation to this effect has already been given. We quote further: "This standpoint is exclusively phenomenological, that is, it is concerned with occurrences, events, experiences, in a word, with facts. Its truth is a fact and not a judgment." (*Psychology and Religion*, p. 3.)

Jung can call Freud a "typical representative of the materialistic epoch" (*Über die Psychologie des Unbewussten*, p. 52). He denies the thesis that the processes of psychic life must be considered as strictly causally connected and determined. "The fullness of life is lawful *and* non-lawful, rational *and* irrational. Therefore, reason and the will grounded in it have only limited validity." And "a man is only half understood when one knows whence everything in him originated." (*Über die Psychologie des Unbewussten*, pp. 83, 89.) Jung certainly knows "that an experience is not even possible without reflection." (*Psychology and Religion*, p. 2). He, too, lays claim to certain leading ideas (motives and symbols) whereby the perplexing variety of psychic facts can be ordered. He calls these motives and symbols "archetypes." They are presented in connection with his discovery of the "collective unconscious" and are rooted in the deepest layers of the human soul. In them the psychic experience of the whole of mankind has been condensed into an immense spiritual inheritance which defines the psychic processes as innermost, central forces. By establishing these archetypes, however, Jung himself approaches the demarcation line where psychology borders on philosophy and a world view. He even crosses the line, for these archetypes "are very close to what Plato understood by ideas." They are, as Jung once said, *"les éternels incréés."* (Jacobi: *Die Psychologie von C. G. Jung*, p. 57.) Behind and above them, however, arises mysteriously and incomprehensibly, as the central expression of the Jungian metaphysics of the soul, the (divine) "self," in which man participates, into which he is himself transformed, since he always is that "self" secretly. Hence even in Jung, the deepest psychic reality is identical with the divine. When man is confronted with inner images and symbols, they exert such primitive power over him that they become idols for him. These idols are ultimately but the projections of his own soul. (Cf. the sharp, but apt analysis of the Jungian psychology of religion which Max Frischknecht supplied in his book *Die Religion in der Psychologie C. G. Jungs*.)

When using psychology, pastoral care will have to be on guard even against Jung, indeed especially so, since Jung is intensely and very personally involved in exploring the subject of psychology of religion. Again, it is true that Jung thereby unearths important findings of a psychological and historical kind. These merit our attention to a high degree. Above all the *history of religion* is revived by his investigations and given a new lucidity from which the dull theories of the many blind and barren theologians and historians of religion could only profit. We can gain from Jung an entirely new appreciation of how religion arises and expands as a psychic image out of the deepest forces of man's inner being. For the understanding of the great world religions, the Jungian psychology of religion renders essential services. Yet it is imperative to keep these psychological and historical insights available from Jung apart from his own *mystical world view* and religiosity implied in their presentation and more or less concealed, but still perceptible. Pastoral care must in no case be infected by them, notwithstanding all it can learn from Jung. The Jungian psychology of religion is a good example to teach us fundamental distinction between a religiosity engendered by man himself out of his inner being and what is true faith, between self-made idols and the true God, between one's own pious words and the Word of God, between religion and revelation.

Lastly, we refer to the books, so numerous today, which do not deal with psychology proper but instruct in the practice of pastoral care on the basis and with the use of psychological insights. This is done by treating problems of the psychic life or reporting on the psychic illness and healing of individual cases. In part these books are written by psychologically trained therapists or psychiatrists proper, in part by people working in the service of the church in the field of pastoral care. The question is to be directed to them whether and to what extent their presentation is colored and perhaps even governed by the philosophical presuppositions of modern psychology. Depending on the answer given to this question, such books are to be admitted or rejected by a thoughtful pastoral care within the church. These books are no longer concerned with the fundamental confrontation with psychology, but exclusively with psychotherapy or the application of psychology in the realm of pastoral care.

In the discussion at the beginning of this chapter some of these books were mentioned and briefly characterized. The wide dissemination of this literature today is a sign of the strong need for a pastoral care that exhibits really sound knowledge of man's psychic state, but also the strong need for a psychology that does not exclude the understanding of man according to faith, that accepts it and is guided by it. Openness to the strength and significance of the truth of the Word of God is not contradictory to psychological wisdom about man; rather one implies the other. In present-day pastoral care, we are again beginning to know about this relationship. It is to be hoped that a new appreciation is shown by psychology as well.

Because man's psychic life is unceasingly threatened and disturbed by sickness, pastoral care becomes pastoral care of the sick. Here it encounters psychiatry and psychotherapy. Pastoral care will define its relationship to them in that even here it follows its given understanding of man and relates illness and healing to sin and grace. The insights of psychiatry and psychotherapy are incorporated and serve to highlight and to communicate the message of forgiveness all the more comprehensibly and powerfully.

11 Pastoral Care and Psychotherapy

The significance of modern psychology for pastoral care calls for a basic reflection on the possibility of its application. In concerning ourselves with this application, we are confronted with *psychotherapy* as the chief form in which psychology is applied. Why this is so, why psychology is applied primarily in the form of an art of healing and thus becomes an auxiliary science to medicine, why psychology turns into psychiatry—these questions can be answered by psychology itself only by referring to the reality and actuality of emotional disturbances and illness. So far-reaching and common is the phenomenon of actual illness of man's inner being that psychological knowledge has come to consider emotional "health" an entirely relative concept, relative to that deep disturbance of normalcy which has come over man's inner being with the invasion of illness. The theological view—the understanding of man according to the Word of God—refers to a quite different context. It refers to *sin* as the root of illness. But what does this mean? How is this reference to be understood? How does illness relate to sin and psychotherapy to pastoral care?

1. *Illness and Sin.* The psychological insight that man is never absolutely, but only relatively healthy, that his actual state is marked by the more or less acute disturbance and diminution of

normalcy comes remarkably close to the picture of man to be gathered from the biblical testimony. There man is considered and called ill not only exceptionally, but regularly and basically. The mark of his existence is not health, but health lost and to be regained through the grace of God. Sickness unto death, whether of the body or of the soul, imminent or already present, constantly threatens him. Sickness actually belongs to the nature of man. To be man and to be ill are not to be separated from one another.

For the Old Testament, it is sufficient to refer to man's subjection to death as expressed in the very beginning (Genesis 2:17; 3:3, 19); to the picture of man in the Psalms, with the unceasing cry of men tormented in body or soul; to the vision outlined by the prophets of the coming Messiah as the Servant of God who will bear and heal man's afflictions and for this reason must himself be burdened and afflicted with illness (Isaiah 53). In the Gospel narratives, men appear from the beginning to the end of Jesus' ministry as affected with every imaginable illness. Fever, blindness, paralysis, leprosy, demonic possession, follow in an endless procession. This expresses the quite definite view that man is ill. Hence Christ is called the Physician. When he says the well have no need of him, but the sick, this means: To Christ, and in his presence, none is well (Luke 5:31ff.).

In the biblical testimony, in contrast to the view of psychology, this sickness of man appears as not merely a natural, biological fact, much as this is always involved. According to the Word of God, man's natural sickness is to be understood as a symptom indicative of a very much deeper, metaphysical disturbance. It is the shadow, the reflection of quite another "sickness" to which man has fallen prey in his total existence. Man is sick because of his *sin*. That is to say: He is sick before God and with regard to God. Because he can live only under the summons of God but still does not heed this summons, because he does not recognize and acknowledge it, because he betrays it, he becomes ill. This is not the place to develop a detailed doctrine of sin. We only assert that sin is a rebellion against God arising from the mysterious depths of man's personal existence. Because this rebellion has taken place and continues to take place, because man is not in order at the roots of his existence, his whole nature is now out of joint. This breaking apart takes the form of illness.

Each of us testifies in some way to the fact that God, so to speak, is hindered from being our God. God cannot exist for us as he is and intends to be, since we do not exist for him in accordance with the purpose of our life. This is the wholly absurd situation created by sin between God and man and which cannot be comprehended or justified. Hence the *illness*. So the Bible sees it. In its testimony, this is apparent in the sick man's confrontation with Jesus Christ. Man's illness becomes evident in his presence. Man's sickness is a sickness in relation to the Messiah, who alone has the power to heal him. This is seen even in the Old Testament and especially in the New Testament. Not without reason Jesus Christ is presented there as surrounded by the sick seeking help. Wherever he appears, the suffering immediately cry out for healing. His presence makes it plain how sick all men are. Their sickness is not only a matter of nature, but has much deeper roots, originating in defection from God. This becomes especially clear in the mentally ill. They cry out when they meet Jesus, "I know who you are, the Holy One of God" (Luke 4:34; cf. Mark 5:7). Such words unmask their illness. It is not simply illness, but a result and sign of man's enduring resistance against God and his Christ. The mysterious but real connection which exists according to the Word of God between illness and sin is exemplified in the demoniac.

True pastoral care is aware of this sickness of man before God. This awareness does not stem from the natural knowledge of man, but from the understanding of man according to the Word of God, i.e., out of faith. Hence the connection between illness and sin as it is established through this awareness exists and is recognizable only for faith. What has biological and psychological investigation and knowledge to do with what the Bible calls "sin"? Only faith can affirm that something is sinful before God and that unforgiven sin, in the words of the elder Blumhardt, may be the "cause" of illness. Exclusively on the basis of this faith, pastoral care links the manifestation of man's illness in body and soul to the spiritual reality of sin. The causality that obtains here cannot be naturally discerned; it is itself of a spiritual kind. Pastoral care can never make use of it to accuse a sick man outside the faith of his sin, quite apart from the fact that it refrains from any such accusation since it proclaims the forgiveness that takes away all sin and makes manifest the "works of God" in Jesus' victory over sin and death (cf. John 9:3). Therefore, we had better not speak of causality at all, but be satisfied with stating the (spiritual) *correlation* between sickness and sin. The Word of God testifies to this correlation when it speaks of sickness as a sign of God's judgment on human life. Illness represents for faith the mark of God's judgment on the sin inherent in human nature, just as man's recovery can become the sign of God's faithfulness in spite of our sin and thus the sign of the forgiveness of sins.

Because faith sees in all sickness (and in all healing as well), quite apart from natural causes and natural developments, a powerful pointer to God the Creator, Reconciler, and Redeemer, pastoral care most seriously fixes its eyes on the footprints and trails so tangibly traced by sin in the form of illness. Specifically, the inclusive picture outlined by modern psychiatry of the sickness of man's inner being is not overlooked but examined with utmost attentiveness. Man's sickness must be understood concretely, because it is to be interpreted to him concretely, not in terms of philosophy but in terms of faith—more yet, because God's healing Word is to be proclaimed concretely to him in his sickness. The specific treatment of the sick in pastoral care reveals how the understanding of man by faith and the knowledge of man in psychology are interwoven. Psychology clarifies the natural extent and development of the illness in which man finds himself. This makes it possible to speak the saving Word in terms of the understanding of man in faith to the human situation so clarified. Since the plight and affliction of the patient is seen concretely and plainly, this plight and affliction can be seized upon in pastoral care, brought before God, and committed to his grace. Of course, this implies humiliation and judgment, but it is wholesome humiliation; there is help in this judgment. If the Word of God is not communicated to the patient, he is left to himself, left to the course of his illness, left to the physicians, dependent on the ultimately limited possibilities and powers of nature which are available to some degree and are within reach. But he does not break through to the source of help. True, he still lives by the grace of God which extends to believers and unbelievers, to the righteous and the unrighteous, to the entire human nature still unredeemed. Only he does not know it; he does not know and cannot grasp his actual deliverance. The word of proclamation is needed to make him comprehend his deliverance, ending the despair of the abandoned, independent man. Thorough knowledge of the human situation, available only to a pastoral care steeped in psychology, is needed if the proclamation is to reach and claim this man.

Let us clarify this interrelation of pastoral care and psychiatry, though in a simplified way, with an example. A psychoanalytic report of an illness shows how a patient suffers from neurotic disturbances which are expressed in inhibitions or perversions of his instinctual life. There follows a treatment in the course of which, through disclosure and clarification of the psychic situation, a perhaps astonishingly sudden liberation and healing occurs. If such a patient comes to us for pastoral care during or after the treatment, we shall endeavor to gain insight into the course of the illness and treatment as much as it is possible for a nonprofessional. Not in order to contribute our own psychological or even psychiatric wisdom! This is not our task. But rather, in order to examine the natural event of illness and healing in the light of faith. It shall gain a spiritual significance for the patient. He shall learn to understand that his illness and its healing have an entirely different dimension—namely, his sin and the forgiveness of his sin. But what does this mean in this particular case? When the physician speaks of neurosis and the pastor speaks of sin, do these connote the same thing? Is it only a matter of different words? Certainly not! The physician and the pastor have not only a different vocabulary, but a different subject. True, both the illness and the sin of the patient are displayed in one and the same scene (man's inner being, his soul), but the one is to be distinguished from the other. Each belongs to its own order: the neurosis to the immanent and natural, sin to the transcendent. Sin is something *toto genere* other than neurosis. Each, however, is related to the other; they are correlated in the way characteristic for the biblical understanding of man. The pastor understands this correlation to mean that the illness called neurosis by the physician is a symptom of that deep disturbance of life which has taken place between God and man. This disturbance is something in itself; it is different from a neurosis. Sometimes, however, it becomes visible in the outbreak of a neurosis; it is disguised as neurosis.

It can happen, even though it does not necessarily happen, that the aberration in man's inner being as uncovered in an analysis of the illness becomes the occasion for discerning and correcting a quite definitely sinful aberration. Psychological understanding of illness and pastoral understanding of man have come to grips with one another. The same is true of the process of healing. In the eyes of psychiatry, healing consists in a liberation from neurotic compulsion. We are not here concerned as to how this is accomplished, how therapy works in such a case. What is important is that for the pastor, healing is actually complete only when the patient can understand his recovery as a gift from God and give thanks for it. This gift is in every case the gift of forgiveness, of grace, as truly as the disturbance of sin is the deepest root of all sickness. But again, the natural event of recovery is not simply identical with the reception of forgiveness. Forgiveness is something in itself, a majestic matter of its own from beyond, to which recovery only points as a sign to be grasped in faith. In fact, it often happens that a man receives and grasps forgiveness without his illness being taken from him. The opposite may happen, too; there are merely psychically healed people who have been set free from their psychic inhibitions without their sins being at all forgiven. Perhaps just because they are again riding high, they feel no need whatever for the Word of God nor any dependency on grace alone. One might almost wish they were not so marvelously well off in order to realize that even enjoying full health we can be sick before God and with regard to God and thus need forgiveness, which alone brings actual "healing," placing man again in the hand of his Creator and Reconciler.

Here that paradoxical idea enters pastoral care which is summarized as the "blessing of illness" and the danger of good health. At this point psychology and psychiatry, as long as they are knowledgeable about ultimate realities, can render an important service to pastoral care. On their part and by their own means they can disclose to the healthy or the healed the constant threat menacing even the healthy and the secure. Our instincts are never wholly subdued and can break forth at any moment. Because of this threat the practice of true pastoral care is indispensable—a pastoral care which refers the healthy and the ill to the one who spoke those words in which illness and sin, healing and forgiveness, are so remarkably brought together: "Those who are well have no need of a physician, but those who are sick; I have not come to call the righteous, but sinners to repentance" (Luke 5:31-32).

2. *The Form of Illness.* Besides considering the natural fact of illness and its relation to sin and to the forgiveness of sin, it is also important to consider the form of illness.

Present-day psychology pictures man's inner being as threatened and rent by conflicts. Something above stands against something below, "mind" against "instinct." Powerful forces are at work. What is below invades what is above. But very subtle remedies come into play. They are automatically operating defensive devices and mechanisms of a psychic kind, intended to protect man against the ruin resulting from this inner conflict, against a complete breaking-apart of his inner life. The consequences are inner obstructions and deformations which can deeply alter the psychic life and give an extremely complex picture of the psychic state of affairs. It is the picture of a state of war mercilessly wavering between victory and defeat. The forces which come into play are irrational, i.e., they are only very slightly influenced and controlled, let alone steered, by human consciousness. Therefore, any rational and moral manipulation or advice can be expected to have very little effect on the complicated working of the psychic process. Perhaps the attempt is made to exhort the person afflicted by emotional disturbances: He should "listen to reason," or he should "pull himself together," and so forth. But this is exactly what he cannot do. His illness is such that he cannot do this. If reason and morality are preached to this patient as is done in such clichés, a law is imposed on him which he cannot fulfill and pushes him all the more deeply into his repression. This knowledge must lead us to seek and find a quite different, new way. The form and power of this repression, its genesis, its course, its foundation in deep, mysterious, but real fixations, indeed bondage of the inner life—these are what this aspect of psychology can show us. Not without reason is it suggestively called depth psychology.

We repeat that this psychological perspective closely approaches the biblical view of man. Long before depth psychology, sin appears there as a rift which cleaves human nature to its depths, splits it into something above and something below, and thus causes an incurable conflict in man's existence. The picture which the biblical testimony sketches of sinful man is therefore mainly the picture of a life shattered by conflict. Something like a front line runs through man, and he is engaged in a daily, even hourly fight. Advances and retreats alternate endlessly. Actual victory, and therefore the actual end of battle, never comes. Man participates in this battle with his whole existence. Even the most hidden island of his inner life is washed by its waves. To be man really means to be a fighter. But this is no proud assertion, for this fighter is not a man of victory but of defeat. He is man who by himself can never arrive at inner unity and inner peace. Harmony of life, "the pearl of perfection" as Chinese wisdom calls it, is denied him. His existence is and remains an existence between the two "dragons," of which the same wisdom speaks so strikingly. He is and he remains "man in revolt" (Emil Brunner), torn, split, and "wretched."

The Catechism speaks of this "wretchedness of man." It gives the pertinent passages of Holy Scripture. We single out Romans 7 for its testimony to the rift and the ceaseless conflict in man. There, as in the Catechism, it is less a psychological assertion than a quite different, soteriological, and Christian view. But even so, Romans 7 contains the whole wisdom of the ageless knowledge of man *in nuce*. "For I do not do the good I want, but the evil I do not want is what I do. . . . Wretched man that I am!" This conflict between the higher and the lower forces in man is what is at stake, under various names and interpretations in psychology. It informs scientific psychology as well as that of the great literary and artistic portrayals of man in secular literature and also that of man's daily and practical intercourse with himself and with others. (For the presentation of this conflict, once again see Emil Brunner, *Man in Revolt*.)

We now state explicitly that this revolt is judged as "sin" in the biblical testimony. In the passage cited above, the Letter to the Romans says very sharply: I do not the evil, but "sin which dwells within me." Here again the Bible reaches far beyond any merely psychological assertion and interpretation. It establishes that new transcendent fact of which we have spoken and must now speak again since the whole form of man's illness becomes explicable only on this basis. Sin—as seen in Romans 7—is not only a rift which splits human nature, but it is that wholly other rift in which man stands before God with his whole being. Remember everything we said about sin as the sickness of man with regard to God and before God. There is a breach which not only separates above from below, good from evil, mind from instinct, conscious from unconscious, in man. Rather it cuts off the whole man with what is above and below in him from the height of God beyond him and throws him into the depth of godlessness which is so deep and radical that no elevation of his mind, of his feeling, or of his will can transcend it. There is nothing so good, nothing so noble, nothing so pure as not to remain with everything human under the evil spell of sin.

Man's godlessness in good is no less real than his godlessness in evil. So seen, what is above and below within the nature of man actually becomes secondary to the primary estrangement of his whole life from God, which represents sin proper. Or rather, this reveals man's internal rift to be a mere shadow, a reflection of this fundamental sin in the nature of man. Man's inner brokenness is not sin itself, or is sin only to the extent that it is its concrete expression. This is naturally not to say that we should take man's inner conflicts any less seriously. The opposite is true; only this view really preserves its whole (in the proper sense of the word) metaphysical seriousness, its underlying depth. Only now does it become the symptom, the irrevocable sign of our alienation from God. And only now do we fully understand the significance of the psychological conception of the form of man's illness and the view of the conflicts tearing man apart and against which the usual rational and moral means are of no avail. How could the inner rift be ultimately healed, how could peace end the battle of good with evil as long as the rift of sin before God is not healed, that rift of which man's own conflict is only the secondary reflection? How could there be peace in the psyche when the whole man in spirit, soul, and body is shot through by discord with God, is surrounded by it like an island by the sea? We can thus maintain even here that the findings of psychology are in no way disregarded or downgraded by what God's Word teaches about sin. On the contrary, they serve to make the rift of sin all the more tangible and comprehensible. There is no better or more striking illustration of Romans 7 than the picture which depth psychology sketches of the inner life of man. The pastoral counselor who faces this estranged man will therefore listen closely to psychology. He will be able to speak differently, more understandingly, to this man if he has himself appropriated the insights of psychology.

It is of decisive importance, however, that we never overlook, much less forget, one thing: The statement about man's sinful estrangement represents only a part of the total biblical view of man, only half of the proposition, so to speak, by which the Word of God describes man. Even less than that, it is only a subordinate clause to the basically different principal affirmation about man. No passage of Holy Scripture places the emphasis on man's sinful wretchedness as such or makes it the exclusive subject of presentation and discussion. Rather, all its affirmations, even those concerning sinful man, testify to forgiveness and forgiveness *alone*. From the first, sin with all its consequences, i.e., the inner estrangement and weakness of man, is placed in between wide and comprehensive brackets. In spite of all the seriousness with which it is discussed, it is regarded as something which is really overcome and taken care of, which now has meaning only in retrospect. The disclosure of sin occurs in the Bible not in the abstract realm of metaphysical speculation about man, but in the encounter with Jesus Christ. Jesus Christ reveals sin very clearly, but he does so by taking it away. Jesus Christ himself steps into the rift between God and man and in so doing brings healing at last even for the incurable inner wound which infects our life. Therefore, while the Bible speaks about the rift of sin with final seriousness, it speaks with still greater seriousness about its being closed and healed in forgiveness. Once again: Man is sick, but in the biblical view he is sick with regard to him who has come as the physician of this illness. He is sin-sick before Christ, who is his Saviour.

This bracketing of sin by grace is the reservation which covers all the biblical statements about man's "wretchedness." This gives them the special bearing and weight that characterizes and distinguishes them from all purely psychological and anthropological descriptions of the fact of human estrangement. Of course, it is still true that this estrangement threatens and afflicts man in spite of, and within the brackets of, forgiveness. Even the man living by forgiveness, even the "Christian" is and remains a sinner. Therefore, the "psychology" of Romans 7 never ceases to apply to us as long as we live. We never leave behind the "wretchedness" described there! Yet it is subject to the power of grace. It is conditioned by grace. It is limited and ultimately made ineffective by it. The *simul peccator, simul justus* is valid, but it is valid granted that incomprehensible preponderance of the *justus* over the *peccator*, of grace over judgment, of election over rejection. We have a frivolous and untruthful understanding of sin if we imagine that some day we will outgrow Romans 7. Such a view partially underlies Pietism as well as numerous doctrines of man displaying a particularly Christian label. Once we recognize the parenthesis of grace so clearly stated in Romans 7 and 8 as encompassing sin, we no longer are in danger of lapsing into this falsehood, and of thinking that only in this way can we testify to the power of grace.

For pastoral care this signifies that on the one hand we have to take seriously the estrangement of human nature, for we know now about the root of sin out of which comes this estrangement. On the other hand, we must maintain the "nevertheless" of grace for the deliverance and healing of man estranged and torn by sin. We must under no circumstances give him up, not even when it comes to the worst case, for we know that the root of sin is undercut by forgiveness. Even when in the case of serious illness the inner estrangement has led to actual schizophrenia, true pastoral care does not give a man up, neither for the world beyond nor for the world here below. Even where, humanly speaking (i.e., from the medical perspective), no hope is left, true pastoral care through faith foresees hope and a future for man. In the strength of forgiveness, it knows about the power of a love that bears all things, suffers all things, believes all things. Therefore, not giving man up is its proper commission and mission. Not that it should entertain and encourage any illusions in people. Psychology and psychiatry will be allowed to demonstrate the inexorable truth concerning the depth, perhaps even the incurability, of the illness. Nevertheless, pastoral care will maintain and proclaim the healing which consists in the fact that God accepts and cares for man in and with his illness, incurable as it may be. In himself man is torn, bewildered, abandoned, but to his irrevocable comfort the outstretched hand of God holds him in his very wretchedness. Almost miraculously, a light from God may enter such a man's life. He may discover some solid ground under his feet upon which he can stand as on the edge of an abyss and continue to live in spite of all his estrangement. And this can have a healing effect down into the unconscious depths of his sick mind.

3. *The Discovery of the Unconscious.* Building upon Freud, the psychiatrist C. G. Jung has presented depth psychology under the title of *Psychology of the Unconscious.* This represents the decisive discovery which has resulted from the study of the neuroses in the exploration of man's inner being and its estrangement.

This discovery may be summarized as follows. Man's psyche includes the two realms of the conscious and the unconscious. The various psychological schools of today agree that the sphere of consciousness, which is under the alert control of reason and volition, is incomparably smaller and more limited than the underlying realm of the unconscious psychic life, which escapes the control and direction of reason and will. Man's conscious life is spread over his unconscious like a thin layer over an unfathomable depth. The unconscious is comparable to a deep cellar vaulted under the bright house occupied by the conscious ego. In this basement, however, dwell and move the really powerful and elementary forces, the drives and affects that make up the obscure, enduring foundation of our conscious existence. Here are the works; here originate the motivations of our whole life. It is the furnace, as it were, in which burns the fire that kindles and enlivens our whole being from within. The unconscious, however, also gives rise to the great aberrations and distortions climaxing in the estrangement from which we suffer. These occur because the control of these unconscious forces and powers has largely slipped from man's ego, his personality.

Man should properly be lord over the whole realm of his psychic life, yet the forces in the depth of his being have "split off" as we say metaphorically but relevantly. These forces, split off from him and withdrawn from his conscious control, break into the realm of the conscious he still controls. Man finds himself confronted with a large part of his being which really belongs to him and yet is no longer under his command. Hence his plight is to be in the grip of these released forces as described above. They oppress him in the form of passions, affects, desires, and fixations that throw him off the track and succeed in disturbing the order of his life. This also makes it clear why reason and will can do little against this invasion. For these forces operate outside the realm of reason and will. A highly paradoxical situation is the result. Man in his inner life is confronted with emotions which belong to him, but which he does not control when they emerge, as though there existed a second, unconscious ego in conflict with the conscious one. This, however, is an impossibility. For how can man envision an unconscious ego in conflict with the conscious one? There is only *one* ego, forced to live with the conscious and unconscious forces of its psyche. But then, what does "unconscious" mean if the unconscious is still to be related to the thinking and willing ego, even representing a part of its life? Here human perception and concepts reach an impasse. It is a sign that we are confronted with the mystery of personal human existence which we cannot master by means of natural knowledge.

In the strictly conceptual, theoretical psychology of Paul Häberlin, the division of man and his life into conscious and unconscious is called "mythology." "This deals," says Häberlin, "not with spheres or realms of the psyche, but with facts and possibilities of knowing and not knowing about the objects of acting. Neither the conscious nor the unconscious acts each in its own way, but the individual acts, now knowingly, now not knowingly. . . . Of course, it may be said that the unconscious acts, but the unconscious must not be thought of as an acting subject. The real subject is always either man himself, the subject of action proceeding consciously or unconsciously, or else the object of action known to the subject." (*Der Geist und die Triebe*, p. 228.)

All this once more vividly illustrates man's inner sickness. For psychiatry, it breaks out in the form of *neurosis* and in the distinctly more difficult cases as *psychosis*. It is not our business to discuss these categories and the prevailing medical theory about them. We only state that all such symptoms of illness are to be viewed as defects of control. Thus the neurotic character is recognizable in the compulsive recurrence of certain emotionally conditioned views or actions. These recurring symptoms indicate that the person acting under compulsion no longer steers his own inner life, but is driven. And because there is no one who does not suffer from such compulsive fancies and acts, perhaps so subtle as to be scarcely noticeable to himself, there is in fact not a person who could not be defined as neurotic in some way. The much discussed "complexes," a rather general mark of the human psychic life, signify nothing but the neural points at which, in ways as varied as the differences in individual men, the compulsive repetition of specific psychic processes sets in.

The basic problem of man's psycho-spiritual existence thus raised may be formulated in a question: Can the human forces be entirely brought under the controlling power of the ego or not? Is it possible or impossible to liberate them from their separate existence and attach them to the conscious center of man's personality in such a way as to restore the steering of its life to the ego? The whole psychic health or illness of a person depends on this. In the last analysis it is the problem of freedom which is posed here in the realm of psychology and psychotherapy as the basic problem of the whole of human existence. Health would mean to be internally free, to be able to control oneself, or simply to be oneself. Sickness, however, means imprisonment, inhibition, drivenness, bondage.

Once again, this is a striking illustration, concretization, and confirmation of what we know and call "sin" from the perspective of the biblical understanding of man. It shows sin as that power which takes the whole man prisoner, a dictatorship to which he is subjugated, even a possession from which he is unable to deliver himself. The splitting of psychic life in the wake of sin is now concretely manifest as a more or less complete loss of inner freedom. This loss involves man's inner wavering and the resulting impossibility of steering his own life. Can the servitude of man as the actor of sin be described more appropriately than is done in a few pages of a current book on psychology describing the evil sway of a neurosis over man as a result of uncontrolled drives and affects? The pastoral counselor will therefore do well to let this perspective speak to him. He will then reread his Bible, liberated from all pallor of thought, and will understand what is meant there by the slavery of sin. Furthermore, he will see men entirely anew and only now really understand the disastrous impact of this slavery. Finally, he will also learn from this to look expectantly for strength and help surpassing this power of sin. By faith, he will learn simply and confidently to count on the liberating power of grace. He will see himself consciously and urgently thrown back to the Word of God and to intercession. Thus there is real gain to be received from a serious study of psychology and psychiatry.

Not only the history of missions, but psychiatric case histories as well, may furnish concrete illustrations of the dark power whereby sin rules over man. They could teach us even more the power whereby grace overrules the bondage of sin appearing in our psychic illness. The Pauline "powers, principalities, and dominions" as the reigning forces and principles of the created world which are estranged from God and therefore arbitrarily push man around are reinterpreted and brought close to home in the form of the powers motivating but also devastating man's inner being. It is certainly thought-provoking when psychology today represents man's inner being as a territory occupied by a hierarchy of powers; it thus almost becomes a kind of demonology or angelology which, under certain circumstances and with certain reservations, may be compared to the biblical view of these things.

4. *Healing as Forgiveness.* Even more significant for pastoral care than the diagnosis of neurotic illness is the concept of the process of healing, the therapy resulting from the exploration of the unconscious. The goal of healing is the recovering of that inner freedom, the loss of which determines the nature of the neurotic and psychotic attack. This is worthy of our attention. When this freedom is restored, when the ego has regained the

most extensive control possible over the inner forces, then the psychic state is attained which we refer to as normalcy or as psychic health.

Most simply expressed, it is the goal of psychotherapeutic treatment that the patient learn to look at himself and, in so doing, step out of his inhibitions, thus again get himself in hand, and build up his life under new perspectives. Of course, the attainment of this state of freedom is always only relative and approximate. Even with the so-called healthy person, parts of the inner being can remain withdrawn from the control of the ego, and the rule of the ego over the territories of the inner world will frequently be called into question. No one is protected against inner fluctuations; fits of anger or attacks of melancholy or other affective threats can suddenly appear even in the "normal" life and entail serious disruptions of inner freedom. Even the healthy or the healed need to maintain unceasing vigilance. "The difference between nervous health and nervous illness (neurosis)," says Freud, "is narrowed down therefore to a practical distinction, and is determined by the practical result—how far the person concerned remains capable of a sufficient degree of capacity for enjoyment and active achievement in life. The difference can probably be traced back to the proportion of the energy which has remained free relative to that of the energy which has been bound by repression, i.e., it is a quantitative and not a qualitative difference." (*A General Introduction to Psychoanalysis*, p. 465. New York: Permabooks, 1953.)

Now, pastoral care is eminently concerned with man's liberation as his true healing. This needs no further corroboration. If sin is servitude, the forgiveness of sin which it is the duty of pastoral care to announce is the end of this servitude and thus the liberation of man. But since illness is a reflection of sin, deliverance from sin promises healing of all infirmity (cf. Psalm 103:3). Furthermore, any liberation from illness, any recovery in the earthly-natural sense, including any therapy, is for true pastoral care nothing but a reflection of that quite different healing of sin-sickness through forgiveness. All sickness points to our sickness before God, yet simultaneously to the promise of our recovery through his power. For just this reason, pastoral care is correlated with therapy. It must establish this reference and announce this promise. Without hindering or at all replacing the function of the physician or psychotherapist, pastoral care has to represent the truth with regard to illness: "The Lord is thy physician" (translation from the German of Exodus 15:26); and "So if the Son makes you free, you will be free indeed" (John 8:36). Freedom and healing are to be understood as the act and miracle of grace.

Here we come back to what has already been said. Seen as a natural development, the process of healing can be demonstrated in physical illness, for example, by the receding fever, in psychic illness, by the receding depression. In both cases the natural vital power which previously seemed to be extinguished flares up again. These psycho-physical processes are the biologically and psychologically comprehensible aspects of healing. Faith receives them from God's hand and gives thanks for them. We encounter sometimes people in pastoral care who say to us: "I experienced God's healing." We can only rejoice in such words. But strictly speaking, this is what happened: These people "experienced" the dropping of their fever, the ceasing of their pains or psychic trials. Not their experience, but their faith, tells them that it is *God* who rendered them this service. In faith, they have placed their experience under the Word of his promise that he is their physician. Thus their natural experience has become the *experience of faith*. The task of pastoral care at the sickbed is to awaken such experience of faith.

If we go on to ask about the form of the healing so understood, we must maintain that it will adopt the form which the illness had assumed. The form of the illness is that estrangement and brokenness of man, that loss of freedom of which we have spoken. Accordingly, the form of the healing is a closing of the wound beginning at the very place of the estrangement; the inner rift in man's life is mended and overcome. It can best and most exhaustively be described by the word "peace," as it has already been suggested in the presentation of what forgiveness of sin is. Healing, regained freedom, means the cessation of all inner conflict, the end of the revolt in which man lives on account of his sin. There arises a new form of life sheltered by the sovereign power of grace and therefore forsaking all strife and revolt. Concretely, i.e., as far as man's psychic life is concerned, such pacification as evidence of the new life will produce visible signs. He who is overcome by peace will begin to move in specific impulses and exhibit the freedom he believes in and experiences in faith. He loosens up, although still in the grip of sinful bondage. It is only a relative and hidden, but nonetheless real, process. Shame and repentance overtake him at the sight of the estrangement and lack of freedom in which he still lives; he struggles and fights against the chains he bears. Nevertheless, despite the continuing brokenness of his existence, the vision of an entirely new and different existence opens up. This new being is promised him in Jesus Christ and he will ultimately be clothed in it beyond the grave.

The statements of *psychotherapy* do not contradict this pastoral understanding of the nature and form of healing. On the contrary, what is to be read in the reports of the psychiatrist about the healing of neuroses rather illustrates and elucidates the view of pastoral care. They thoroughly explain how the inner brokenness is overcome and eliminated and how the integrity of the personality is restored. There we see how a patient caught in severe psychic conflicts undergoes a liberation through the treatment; he shakes off his inhibitions, his shortcomings, his repressions and compulsions, thanks to the analytical examination and clarification of his inner situation, and again becomes a man who feels and acts freely and normally. Such treatment and healing may indeed provoke that movement toward freedom to which we are called by God and which is promised and granted us in pastoral care.

Pastoral care, therefore, has no reason whatever to doubt, to suspect, let alone to replace with a "pious" therapy of its own, the results of psychotherapeutic healing. It will acknowledge therapy, provided, of course, the latter does not propose any philosophical interpretation conflicting with faith. It will not hinder the people in its care from seeking psychiatric treatment. Rather, it will co-operate with the psychiatrist whenever feasible. It quite consciously includes psychotherapy in its own comprehensive and encompassing understanding of the nature and form of true healing. Of course, psychotherapy develops its methods on the basis of purely natural presuppositions. Nevertheless, is it not an indication of the fact that man, for the sake of the promise of God's Word established over him and thus of his innermost destiny, shall not remain a prisoner of the estrangement which has befallen his nature on account of sin? In its worldly way, does not therapy signify the conquest of sin by grace? By accepting and recognizing psychotherapy in this way, pastoral care attests from its own presuppositions of faith the victory and the lordship of Christ even over the province of nature and natural knowledge. God makes even the physician his servant (as he does the statesman; cf. Romans 13:1ff.). Thus true pastoral care takes a positive stand toward a scientifically oriented psychotherapy. (Cf. Maeder, *Ways to Psychic Health*, or the books by Tournier.)

The great proviso of forgiveness under which all pastoral care works obviously elicits at the same time a delimitation of every kind of therapy. For this proviso implies that the final concern is not physical or psychic recovery as such. The final concern is the withdrawal of the bolt between God and man, as indicated by sickness. Whether this drawing of the bolt of sin occurs alongside physical and psychic healing, whether God is acknowledged, whether the healing itself is received as ultimately wrought by him as a sign of his grace—this is the question of pastoral care to the sick, first, last, and always. The concern for recovery may even become secondary. Maybe the illness does not yield, yet man in his illness breaks through to faith and accepts even his illness as from God's hand.

Pastoral care must lead to an "acceptance" of illness. This is its first responsibility. Acceptance consists in one's learning to understand illness as a crisis in accordance with the will of God, designed to make man face the ultimate question, the question concerning his God. Illness thus becomes the battleground where even much more than in so-called health the struggle for faith in God's power and presence is fought. What we called the "blessing of illness" is based on this. Essential comfort will come to the ill through the concrete assurance of this blessing.

Furthermore, we may make the paradoxical statement that as pastoral care places spiritual healing ahead of natural recovery, it actually aids this natural recovery. The attainment of inner relaxation plays a significant role in the therapy of psychic illness. The accepting of illness, the entrusting of oneself into God's hand, is concretely accomplished when the patient gives up the ambitions he has compulsively striven for, and which remained yet denied him. In fact, they are often enough the real though hidden cause of the illness. Pastoral comfort frees man somewhat from his ego with its desires, its bondage, and the disquiet these engender. He no longer tugs and shakes the chains of his illness so defiantly and so despondently. He begins to learn what it means to expect everything from God. He begins to believe and to pray. This brings about that relaxation which is a prerequisite to healing, which indeed in itself already represents a partial healing. To be sure, it cannot be the primary purpose of pastoral care to further such relaxation. On the contrary, it must forsake any such intention, any flirtation with natural healing, for this would be a flirtation with false gods. There is nothing worse than spiritual therapists that, like pagan medicine men, use faith and prayer as *means* to gain healing results! Such manipulation leads directly to magic. But where complete openness reigns; where nothing else is intended and sought than the service of God to the sick; where we really seek first after his Kingdom, according to the words of the Sermon on the Mount, a peace descends on the sick that may well have a healing effect. This is why knowledgeable psychiatrists request the service of pastoral counselors for their patients.

The miracles of Jesus Christ with the sick reveal that illness and healing point to God's work and its discernment. This is made explicit prior to the healing of the man born blind in Jesus' answer to the disciples' question about the cause of illness: "That the works of God might be made manifest in him" (John 9:3). This is why he is ill and why he will be healed. Ask no further! To teach rightly "to accept illness" out of the hand of God as a fundamental prerequisite for healing is undoubtedly also the purpose of the well-known book by the Genevan physician Tournier, entitled *Médicine de la Personne*. But this book also exemplifies the ever-present danger of abusing faith and prayer as a means of restoring health. If this is done, everything is spoiled. This explains the inherent ambiguity of so much of spiritual therapy. It transgresses the third commandment. A case in point are the healings of Christian Science, which on this account largely represent a pagan aberration. The popularity it enjoys and the results it exhibits are dearly bought and should not delude us about the thoroughly wrong way of Christian Science. The same twilight overshadows the widely read book by Weatherhead, *Psychology, Religion, and Healing*. In contrast, the little book by Rolf Eberhard, *Von der Tröstung der Kranken* can show what pure, unpretentious, evangelical pastoral care of the sick looks like.

5. *The Psychotherapeutic Means*. First among the means applied by present-day psychotherapy in its healing method is the psychotherapeutic conversation. Though probably no psychiatrist will renounce the use of medication, hypnotherapy, or shock treatment, the decisive means will always be mental conditioning through psychiatric discussions conducted with the patient.

No strict distinction between somatic and psychic conditioning and treatment of psychic and nervous disorders is possible because man's inner and outer being are inseparably related to one another, indeed both must be seen as a unity in their relationship to man's ego. We have repeatedly touched on the problem of the relationship between soul and body. The discussion of it shows that it has not yet been solved at all or even clarified. In fact, no solution is possible on the basis of purely natural knowledge since the problem borders on the mystery of man's personal existence, which is ultimately comprehensible only out of the Word of God and of the understanding of man in terms of faith. But present-day medicine and psychology does make it clear that one must see, and correspondingly treat, the patient as a psychosomatic unity and entity. This acknowledgment is truly one of the forward steps taken by modern medicine in the field of therapy. (Cf. Richard Siebeck in his *Einleitung zum Lehrbuch der innern Medizin* on the "concept and position of medicine," published by Julius Springer, Berlin.) Every psychotherapist must master the basic tenets of general medicine; conversely, no general practitioner can properly function without psychological and psychiatric training. This tight rule is a warning signal to the pastoral counselor never to indulge in medical and psychiatric dilettantism.

The psychotherapeutic conversation is not only indispensable for diagnosing a psychic disorder and thus for the analytic investigation and detailed examination of the psychic condition of the patient, but it has also been shown that a systematic analysis in itself can have a healing effect. The analytic conversation advances into layers of psychic depth, thereby uncovering and releasing the psychic disturbance moored there.

This discovery of psychoanalysis, though substantially modified in its primary form developed by its founder Sigmund Freud, has found general acceptance as the outstanding healing method in present-day psychotherapy. It employs dream analysis as a prominent means to its accomplishment since the unconscious becomes tangible in the dreams. Besides dream analysis, however, other means are available (tests) which serve the same end. Their results are not to be contested. A responsibly conducted talk pressing into the most subtle ramifications of the unconscious and consequently a clarification of the genesis of psychic errors can bring healing to the patient. Conversation, the verbal interchange between physician and patient, plays a decisive role here. This is a reasonable assumption if we consider again that everything psychic is concerned with the whole person, with man's ego. Here, the ego is morbidly bound, threatened, and torn by its dividedness, and must find freedom. This ego in its personal identity can ultimately be touched, reached, and awakened by no other means than the word. Psychotherapeutic conversation aims at this touching and awakening, as does pastoral conversation, though in its own distinctive way.

It is noteworthy that psychoanalytic treatment in the course of its development abandoned the previously prevailing therapy by hypnosis. (Cf. Freud, *A General Introduction to Psychoanalysis*, pp. 453-461; and C. G. Jung, *Über die Psychologie des Unbewussten*, pp. 21ff.) Hypnosis, too, succeeds in clearing away inhibitions and in releasing and setting into motion forces and impulses in the deep layers of the psyche outside of the patient's control. Man's ego is thereby enabled, momentarily at least, in a truly extraordinary, artificially heightened freedom, to undertake actions and steps of which it would never be capable in the non-hypnotic state. The somehow unnatural experiments which clever hypnotists are accustomed to trotting out rest on this possibility. The freedom thus achieved, however, is only a caricature of genuine freedom. In the process of hypnosis, the individual is transposed into a kind of psychic trance by suggested removal of his inhibitions; but it is only a state of intoxication and dream, soon enough to vanish. The ego has accomplished some unconscious tricks with closed eyes, but it was enticed to an unworthy fool's play. Genuine freedom can never be suggested. It is a wide-awake dominion of the ego over its psychic forces. And the road to it does not lead through states of twilight, sleep, and intoxication. On the contrary, it leads through clarification of the obscure unconscious, a switching on of the control, a mastering of the inhibitions. This is achieved through addressing and calling the ego as it is done in conversation where the call is consciously heard. Psychotherapy recognized this and, turning away from hypnosis as the chief means of healing, perfected the analytical conversation instead. Hypnosis may still be used to produce certain transformations in particular cases. It is, at any rate, an extraordinary means which belongs in the hand of the responsible physician. Pastoral care must beware where it finds hypnosis used as a trick and for the sake of entertainment.

If we compare the analytic conversation with our pastoral conversation, we find that they are *toto genere* and unexchangeably different. In contrast to the psychoanalytic conversation, the pastoral conversation proceeds in strict and fundamental dependence on Holy Scripture. Prayer is an indispensable ingredient. These are sufficient marks of its distinctiveness. There are no doubt psychologists and even pastors (though bad ones!) who fail to discern the fundamental difference between the two kinds of conversation. They believe that in his own admittedly unscientific, possibly naive, and nonprofessional way the pastoral counselor does the same thing as the psychoanalyst. This may happen here and there, but when it happens, it is surely something else than true pastoral care. All true pastoral care is concerned with proclaiming the forgiveness of sin. And forgiveness of sin is never to be likened to the detailed inner examination as practiced in psychoanalysis and the resulting changes and liberations in man's psychic life. True, forgiveness, when it is effectively communicated in the Holy Spirit, can and will achieve such change and liberations of man's inner being as psychotherapy produces, but important as they are for the beneficiary they signify only a side effect in the pastoral conversation and cannot be regarded as the proper goal. They are signs which indicate and accompany the real transformation sought by pastoral care. This transformation consists in the change of direction called "repentance" to which man is led by the Word of God, so that he rises and stretches out his hand for grace. This turnabout has nothing to do with psychoanalysis. The communication of forgiveness can never be replaced by analysis. For we must never be misled into thinking that the psychotherapeutic solution of the problem of psychic healing in itself disposes of the crucial question of sin in pastoral care. We repeat what has been said earlier: Through analysis, a man may well succeed in clearing up his psychic conflicts, and yet remain the old, sin-sick man he has always been. Let us beware of confounding a successful psychotherapeutic cure with repentance. The barrier of sin cannot be surmounted even by the best analysis. Forgiveness is needed and hence proclamation in the true pastoral conversation.

The psychiatrist himself, for that matter, frequently runs up against the possible existence of a frightful final barrier, a last morbid resistance in the emotionally disturbed and sick person which no psychiatric art can eliminate. So it may happen in analysis, as it presses deeper and removes more layers covering up the true condition of the patient, that a deep-seated and insurmountable inner estrangement comes to light. And in severe cases, the patient's bewilderment at this disclosure of his deepest psychic schism is such that he is no longer equal to it and breaks down. At times the analysis ends in a deep depression that can lead to suicide. The statement by a leading physician is not unfounded: "The more deeply the physician probes into man's innermost being, the more unmanageable destructiveness threatens, even to the point of suicide during the analytic treatment." (Richard Siebeck, *op. cit.*, p. 637.)

This innermost being is man's personal identity, his psychic self as it confronts an inner situation which it is no longer able to master, since the inner strength that might force a way out is lacking. To submit to analysis is therefore always a matter carefully to be considered. The healing means of the analytic conversation can become a dangerous poison. But it can also happen that the patient, in the dangerous moment when the whole abyss yawns before him, can seize upon something that saves him. With Freud, one may call this, somewhat vaguely, "an array of available psychic forces" (*op. cit.*) emerging at the right moment; one may speak of reserves of healthy psychic substance, still present, of a yet undestroyed remnant of personality. Nevertheless it remains strange, even borders on naiveté, that Freud's thoroughly mechanistically and naturalistically conceived psychoanalysis, indeed all analytic therapy counts at the decisive moment on the presence of such "psychic forces," such a healthy substance. It is the great *as-if*, thanks to which the illness can finally be conquered, when the inner resistance against the therapeutic conversation is given up and the healing process sets in.

Behind this somehow presupposed reserve of psychic forces available in the critical moment hides the simple fact that man should be able to find in himself a last refuge and confidence which provides precisely in the extreme peril that support to his tottering self without which he must sink into the abyss. Man lives then in all his brokenness and estrangement as if he had ground under his feet, as if a protecting hand existed, as if there were wings that cover him, a wall that shelters him. But where does analysis get the right to such confidence? How is it entitled, on the basis of its presuppositions, to count on such a power reserve in man as if this were self-evident? It is quite another matter when pastoral care proclaims and mediates this confidence. It knows and may testify on the basis of the biblical understanding of man: This confidence is no mere illusion; these inner forces are no mere as-if! The ground that bears us, the hand that covers and leads us—they actually exist! We may and we shall count on man's preservation as by a miracle even in the most extreme peril to his inner existence. We stand again before the reality and power of God's mercy in Jesus Christ. Whether men know it or not, if we do not break down under the oppressing psychic conflicts but come through because our self, perhaps through treatment with the help of a physician, learns to find itself, to rise and recover, then this process of our healing, psychologically seen, may seem like a manifestation of anonymous psychic forces. In fact, however, our healing is grounded in the reality of faith and in the knowledge of man's preservation in the hand of God. And this perspective of faith is the true and proper perspective, the view from within, against which psychological consideration, with all of its importance, still represents only an outside view. As man appropriates this perspective, as he begins knowingly to serve his God, to whom he belongs even unknowingly, he learns to tread the ground on which he finds support and strength even in the severest peril. He begins to live out of *faith* and out of faith to *live*. Here lies the task of pastoral care. It must certainly not intend to supplant or to replace the psychotherapeutic healing conversation, but it is of the highest importance that it undergird and accompany it with its own conversation in order to induce true healing in the forgiveness of sins. The danger inherent in analytic treatment of opening the wound in man's inner life without the merciful protection of pastoral care will then be banished.

6. *Healing as Miracle.* A final question arises. If healing depends on the forgiveness of sins, then why resort to the application of human means of healing at all, on psychotherapy and medical interference, on the analytical and not on the pastoral conversation *alone?* This question is identical with the question of the possibility of miracles.

On the presupposition now familiar to us of the connection between healing and forgiveness, every recovery, even if achieved by means of medical help, is a gift of God. There is no healing of physical or psychic illness that in the eyes of faith does not bear the mark of the miraculous. Miracle in the proper sense, however, is differentiated from the above. A miracle is a signal event whereby the connection of forgiveness and healing comes to light without any kind of natural mediation. In the miraculous sign, the divine power of forgiveness forsakes each and every therapeutic means and exclusively employs its own means, the means of the Word and of faith. Alone and free, the Word of God and the faith bestowed upon man through the Word steps into the arena and knocks the illness out. Whenever this happens, it serves as a reminder that even in what might be called regular cases where the natural means of the healing art remain in force the power of forgiveness *alone* heals and saves. This makes it plain that behind the appearances of illness and death stands something entirely different from the injuries and destructions of body and soul affecting the nature of man, namely, the power of sin. Recovery is therefore never concerned only with regeneration of man's inner or outer being, but also with deliverance from the corruption of sin by forgiveness in Jesus Christ.

This is the meaning of the healing miracles of the New Testament, and, consequently, those of the Old as well. They are without exception messianic signs, i.e., signs which announce the victory of Christ over sin and death and thus confirm the power of his Word. This is particularly convincing in the reports of miracles in the Fourth Gospel. Yet the Fourth Gospel simply discloses what is meant and shown in all reports of miracles. Our question is now whether such miraculous events according to the testimony of the Scripture are confined to the biblical revelation, or whether they continue to occur even here and now. We must answer that of course the miraculous events at the time of the biblical revelation share in the special dignity wholly its own, as it befits the words of the apostles and prophets in distinction from the ongoing proclamation of the church. But it is forseen and promised in the Word of God itself that an image and reflection of the miraculous events of the Bible can and will accompany the ongoing proclamation of the church (cf. I Corinthians 12:10, et al.). To the extent that the prophetic and apostolic Word truly continues to be proclaimed in the church and lives and exists ever anew in the Holy Spirit, the sign accompanying this Word is in the eyes of not only a fact of the past, but a new reality in the life of Christian community.

Wherever the miracle of healing takes place, it is a unique event. It represents an exceptional and divinely free act, both in the course of natural events and within God's dealing with man which is accessible to faith. Miracles do not happen every day. Even for the believer, they are treasures; he must wander a long time without any miracle. It can be denied to the Apostle himself, and he must put up with his own mysterious illness without any reliance on healing; yet he remains certain of the grace of God (II Corinthians 12:7-9). But then suddenly and unexpectedly the promise of grace is confirmed by a miracle, and the believer may go his way comforted. So seen, the miracle is comparable to the comfort, indeed healing, flowing from the sacrament without, however, the one being replaceable by the other. (Cf. I Corinthians 11:27-32 and the exposition by Werner Meyer in *Der Brief an die Korinther* in the series of *Prophezei*, Zurich.) Furthermore, if it is true that every act of God remains imperceptible and incomprehensible to natural reason, this is especially true of the extraordinary act of the miraculous event. This is to say that it is accessible only to faith, whereas outside faith it is an incident defying any attempt at clarification; most people will pass by with a shrug of their shoulders, if they do not openly question its factuality.

We think of the countless, but completely erroneous, attempts to explain the biblical miracles by tracing them back to natural or so-called supernatural forces. But we also think of the ambiguity and twilight surrounding the miracles occurring and witnessed here and there in the church. Was the healing of Gottliebin Dittis in the ministry of the elder Blumhardt actually a miracle (cf. Zündel in his biography of Johann Christoph Blumhardt)? Or can it be explained naturally? We shall never agree about it as long as we proceed from purely natural and rational presuppositions. Perhaps this very ambiguity is strong indication of a genuine miracle in this case. In the more recent theological literature, both exegetical and systematic, the problem of illness and of the miracle of healing is to some extent neglected. For example, the entry under ἀσθενής in the *Theologisches Wörterbuch zum Neuen Testament* is inadequate.

The freedom in which the true miracle occurs reflects the freedom of grace itself, from which the miracle proceeds and to which it refers. On account of this freedom, the miracle of healing can never be changed into a procedure or a method at the disposal of pastoral care. In the church, of course, we shall not cease to count on the divine possibility of miracles, to expect it, and to pray for it. In this connection, we are reminded of the prayer for the sick attested in the New Testament church and to the related laying on of hands in the expectation of a miraculous intervention of divine help. Where does this exist with us? What has come of it? Nevertheless, as pastoral counselors we shall not intend to become miracle workers. For the miraculous signs in the Bible did not occur and are not transmitted to us in the testimony of Holy Scripture so that we should shun the ordinary course of divine action, pay it slight heed, and thus ignore or discourage the use of the truly God-given natural means of healing. This would be an impasse. Whenever we enter it, the danger immediately arises that the extraordinary gift of God in our hands becomes a usurped means, prayer a compulsion, and the laying on of hands a magic trick. Miracles are attested and promised in order to impress upon us the power of God and his condescension to us in the forgiving of sins. We shall keep them before our eyes and be mindful of this power whenever we bear witness to him. But they shall not entice us to strive inappropriately for a miracle which we might arrogantly desire or effect by ourselves. Only where forgiveness is purely communicated, faith, if God wills it, may be given as an extraordinary sign confirming God's promise. Such is to be interpreted, accepted, and kept sacred as a miracle.

If the church dares to profess the Word of forgiveness in prayer for its renewal in the Holy Spirit, the signs accompanying this Word will never entirely lack in its midst. At any rate, pastoral care must not be suspected of blind enthusiasm if it again becomes biblical in believing God's Word capable of working miracles. On the other hand, the warning must be sounded against those dubious prayer meetings and prayer movements featuring spiritual leaders and guides with a reputation of being especially "effective intercessors." The prayer healings they promise and perhaps even accomplish are distorted and corrupted inasmuch as they divert man's attention away from the act of God to the human act, to the effect to be obtained, and to the psychic dynamics producing this effect. The gathering focuses on "effectiveness" of the prayer of the pastor or leader of the assembly in question. In the resulting sultry air, psychic high voltage is confounded with the power of the Holy Spirit, and all kinds of demonic temptations linger around. He who once took part in such meetings or assemblies knows about this danger. They fall short of the pure praise of God and his power, the proper mark, intention, and consequence of biblical healing miracles. They fall short of lifting up the forgiveness of sin before men and of giving glory to God alone. But what do healing miracles signify if this does not come to light? The church must not be seduced by the success of these faith healers. Much as they may keep the name of Jesus on their lips, they do not really act in his name! Even Pharoah's magicians were able to change rods into serpents; Lourdes can boast astonishing healing records. However, that lady to whom Löhe wrote the letter we quoted (see chapter 4) and who then went to the elder Blumhardt in Bad Boll did not receive complete healing from her suffering, but rather the peace in the forgiveness of sins and with it the praise of God in her heart, and this is by far the greater thing. As pastoral counselors we must not hesitate at this point. We must know what is at stake in all sickness and recovery, or even continued illness: At stake is grace and only grace. This assurance is our unfailing help.

In conclusion we cite as an example of good pastoral counsel a letter by Christoph Blumhardt which sums up all that can be said in this matter:

> My dear lady:
> I have received your letter and am sorry not to have written earlier. I prefer writing through you to that sick person and would send her hearty greetings and assure her of my sympathy. I bear such human misery continually on my heart and shall also commend it to God. Yet I increasingly feel we should not pray too urgently for health and help in illness, but rather for our right attitude toward God in order to make the streams of living water flow more richly. God is often hindered from doing what he would gladly do if we were more his people serving him. Now that God has caused me to experience so many and such great things for the benefit of the downcast and sick, I long for the experience of seeing men care more for his Kingdom and take a back seat for themselves. In this way, even illness can become a service for God, and God is again close at hand. I shall faithfully think of your sick friend, but am grateful if she in turn also helps me and wishes even more than her health that God's right be acknowledged on earth and his will alone be done. This is certainly how we are well-pleasing to God.
> Greeting you and your parents with heart-felt love, I am your devoted
>
> Christoph Blumhardt
>
> Bad Boll, August 8, 1890

III The Implementation of Pastoral Care

The concrete practice of pastoral care consists in the true ordering of gospel and law, of justification and sanctification. The gracious assurance of the gospel must become the claim which commits man to his Lord. This means that the gospel goes forth in the form of commandment, but also that the commandment must never be anything else than the communication of the gospel. The dissolving of the unity of gospel and law, of justification and sanctification, as it takes place, for example, in the pastoral care of the Catholic Church, is to be considered a mortal threat to true pastoral care.

12 Gospel and Law in Pastoral Care

True pastoral care has impressed us in its form as conversation, in its content as forgiveness, in regard to the recipient as message to sin-sick man. We now turn to the proper implementation of pastoral care and understand by this the specific act of communicating forgiveness in the pastoral conversation. If this conversation is comparable to the way in which pastoral care proceeds, we now deal with the specific steps to be taken in order to reach this goal, namely, the addressing and claiming of man by the saving Word.

It is essential to the claim made by the Word of God and hence essential to the practice of pastoral care that it be a call capable of reaching and arresting man. The idiom "to have to do with" expresses here most pointedly what is meant, both for the counselor and for the counselee: Pastoral talk has to do with me, i.e., it approaches me, it lays hold on me; I cannot shun it. But this signifies that it proceeds in the form of an admonition, an instruction. True, its content is nothing but pure compassion, for it is concerned with the forgiveness of all my sins, but this content imposes itself in the form and with the power and strength of a commandment that requires obedience. Pastoral care, as Romans 12:1 calls it, is an appeal by the mercies of God. Not a single pastoral conversation can do without admonishing, even rebuking and chastising in some way. This does not exclude the fact that this conversation ultimately aims at comfort, the real content of all pastoral care. The nature and substance of this comfort is rightly to admonish man. For what else do we expect from a pastoral conversation than that the counselee leaves it repentant and in the power of this repentance returns to his life as a new man? He is put back on his feet and given a sense of direction; formerly confused he now sees clearly; formerly bound, he is now free; formerly insecure, he now confidently goes his way. This change is always prompted by a commandment, an instruction, which is in the form of law. This is what we mean when we understand pastoral conversation as admonition out of compassion.

This poses the foremost problem in examining the practice of pastoral care: the problem of the right relationship of consolation and admonition, of gospel and law in pastoral care. We formulate it in the following question: Is there an admonishing which, while it is nothing but admonition, at one and the same time is the merciful communication of good news? Does this not mean contradiction, even conflict? Or if not actually conflict, then at least supplementation, since the admonition is delivered, yet in such a way that it is added to the merciful communication of the message of forgiveness as a second thing following a first, or as a first thing preceding a second? Is this the relationship of gospel and law? We confronted this question previously when we spoke of the forgiveness of sins as the content of the pastoral conversation. We saw there that the relationship of gospel and law can under no circumstances be conceived as one supplementing the other. Forgiveness is either everything, the whole message, or it is not forgiveness at all. But how does this agree with the assertion just made that pastoral care has to do with admonition, with establishment and communication of a commandment? Speaking now of forgiveness and now of commandment and obedience, must not the one almost necessarily limit and encroach upon the other?

Of course, the counselor often resorts to alternating the two in the implementation of pastoral care; he now admonishes and now comforts, thereby inducing mutual distortion. Let us beware! This is no mere distortion, but total destruction. This is a clear-cut either/or. That is, if gospel and law do not really coincide, are not entirely identical, the one can only annul and destroy the other. This destruction of gospel by law or of law by gospel (and this always means mutual destruction) is what happens so easily in pastoral conversation. It has catastrophic implications and must be avoided at any price. Everything is at stake here. We may have concluded ten times that the forgiveness of sins, and nothing else, is at stake. Yet if we do not know how to administer gospel and law in the right way, we have gained nothing. The conversation, however well meant and begun, perhaps with prayer and serious intentions, inevitably degenerates either into an insipid, quite unreal babbling of grace and forgiveness which does not reach the person and therefore cannot comfort and strengthen, or—what is no better—into a seemingly very gripping, yet only moralistically gripping, address which leaves man ultimately alone in his deepest distress.

The solution of the problem lies in the opposite question: Can forgiveness be communicated in any other form than admonition? We must recall that the Word of forgiveness is essentially a Word which sovereignly lays hold on man's life. It is a Word, to employ an expression already used, which lays a total claim upon the person it reaches. Forgiveness is a liberation of man. It leads him out of captivity. This is proclaimed in ever new expressions in the biblical testimony itself. But this liberation in turn operates in the form of an imprisonment, an arrest. A change of regime takes place. Formerly, man belonged to sin and death, but now he belongs to him who approaches him as his liberator and wants to become his new Lord. "Thy sins are forgiven thee!"—where these words are voiced, a hand is laid on the one imprisoned in his sin. He is told, "With body and soul, both in life and in death" you are now subject to your new Lord, who is your proper, your legitimate, Lord. For he has dearly bought you for his own. The power of sin and death is broken; the power of Jesus is established over you.

If this is forgiveness, how is it expressed except by the summons to man: Come out of your sin! You can do it, for sin has lost its spell over you. But this is in every case a formal commandment; it is a law being established over us. But as the law it is, it is joyous news. For this command announces liberation. It is and remains forgiveness, nothing but forgiveness which is granted to man. But this forgiveness cannot be granted except in the form of such command. The simple fact is once again expressed here that the forgiving Word is no empty word, but a Word that possesses power and strength. For this is our comfort, that we know ourselves summoned by our Lord. The more severely, the more mightily the commandment is addressed to us, the more complete is the claim by the hand of this Lord, the more complete also our protection in this hand.

Not without reason is the Decalogue introduced by the gracious words, "I am the LORD your God, who brought you out of the land of Egypt, out of the house of bondage" (Exodus 20:2). In this affirmation are all commandments rooted; to this alone they give expression; their substance is to proclaim the gracious action of God, who asserts himself as our Lord by leading his people out of lawlessness in Egypt and placing them under his new law and commandment. The preamble before each individual commandment serves as its basis: "I am the LORD your God" —*therefore*, "you shall . . ."; in this way, the commandment becomes the proclamation of the gracious will of God. The whole Sermon on the Mount is to be understood in this perspective. Jesus is shown to be the Christ by placing his people under the new and better righteousness of his new commandment as he fulfills this righteousness himself in the midst of his people and for his people (Matthew 5:17-20). Grace and commandment are one in him. The commandment of the Sermon on the Mount becomes the proclamation of the new life in the Kingdom of the Father which Jesus came to bring. Furthermore, we recall the vehement conviction with which this unity is defended in the Pauline testimony, above all in the Letter to the Galatians, where the battle is joined to overcome the divorce of gospel and law. Lastly, this fundamental relationship of gospel and law is the focus of the message of the Reformers. "The question of the right relationship of gospel and law is *the* question of the Reformation." (Alfred de Quervain.) The Catechisms of Luther and Calvin and especially Luther's "Sermon on Good Works" may be cited here. The whole problem is taken up and completely rethought for our day by Karl Barth and also by Alfred de Quervain. (Cf. Barth's important essay on *Evangelium und Gesetz* and his foundation of ethics in *Church Dogmatics*, II, 2, 8, and Alfred de Quervain in *Die Heiligung*, Part III. The question of the right understanding of the Sermon on the Mount may be looked up in my own work, *Die Bergpredigt*.)

This explains how pastoral care in itself is call to repentance, call to conversion. We give no new content to the concept of pastoral care, we add to it nothing it does not already contain when we liken true pastoral care to the call to repentance. We only repeat that pastoral care is concerned with forgiveness of sins, but we now understand the forgiving Word explicitly as a powerful Word, actually reaching and arresting man. We underline the concept of forgiveness; we underline its actuality and powerfulness. It proves to be a powerful claim on man. In this it is the great deed of Christ for which the church is so impressively urged to give thanks in the communion prayer.

Expressed in the theological language of the Reformers, what we have developed here is the relationship between justification and sanctification. Justification of the sinner before God by grace alone is the content of the message of forgiveness. But sanctification is always joined to justification. Sanctification, however, does not appear as an independent act, subsequently added to justification and joined with it by the conjunction "and." On the contrary, sanctification is once again the same as justification, but in such a way that it confirms in a specific direction what is already fully given in and with justification. What is given with justification? We answer with the words of

Luther's Shorter Catechism and of the Heidelberg Catechism: We have become God's "own." Our santification seals this surrender of our life into God's hand; it definitively seals Christ's taking possession of our life as proclaimed in justification. Yes, it is true, sanctification tells man: You belong to God, for you are truly justified. You can do no other but be willing and ready to live henceforth to the Lord whose own you have become. In fact, the literal meaning of the concept of "holy" is belonging to God. The basically very simple fact prevails that because of its efficacy and validity forgiveness cannot be communicated except by declaring the addressee to be entirely God's own. Therefore, forgiveness must proceed in the form of a binding summons; justification must become sanctification; comfort must be claimed, or else it would not be the mighty assurance of grace. This is the relationship of gospel and law, of justification and sanctification. Accordingly, ethics is based on grace, but grace, if it is rightly proclaimed, leads from itself to the commandment and to the keeping of the commandment.

Because this is so, because there is no forgiveness without sanctification, the commandment must be established in each pastoral conversation by the very nature of the case. Pastoral care without sanctification would be a wooden horseshoe, a ship on the sand, a contradiction in itself. With forgiveness, commandment and obedience must also be communicated, yet in such a way that even commandment and obedience on their part only underscore the truth and actuality of forgiveness. To reduce it to the lowest denominator: Where commandment and obedience are rightly proclaimed, Jesus Christ is proclaimed, who stands for the unity of grace and law since in his incarnation he is the fulfiller of the law. Hence, the gospel must be proclaimed, nothing but gospel even where law is proclaimed; law must be communicated, but law whose one and only content is gospel; justification, but justification as sanctification; sanctification indicating the actualization of justification.

Here it becomes clear what a dangerous thing happens when that separation is made between gospel and law against which we previously warned so forcibly. It is imperative not to proclaim a law which is separated from the gospel and which preceding or following forgiveness, has special significance in itself. Neither must a gospel devoid of the law be proclaimed. Where this happens, the gospel is robbed of what makes it powerful as gospel. It no longer really places man in God's hand and possession. Man remains emancipated, but this means he continues in sin. Conversely, the law split off from the gospel becomes a matter man seeks to settle by himself, a mere moral code he thinks he can live up to on his own, without grace.

We ask at last: How does this dangerous separation of gospel and law happen in the first place? Why does it always irresistibly tempt us? The answer is plain enough. The permanent threat not only to pastoral care but to the whole proclamation of the church flares up here. Man's old and ever-renewed struggle against grace becomes visible. This struggle in itself represents man's sin in its proper and dreadful form. Man rejects and fights the very purpose of true pastoral care as it is achieved within the good order of gospel and law, namely, the submission of his whole life to the grace of Christ. And because he does not want it, because he strives against such ordering of his life, because he refuses to live from forgiveness, he goes ahead and separates the gospel from the law and the law from the gospel. He severs gospel and law in such a way that the gospel appears as the proper Word of God rooted in revelation, whereas the law is only indirectly God's Word, imparted to man and indwelling him from the creation; albeit with the help of God man is capable of fulfilling it. But this view leads to the emasculation of forgiveness, to the great corruption of the proclamation. It also corrupts pastoral care. In this kind of counseling, the strong message of the justification of the sinner by grace alone is superseded by a feeble both-and, both God and his help *and* man and his ability to help himself, both grace and good will. The gospel is not completely lacking, but it is no longer the living center from which everything flows and to which everything streams. The law is indeed established, even severely and categorically, but it is no longer rooted in the gospel and therefore hangs in mid air. Sin is still discussed, but the fact that we are lost in our sin is no longer taken seriously. Forgiveness is still proclaimed, but it is no longer the one and all-sufficient help. And what kind of forgiveness is this! Pastoral care of this type can look very superior and tempting, yet one might wish to have tongues of angels to warn against it.

The danger of this corruption of pastoral care was already the target of Vilmar and Löhe. They warned against the use of pastoral care as a complementary, extraordinary means to be added to the ordinary means of sermon and sacrament. They also rejected a certain Pietism because of the inherent danger of shifting the emphasis away from what Christ has done for us to what we do for Christ. This is also the target in our critique of that false independence granted to pastoral care in the modern movements of awakening and penitence; the faithful are called away from the ordinary hearing of the Word in the preaching of the church to accomplish on their own an often very arbitrary repentance in special meetings. This is the target of our objection to the psychologizing and rationalizing of pastoral care in the secular spiritual direction of modern psychotherapy. The mystery and the actuality of forgiveness are devaluated and finally vanish, and what is left are natural laws and methods in the psychic realm whereby man is to regain his balance on his own strength.

The classic expression of the corruption of pastoral care through establishing the law without forgiveness in Christ is and remains *Judaism*. We know from the testimony of the New Testament that Jewish pastoral care, built entirely on the law, was bound to become dreadfully and mercilessly severe. Matthew 23 suffices to remind us that this Jewish legalism was the real issue with which Christ Jesus had to contend in continuation and fulfillment of the battle of the prophets and which brought him to the cross in the midst of his people. This fight for the freedom of grace against a falsely understood law without Christ continues in the apostolic letters. We think in particular of the Letter to the Galatians.

No other writing in the New Testament ought to be understood more deeply and accepted more fully for the benefit of true pastoral care than the Letter to the Galatians. On the other hand, for the benefit of a lazy Christian church which proclaims the gospel without the law, the Letter to the Galatians is to be counterbalanced by the Letter of James. It is the great reminder of repentance to be born not from the law itself, but from the law as heard in faith in Christ, since faith without the law can be no more alive than the law without the gospel. Both the Letter to the Galatians and the Letter of James must be our guides if we want to remain in the right order of gospel and law. We must even affirm that right pastoral care rests upon the interplay of both testimonies; or expressed differently, it is imperative in pastoral care to hear Paul with the underlining of his message by that of James. (Cf. for the understanding of the Letter to the Galatians once again the study already cited by Karl Barth, *Evangelium und Gesetz;* also Karl Ludwig Schmidt, *Ein Gang durch den Galaterbrief;* further, the newer exegesis in the commentaries by Günther Dehn, Hans Asmussen, and Christian Maurer; for the understanding of the Letter of James see my exegesis, *Der Brief des Jakobus.*)

In order to know more precisely what Jewish pastoral care is like today, we would have to gain a much deeper insight into the synagogue and its spiritual direction than is usually possible. What we know of literary testimonies, of Jewish sermons, and of presentations of Jewish piety indicate that the synagogue's relentless battle against grace still engenders a purely legalistic style of life and spiritual direction. It may be mitigated and softened by humanistic and idealistic trends, above all by mystical influences as represented by the significant writings of Martin Buber. (Cf. the interpretation of Buber's anthropology in *Church Dogmatics* III by Karl Barth.) But it is fundamentally unbroken and can suddenly impose itself again in all its ancient severity. This will not change unless the veil of which the Apostle speaks which covers (and promises!) the Christ is lifted from the eyes of Israel.

Within the Christian church, pastoral care by the law continued, though in an extraordinarily altered and deepened form in the pastoral direction of the Roman Catholic Church. The Catholic pastoral care and its corresponding piety rest upon a synthesis of gospel and law. No doubt it cannot be reproached for being purely legalistic; still less can it be said to be truly evangelical. The evangelical message of the grace of Christ is certainly accepted and exalted. And yet it is no longer the message of free grace. For the message of grace is subject here to a quite specific interpretation robbing it of its sovereignty and strength. A system of thought is presupposed and the message of grace is incorporated and developed within this framework. The principle and content of this system is the co-operation of nature and grace. It is presented as a truth taking precedence over the Word of God. Thus, unbiased reading and receiving of what is written in Holy Scripture is ruled out from the start. Given the interpretation as necessitated by this system, the biblical message of grace can no longer be really heard or make itself heard. God's Word can no longer say what it properly intends to say; it is not communicated (as it should be) on the basis of pure, factual exegesis, but on the basis of one that is dimmed by speculative thought and therefore falsifying. What is taken from the Word of God is not its own truth, but that speculation on the co-operation of nature and supernature. Of course, Jesus Christ is still proclaimed and put in the center. He is called and depicted as "the Heart of the world" (H. U. von Balthasar). His actuality and efficacy are deeply and greatly seen, yet solely for the sake of the significance he has as the main figure in this interplay of nature and grace. This co-operation is the heart of Roman Catholic christology.

This was recently confirmed in a Catholic work which sets itself the task of describing the counseling activity of the church within the sphere of the grace of Christ. (*Wesentliche Seelsorge,* "*Grundfragen und Zeitaufgaben wirksamer Seelsorge in der Verantwortung der Gegenwart,*" edited by Xavier von Hornstein, Lucerne.) Christ is very highly revered and praised here, nevertheless he is immediately used to gain the "metaphysical position" from which the church can carry out pastoral care.

This co-operation of nature and grace has as an inevitable consequence the fatal rending of the unity of gospel and law characteristic of Roman Catholic thinking and practice. The law related to "nature" and based on it becomes a relatively independent factor. It co-operates with grace, yet thereby limits it, so that grace no longer rules in absolute freedom. Everything is called into question. The message of grace can no longer be proclaimed purely, i.e., evangelically; if it still happens, it is due to a fortunate inconsequence. Ethics and pastoral care, however, slide off into casuistry.

An example of such casuistry is found in the great book of Roman Catholic pastoral care just cited under the section "Modern Surgery and Pastoral Care." Exhibiting thorough surgical knowledge the author discusses in detail which gynecological operations are to be permitted and which forbidden by the pastor.

Seen in a historical perspective, one could say that the Roman Catholic Church has from the beginning thwarted and broken the message of grace by the Pelagianism it never entirely conquered. Augustinianism, to be sure, counteracted this trend, yet not so thoroughly as to actually prevent the invasion of legalism into the sphere of grace. Only the doctrine of grace in the Reformation, with its interpretation of Augustine, conquered and overthrew Pelagianism within the Christian church.

The conflict of law-inspired piety with grace in Catholicism has made of the province of pastoral care a very sublime, but nonetheless triumphant, climax in Jesuit pastoral direction. Jesuit pastoral guidance is admirably and classically expressed and exemplified in the *Exercises* of Ignatius of Loyola, the founder of the order. In fact, it is fitting explicitly to expose the *Exercises* as the great opponent of true evangelical pastoral care. As in no other example we can learn here what it means to pit the law against the gospel. This is done in the subtlest, the most sophisticated, but consequently in a truly seductive way in the

Exercises. This work, unbeatable on its own ground, demonstrates what false sanctification means and really is, a sanctification accompanying forgiveness as an independent possibility.

Ignatius' appeal lies in his anticipation of the whole modern psychologizing of the law. For him, there is no question of the law intruding on us as a rigid, severe reality alien to our psychic life. Rather, instruction in the law is disrobed of all severity; converted into pastoral direction stemming from the deepest knowledge of man, it is displayed in the form of wise counsel and earnest exhortation to repentance and wholly internalized conversion. Through such advice and counsel, man is indeed seized with a firm hand, but at the same time feels himself marvelously understood in his deepest longing for direction and support.

First, this approach recognizes that a firm hold on man is assured only by cultivating and training his imagination and his intuition, so as to subjugate him entirely to suggestion and to the spell of a compelling image of what true humanity is. By this the person is to be induced to realize this image in his own life.

The illustrations—and this is the *second* characteristic—are entirely taken from the testimony of the Holy Scripture on the earthly life of Jesus Christ. These object lessons proceed in four main steps. The *Exercises* begin by confronting man with his sin and the infernal punishments following this sin. Next comes the description of the life of Jesus; as an encouragement to the person to tread the way of Jesus, so to speak, experimentally at first and, when at last he faces the "choice," to decide for this way himself. This is followed by the picture of Christ's suffering and death where Christ appears to us as the model of a man who obediently chose God. And in the fourth and final step the victory of Christ is exalted as the reward beckoning to him who, in imitation of Christ, has likewise made the right choice. There can be no doubt: These four steps focus on the concept of the way and the choice. Yet it is not the way which the Christ goes for us, to cover us with his grace by virtue of this way, nor is it the choice he made for us and of us; it is our own way, our own following of him, and it means the choice we make for him.

Consequently, the examination of this picture of the life and suffering of Christ always aims at man's contrition and at the decision he is to make. However, not abstract truths but imaginative visualizations are used to stimulate man's moves. It is recognized that such impressions and images can excite and transform man much more than mere abstract thought.

The *third* characteristic of this pastoral direction is the secret and sweeping presupposition of man's soul concealing in itself by nature the power which enables man to walk this way to repentance and decision. This power needs only to be released. And this occurs precisely through these mental exercises.

Fourth and last, another human being is appointed the guide of my soul, my helper and human example so that I go the way he leads me. This is based on the insight that we do not easily get going by ourselves, that we need kindling by a neighbor in whom we see our ideal already realized by a kind of transference.

There is certainly no more assured, it might perhaps be said no more demonic, way to bring man under the law and thereby —supposedly!—to lead him to healing and salvation. This goal of healing and salvation is also called *grace* by Ignatius. Even for him, grace is highest and last of all realities. He wants to lead man by his exercises to the church, and this means quite concretely to confession and to receiving the sacrament of the altar. There flows the source of grace! And yet, not grace but law, and only law, has the last word here. For grace stands not at the beginning, but only at the end. Before grace comes the way I must walk to grace, my training, my fulfillment of the law, whereby I must work my way up to grace. Significantly though, Ignatius scarcely talks of grace, of the church, of the sacraments in the *Exercises*. This silence naturally does not mean disregard of grace and of the means of grace. Rather, these are self-evident, and he wants to lead to them. But is this legitimate? Can grace assert itself if the whole emphasis falls on the way man must travel to this grace? This way of man as a law preceding grace, however sublimated, at any rate covers the whole realm of piety in Ignatius' *Exercises*. What is enjoined here is a spiritual *lex naturae* ultimately separated from grace, a commandment, though developed on the example of Christ, yet separated from him. This emancipation and independent existence of the commandment, this abstract use of the law, this fundamental dualism of nature and grace is the trade mark of this penitential teaching and pastoral direction. It is at the same time a mark of corruption, because the grace of forgiveness is destroyed. True, this method had astounding results, and has them even today. Ignatius shows that people can be manipulated. He shows that they actually expect such manipulation. They want to be taught to achieve the goal by exertion of their own psychic forces. For they want to be saved by their own spirituality, without grace. They do not want to live as people who depend on free mercy. They want nothing on a gratuitous basis. They do not want another to take their place and pay with his life. They do not want to be saved by Christ alone.

The pastoral approach of the *Exercises* is not simply an accidental, subordinate example of Roman Catholic pastoral direction. It is rather the characteristic and authoritative expression of it. It represents the final consequence of the interaction of nature and grace in the theology and in the practice of the Roman Catholic Church. Ignatius' pastoral letters are instructive illustrations of the *Exercises*. (Cf. Ignatius von Loyola, *Geistliche Briefe*, edited by Otto Karrer.)

In present-day Protestant theology, Karl Barth sharply recognized that the fundamental issue in the debate with the Roman Catholic Church centers in this dialectic of nature and grace. (Cf. his statements about nature and grace in *Church Dogmatics* I, 2 and II, 1.) It is surprising how innocently the rest of Protestantism continues to admire and acknowledge the pastoral care of the Catholic Church. (Cf. the remarkably uncritical appropriation of elements of Catholic pastoral care by Benoît in *Direction Spirituelle et Protestantisme*.)

The pastoral care based on the law and given its classical expression by Ignatius of Loyola found various imitations outside the Catholic Church. We refer once again to the Anthroposophy of Rudolf Steiner and the education and pastoral guidance derived from it. Though alienated from any ecclesiastical tradition, it is yet inconceivable without the background of the pastoral guidance of the Catholic Church, in which Rudolf Steiner was brought up.

The magic spell of Anthroposophy on our unchurched contemporaries cannot be explained away by tracing it back to the purely scientific urge for knowledge and its satisfaction through the esoteric teaching established by Steiner. Of course, metaphysical projection and deepening of the world view plays an important role in Anthroposophy. But just as important is what might be called the pedagogical, therapeutic use Steiner makes of his insights. Specifically, he promises to lift man up, even to redeem him by disclosing and unfolding transcendental and metaphysical realities and forces. With this purpose in mind, he develops his instructions for the attainment of "knowledge of higher worlds." By virtue of this knowledge, man shall be enabled to reopen the buried access to upper worlds and the spirits that dwell there and thus to become himself a "spiritual being." This promise makes for the attraction which Anthroposophy has. In pastoral care, we continually meet people who are strongly influenced by it. They are fascinated not so much by the purely intellectual interest in new and mysterious explanations about the world and man as by the prospect of coming into the hands of the pastoral guide and educator who can reshape and renew their whole nature and life. But this happens by way of a training at least formally resembling the Jesuit. By means of contemplation and practice, man shall ascend to a higher level of spiritual existence by virtue of which he can penetrate as through a narrow gate into a world beyond sensory perception. There is no need to contest the anthroposophist world view. Much of it may correspond to reality, though perhaps with a different interpretation. Our opposition rather sets in as soon as the Anthroposophists apply their insights to the disclosure of a new way of salvation upon which, by practices of concentration, perhaps by eurythmics or some other means, man strides beyond the earthly, sinful life and matures to a higher, purified being—all this without the forgiveness of sins by Jesus Christ alone. (We may refer again to Georg Merz, "Der Einbruch des Mysterienglaubens in die Kirche der Gegenwart," in the Kirchliche Verkündigung und moderne Bildung, one of the best Protestant studies of Anthroposophy ever written.)

Finally, we consider the numerous offers within the church itself of ways and means whereby men attempt to change and renew their lives. They are manifold, and even permeate to some extent the pastoral counseling of the church itself. This is shown by strong tinges of both legalistic and mystical-contemplative advice given in our pastoral care. Of course, evangelical pastoral care, even in such a legalistic form, is distinguished from the manner of Catholic pastoral direction by numerous mitigations and refractions of its legalistic-moralistic or mystical-contemplative attitude. These mitigations and refractions are caused by the never entirely forgotten message of forgiveness. Yet it is no longer a pastoral care built on free grace alone.

For example, we may point here to the frequent use in pastoral counseling of biographies as a source of wisdom and a model for imitation. This is not to forbid once for all the reading of such descriptions of exemplary men. Caution is nevertheless indicated. Are these presentations not remarkably close to the pictures of the saints in the Catholic Church? Their interest for church history is uncontested; the danger lies in the legalistic use one so easily feels tempted to make of them. Who does not know that feeling of self-rejection whenever he takes up such a more or less victorious account of the life of a pious man? We stand as at the foot of a high mountain and look at the climbing man presented in the biography. We silently sigh: I shall never make it! My life will never look so pious, so righteous, so radiant! I shall never leave behind such bright imprints! Even so, we try to climb in turn. But this is indicative of our legalistic interpretation of this biography. This makes it spiritually dangerous. Here is the questionable aspect of recommending such books to the spiritually insecure reader. There are biographies which do not contain this danger because the main character meant to be and was nothing but a human being accepting free grace and appears as such in the presentation. Such biographies can be most helpful. But they do not abound. The great majority of Christian biographies move in the legalistic direction. And therefore, there is less joy in heaven about them than on earth.

In this connection, the pastoral care of Moral Re-Armament merits mentioning again. All to the good, it freshly reaffirms the power of salvation in the forgiveness of sins over against a church which to some extent is no longer open to the grace of God. Moral Re-Armament in turn did not escape the danger of lapsing into legalism. We refer to what was already said: to the assertion of the four "absolutes" by which one has to measure himself; to certain characteristics of an order which the movement has assumed; to the exemplary, public giving of testimony; to the legalistic demand for confession and surrender to Christ. Here a new kind of manipulation of man's psychic life by imposing specific operations suggests itself.

In fact, the success of the movement rests in part on such more or less legalistically applied operations. In this, it meets half way man's desire for manipulation. More people than we might think are driven by a deep desire for specific instructions to follow in order to gain peace. We must immediately concede that the lack of relevant pastoral care, definitely and clearly communicating the gracious commandment of God to me, actually called for Moral Re-Armament and gave it its significance. We must further concede the practice of genuine and unexceptional pastoral care in Moral Re-Armament.

All these deviations from the way of a pastoral care of free grace could not have occurred if the church on its part had respected the right use of gospel and law. The church no longer knew that justification without sanctification is nothing. A preaching of forgiveness spread which lacked the seriousness of the law. This weakened preaching of forgiveness came under attack. It dawned on some that forgiveness brings sanctification with it, or else it is not forgiveness. But this corrective, in itself necessary and wholesome, unfortunately prompted an independent preaching of the law which set itself alongside, and even above, grace. An actual dictatorship of the law was established. Forgiveness and grace were made dependent on man's obedience in fulfilling the law. This is the beginning of those movements of awakening and repentance which certainly have a mission with their preaching of sanctification. They shake the church, but they fail to build it up. Granted all the seriousness of their effort and all their rightful significance we still have to caution against them. For they get entangled in false legalism and therefore do not break through to the proclamation of free grace which alone saves.

But who dares to throw the first stone here? We are daily in mortal danger of preaching the law instead of the gospel in our pastoral care. How different the church would look if God's healing and saving claim were communicated in every pastoral conversation! Then clear evangelical confession, conversion, and awakening would result from our pastoral care. Then the preaching of forgiveness would become a liberating event. Then good care would be taken of the souls of those requesting our pastoral care.

Such pastoral care certainly happens in the church even today. But we have every reason to ponder how it may happen more often and better. We are perhaps not so much in danger of an oppressive establishment of the law as—what is no better—in danger of a feeble, sapless, powerless, lifeless pastoral care. We no longer dare to communicate the commandment powerfully because we no longer proclaim grace unconditionally. By this failure we call into existence that other pastoral care of the law, which works with strong means and not only grasps, but whips, men. What ought to occur is this: communication of forgiveness, but powerful forgiveness, a forgiveness joined by the commandment. Sanctification must be wrought, but a sanctification that wants to be nothing but justification, thereby becoming real sanctification. The lost would have to be won, souls to be saved in the church. We do not have to be ashamed of such catchwords and leave them to Methodism and the Salvation Army. Let us recall how strongly Luther expresses this: ". . . who (has) gained and won me . . . from all sins, from death, and from the power of the Devil, not with gold or silver, but with his holy, precious blood. . . ." This wresting us from the spell of sin and the power of the Devil will take place where Jesus Christ is clearly and expressly confessed and proclaimed to be both Lord and the Merciful One, the one not without the other. Then the praise and thanksgiving of the saved will be sounded again in our pastoral care, and the Lord of the church will no longer miss the fruit in us which he seeks.

The communication of the gospel in the form of commandment leads to repentance understood as the concrete change of direction in man's life as a result of forgiveness. At the very point of his sinful act, man is pardoned by the Word of forgiveness and thereby judged and placed in obedience to Christ. This is his regeneration and his conversion. Since only the gospel can bring it about, repentance, notwithstanding the seriousness of the judgment, is a joyous repentance.

13 Evangelical Repentance in Pastoral Care

How is the law rightly and evangelically communicated in pastoral care? This is the question to which we now must turn. It is equivalent to the question of true, evangelical repentance.

The English word "repentance" is the translation of the Greek word in the Septuagint and the New Testament which means "change one's mind," "rethink," and of the Hebrew word which means "turning around." It is a question whether this is an adequate rendering of what is denoted in these biblical words, for it is also closely related to the Vulgate word *poenitentia*, and something of the legalistic character of this medieval word adheres to it. But the word "repentance" is now customary and signifies *sanctification as an act*, as a real occurrence in man. Man hears the promise of forgiveness, and now this promise becomes effective as a claim on him. As we have shown, he comes under forgiveness as a power which seizes and moves his life. The term repentance can express the objective content of the promise and is then to be understood as call to repentance, as well as the subjective reception of the call by the listener. So understood, repentance leads to regeneration and to conversion. As a whole, it is a change of direction and renewal of life brought about by the Word of God; the concept of regeneration emphasizes that it is effective from above, whereas the concept of conversion implies man's total participation in it. (Cf. the brief [indeed, all too brief] pertinent statements in Alfred de Quervain, *Die Heiligung* I, pp. 104 ff.)

Repentance has to do with a separation and decision—it is called "crisis" in the New Testament itself—between the sphere of the rule of God established in Christ and the sphere of our life, which opposes this rule (even if in vain), between the world above and the world below, between spirit and flesh, between obedience and sin. Proclaiming forgiveness, pastoral care accomplishes this separation in the lives of those whom it calls to repentance. It promises and brings regeneration and thereby requires and accomplishes man's conversion.

Reference is made here to the preaching of the Prophets, according to which the sanctification of God's people is always to be understood as a singling out from the godless world and therefore as a separation from and renunciation of this world and its false gods to be accomplished by this people. To this preaching corresponds the announcement in the New Testament of the coming of the Kingdom of God as a change in government: The old government is overthrown, the new government of Christ is established, and the faithful are gathered as the band of people who let themselves be cut off from the old aeon in order to be sanctified for the new. (For the whole New Testament proclamation of the kingly rule of Christ and of the singling out and preparing the Christian community, see the exceedingly significant essay by Oscar Cullman, *Die Königsherrschaft Jesu Christi in Neuen Testament.*)

Because true, evangelical repentance deals with this crisis, with the singling out of those who let themselves be seized by grace, the fight against false legalism is waged here most fiercely. Legalism now is the attempt to work out one's own self-sanctification instead of surrendering to the holy separation by the gracious call. Repentance is seen as man's own achievement rather than as regeneration from above. Man wants to make his own decision and disentangle and liberate himself from the sphere of the flesh. Repentance, of course, always involves a decision and return to be made by man. Yet it consists precisely in man's renouncing all self-sanctification and self-help and trusting with all his strength the decision made for him in Christ. Man repents, not as his own act, but as that "alien work" which comes over him from God. It is in no way man who converts himself; regeneration by the Holy Spirit becomes his conversion. It is Christ who turns man about, and that so completely that he walks from now on in a new life.

We recall the passionate warning sounded by the Apostle at the beginning of the third chapter of the Letter to the Philippians, where he talks of the "dogs" that break into the Christian community to bring it again under the law in that profligate, Jewish way, instead of calling it to Christ and to his grace alone. But did not these dogs again break into our churches? Are we not ourselves permanently engaged in slovenly and corruptly confounding conscience and morals instead of placing them under grace and the repentance based on it? (Cf. my exegesis of the Letter to the Philippians, *Der Brief des Paulus an die Philipper;* also Alfred de Quervain, *op. cit.*, pp. 105 and 109 ff., where thought-provoking utterances of Luther and of the Reformed theologian Kohlbrügge are found pertaining to the matter of true sanctification, repentance, and conversion.)

Our pastoral care would acquire quite a new countenance if it summoned men to such evangelical repentance and conversion. This would mean the rejection of every kind of the ever-tempting moralistic rearmament. Where this happens, the penitential conversations, however unostentatious they may seem to the outsider, become the place of liberation and of vital help. They lead to decisions in the lives of those with whom they are conducted. But instead of this, pastoral conversations all too often deviate into some kind of legalism, which enslaves instead of releasing and which encourages self-help instead of true repentance.

A practical example may make this clear. In numerous Sunday school rooms and pastoral studies, one can still see a picture representing Jesus' words about the narrow and the wide way (Matthew 7:13ff.). These words intend to guide us to the repentance preached in the Sermon on the Mount. But how is it understood in this picture? It shows the wide way as a street of this world. It is lined with taverns, dance halls, theaters, and the like. Today, the cinema and the stadium could not be absent. And all these places are full of people who live merrily, apparently without giving thought to anything eternal or divine. We also discover the Devil at work, leading men to corruption on this street. It ends in open hell with its fire. On the other half of the picture we see the narrow way, bordered by preaching stations, churches, chapels, and their social halls. Not many, only a few, go this way, for it is steep and leads high up through a narrow gate. There are poor, bent figures that walk this narrow way, the cross-bearers and the tormented. But above, at the end of this little street, the heavenly city in its splendor awaits them as their high reward. The whole picture, in dependence on Bunyan's *Pilgrim's Progress* and its still older models, is possibly conceived as advice for the care of one's own soul and those of others. But must we not say that both ways are approximately as the earnest and pious Jews of Jesus' time imagined them; the frightening wide way of the despisers of the law, and the steep and narrow way of those who take pains to keep the commandments down to the smallest detail.

By preaching true repentance for the Kingdom of heaven, Jesus opposed this moralistic, religious interpretation of the work of penitence with all his might. Of course, he also called men away from the world, from mammon and all false desire, but unlike the scribes and the Pharisees who stressed the letter of the law, he stressed the forgiveness of sins. He did not burden men with commandment after commandment, thus placing them on the narrow way and separating them from those who rush to corruption along the broad way of lawlessness. Rather, he strode himself the narrow way of obedience unto death for all, in order to open the way to the Father by the road he walked for us. The wide way of which the Sermon on the Mount speaks is not the way of the children of this world, but precisely the way of the falsely pious, of the scribes and Pharisees. It is the very way of those who so readily see themselves on the narrow path of strict and strenuous fulfillment of the law. The narrow path signifies the way which turns away from all human fulfillment of the law as it is probably understood in that picture, whereby human beings are summoned to pious self-help and led away from the gospel.

We continue nonetheless to recommend and walk "narrow ways" in this false, legalistic sense. As a result, the highly questionable lines are still drawn between those who consider themselves awakened and converted and those who in some sense live sluggishly and unredeemed. This can happen even in a highly modern and liberal manner—for example, by depicting Jesus as a noble man to be emulated, or by projecting an ideal of high personality development to be achieved by one's own strength. We find such instruction "to the venture of personal life," for example, in the religious writer Johannes Müller already mentioned several times. As a sure signpost of the narrow way of true evangelical repentance the undoubtedly necessary separation between world and piety will be marked at quite another point. The pious will recognize himself as belonging in his piety to the world, as one whose sins must be forgiven like those of any other child of this world. By such recognition, the truly penitent is separated from the world; he is separated from the false piety which strives against grace and therefore nails Christ to the cross. But to the world he proclaims the gospel which saves him and the world, and thus calls it to the repentance which is his own repentance.

But how does the true call to repentance go out? How is it accomplished in pastoral care? Is there any pertinent counsel, any rule? Were we to effect man's return by way of legalism, detailed methods could easily be developed. To preach legalistically means to give instruction as to how I can avail myself of the true life by specific acts and practices. To communicate the gospel, the forgiveness of sins signifies, on the contrary, the recognition that this method is doomed. Even our best act is nothing. Help only comes on the way which we do not go ourselves, but which Jesus Christ has gone for us. And to repent in the evangelical sense means to set this way before the soul and to see the sole deliverance in it. It means to love Jesus Christ "with love undying" (Ephesians 6:24). Hence, evangelical repentance cannot consist in choosing a way of the law or insisting on a manipulation, perhaps still more earnest, more pious, more spiritual than all those preceding. If advice must be given as to how to proceed to achieve repentance, it can only be: Communicate the forgiveness of sins and this alone and abstain from everything which hinders, limits, or endangers the delivery of this message. This is the rule of all rules. The right rule here is to make and keep free the way in the pastoral conversation so that the sinner may truly grasp the grace of God, which alone leads to repentance.

We now recall the special function devolving on the pastoral conversation in communicating the Word of forgiveness. It must not try to complete or even replace the sermon or the sacrament, but it is the necessary repetition, underlining, and clarification of the Word communicated by the ordinary means. It wants to bring about the overtaking and confronting of the individual by the Word of forgiveness. A person perhaps tolerates a general sermon on grace, but tries to overhear the personal call. The pastoral conversation bars this possibility of escape. Noncommittal assent to the gospel is not enough, for this allows man to abide with some self-chosen law and forfeits the true help and deliverance.

But what does it mean concretely to affect a man with the Word of forgiveness? It means that a quite specific, *real sin* is hit and disclosed, but also taken away and forgiven by this Word. Let us take up once again the repeatedly used picture of an arrest: If a person is arrested, he is not arrested in general, but, for example, he is arrested as a thief or as an adulterer. It is not otherwise with the Word of repentance. It is always a specific sin, a *sinful act*, which becomes the occasion to call man to repentance in pastoral care. His disobedience, but also God's mercy, is set before him in this specific sinful act. Each individual sin involves man's total existence. There is no individual act of sin that does not spring from our human sinfulness—in which we attempt to live our lives without God and his grace. But this common sinfulness, this wrong way on which we tread is now disclosed to us by a single sinful step in which we are engaged. We are overtaken by repentance at the specific point of a sinful deed. In shame and contrition we recognize our aberration, but at the same time are shown the Saviour, who will rescue and liberate us.

If the pastoral conversation is to lead to such concrete repentance, it must very plainly deal with the concrete sin in which the individul to whom we speak is enmeshed and which is to become the occasion for him to grasp forgiveness. We must therefore insist on actual *acknowledgement* of sin. We must examine most scrupulously and conscientiously the concrete lostness, bondage, and imprisonment in which the great, common sin of mankind is expressed by this specific person. Yet we must always regard it as a sin to be forgiven in Christ. This alone releases man from his sin. This does not exclude, but rather includes, man's responsibility for his sin. He did not simply suffer ill fate when he sinned, but he yielded to his corrupt nature and stands guilty and convicted before God. But since this responsibility is held against the background of forgiveness, it is completely enveloped in mercy. Man is made responsible for his sin in order to be told: You can and you may become free. You are a prey of your sin and now shall be released. You are sentenced and now may look forward to your acquittal. We now talk of your sin with the sole purpose of pronouncing the absolutions. And finally, this absolution in itself signifies man's freedom to *obedience*. The released prisoner knows from now on: Sin no longer belongs to me; I no longer belong to my sin. A struggle now begins in him against sin, a departure from the fields of death toward a new life. The summons to such striving, however, goes out in the form of admonitions and instructions of a correspondly concrete nature. He who is touched by the Word of repentance is pledged according to his specific sin to a specific, new obedience. He is exhorted to leave undone this or that previously committed sin, or finally to do what God commanded him and he had left undone. However, this summons to obedience is not a new law to be fulfilled by human strength; even when it goes forth in specific instructions and orders, it is new freedom. Man no longer must, but may and can, do what he formerly could not and might not have done because of sin. The message of grace has become the driving force in which he walks and does not grow weary. Sin is not simply gone; it still tempts him, yet he may now withstand the temptation. He sins and yet sins no more, for he no longer fights against grace which overcomes the sin in him. This is evangelical repentance.

The Scripture passages which might be quoted here are countless. Holy Scripture proclaims such repentance throughout and grace and obedience always appear as one fact even if they are expressed in two words. It is always proclaimed in a concrete application, e.g., Romans 6:1-11, where the great question is raised whether grace can lead us to laziness and more sin because we are sure of forgiveness. The answer is clear. He who understands grace in this way does not understand it at all. For grace means to be put to death by Christ so that we may rise through this death as men who walk in a new life. This new life is very explicitly mentioned in all the admonitions that fall like hammer blows in the apostolic letters. They are nothing but the great confirmation of the fact that forgiveness is a concrete arrest affecting man's life. But this arrest, this being admonished no longer to be angry, no longer to lie, no longer to steal, no longer to indulge in hate and wrath (cf. Ephesians 4:25ff.), is nothing but pure grace. For these admonitions one by one say to us: You are God's child; therefore, you can no longer give room to the evil one! And this is truly a joyous, gracious message.

The Letter of James must be mentioned again. It is a sharp letter and yet also one that is filled to the brim with mercy, if only we know how to read it rightly. It is a single great warning against separating faith and obedience lest faith lose the liberating strength, its true attribute. So understood, it is a letter which one cannot employ often enough in pastoral care. Lastly, the Sermon on the Mount needs to be quoted. It again proclaims the grace of the Kingdom of heaven in the form of admonition, the admonition opening the door to the transformation into the freedom of the children of God. (Cf. Karl Barth, *Church Dogmatics* II, 2, 38, 2, where the way is paved for the right understanding of the Sermon on the Mount; also my work, *Die Bergpredigt*.) We consider, finally, that in the New Testament, repentance is linked to baptism. But baptism is baptism in the blood of Jesus; it brings the great transformation over the whole world, that transformation from death to life which comes to light in the resurrection of Jesus Christ. This is to say that Jesus in his death snatches the prey from the power of sin. From now on the world is by his death sentenced and called to repentance, but by his resurrection declared saved in the same repentance. This salvation manifests itself in the great transformation affecting all things on earth. To repent means thenceforth nothing else than allowing this judgment and this salvation to become effective in our lives.

We summarize: Evangelical repentance stands and falls with its roots in forgiveness. From the vantage point of forgiveness and on account of forgiveness, pastoral care must be thoroughly and unhesitatingly talk of sin and call to obedience. But this talking of sin and obedience must not for a moment be cut off from forgiveness. We must admonish and punish, but only in the name of Jesus Christ and therefore in mercy. If this connection is sundered, if in the pastoral conversation we allow only for a moment the great recollection of the mercy of Christ to vanish, then all is lost. We then indeed admonish, disclose, and punish, but we do it in a legalistic, harsh way. This sundering of the connection between repentance and faith can happen in a very subtle way, perhaps by letting ourselves, without noticing it, be misled in the discussion of a life situation where Christ and his victory over all sin is disregarded. It may be a purely moralistic or purely psychological or an oppressively pious consideration. Once treading on alien ground, we automatically fall into the trap of a false severity or, what is no better, a false leniency in the instructions to be imparted. True comfort is not given; the person we address is not exposed to the power of forgiveness. The sure sign that true evangelical repentance is carried on lies in the fact that our conversation is no doubt severe, but in all its severity it is a liberating, joyful conversation. Evangelical repentance is *joyful repentance*.

Observe how this note of joy breaks forth in the gospel reports of repentance! Jesus is called the master of joy in spite of, indeed because of, the great repentance he imposes on men. This irritated the pious of the time so much that they rebuked him for lack of seriousness. His repentance was to the serious not serious enough, to the pious not pious enough, because he did not bend men under a new law. Around Jesus, men also wept tears of repentance; they were so bitter because he who wept them had to recognize how much he had drawn away from the joy of the Kingdom of heaven as he wandered far from Jesus.

To be sure, the joy of true repentance cannot be artificially awakened. The often tense and affected cheerfulness so frequently found in so-called awakened circles has little to with the true joy of evangelical repentance. True joy is a very hidden and personal matter. It does not even exclude the sadness we feel in bewailing our sin. But this is that divine sadness of which the Apostle says that it works repentance for the Kingdom of heaven. It is the outer garment in which deep and pure peace is concealed, that "great peace," which according to the words of the Psalm is bestowed on those who love God's law (Psalm 119:165). Consequently, evangelical repentance is a serious yet at the same time a joyful repentance. Our pastoral care will shake men as it leads them into a wholesome terror at the depth of their sin; however, it will not harass them, but it will set them free. For it stands where the Lord of the church stands with his gracious call to repentance.

Repentance is the act whereby I allow the Word of God to disclose my sin to me and lay it before God, so that he may take it from me. This laying of my sin before God is my confession. It is realized in the individual prayer of each person and in the corporate prayer of the church at worship. Such repentance before God and Jesus Christ against the opposition of the power of sin is made possible by confessional conversation where sins are confessed to one another, forgiveness proclaimed, and wholesome admonition given. Evangelical confession is sharply to be set over against Catholic confession; yet it is indispensable and represents the helpful and liberating center of all true pastoral care.

14 Pastoral Care as Confession

We have found that pastoral conversation is penitential conversation. That is, man's sin must be spoken of very concretely in pastoral care. How shall forgiveness be announced unless we enter together the place of sin in order that it may become the place of forgiveness? For sin is disclosed not in order to charge man, but to discharge him, to confront him with God, whose Word awakens repentance in us and in our repentance absolves us from sin.

By requiring the pastoral conversation to be penitential conversation in which sin is disclosed and forgiven, we transform it into a confessional conversation. What this means and how it may be conducted needs to be explained at this point.

The concept of confession is loaded for us because it is employed in the Roman Catholic Church to denote the sacramental act of penance. But this is no reason for not accepting it. What we reject in the Catholic confession is not confession as such, but the fatal, sacramental use which is made of it. The verb "to confess" means to affirm something, to stand for something, to acknowledge something. The object which is acknowledged in confession is sin. Confession is confession of sin. To confess means: I affirm the specific act I have committed as something for which I am responsible. I affirm it as distinct from fate which I endure without accepting responsibility for it. I affirm it as my deed in such a way as to make plain that I have done it under the spell of sin. My act is marked by sin just as an object bears a trademark indicating its origin.

Whether small or great, subtle or gross, inward or outward, secret or public, sin has the peculiar force of laying hold on me like an alien power, carrying me along where I do not wish to go. Yet I accept its sway; I let myself be carried along by it. Thus it is described in the basic passage, Genesis 3. This acceptance of sin is the decisive act. *I* do the sin. I cannot shift the responsibility to the alien power. The alien power, sin, so to speak, takes quarters in me under the cover of my own deed. That here something happens to me and in me without my willing it, and yet it is I who do it—these two things are one and the same. Remember the presentation of this factual situation in the second decisive passage, Romans 7: "I do not do what I want, but I do the very thing I hate" (verse 15). Still, *I* do it. This is sin. And this sin is the object of confession.

He to whom confession is directed, its recipient, is *God*. Rightly done, confession is no monologue; it is not even merely a dialogue between two persons; it is, perhaps in the form of such a dialogue, a confessing and affirming of sin before God. It is an admission that we have sinned against him. The word "God" belongs to confession as self-evidently as the word "sin." There is no true confession unless it places us before God. There is no confession which does not turn into prayer, indeed which is not a prayer in itself.

We refer to the penitential Psalms and among them primarily to the Fifty-first, which is one great confessional prayer. The proper purpose of confession is to encourage me to bring my sin before God. For sin is essentially an event between God and me. True, specific acts of sin are at stake each time. Yet only because they represent transgressions of the commandments of

God and are committed in the attempt to live our life without God, are these acts called sin. This deviation from the will of God is what makes the sinful deed sin. "Against thee, thee only, have I sinned, and done that which is evil in thy sight" (Psalm 51:4).

The goal of confession can therefore be nothing but attaining forgiveness. I confess for the sake of forgiveness; confession itself is prompted by the promise of forgiveness. Or what could decide us to bring our sins before God if we did not know that he is merciful to us? Behind each true confession there looms Luther's urgently burning question: "How do I deserve a merciful God?" God's merciful intention is the presupposition of confession and at the same time its driving force. If it is true—and it is true—that we are sinners and that therein consists our whole misery, but that God intends to abolish this misery in his Son—and he so wills—can there be any other way open to us but to go and repent, confessing our sins to him?

If this is true confession, then it cannot be understood as an isolated act, a work accomplished alongside and in addition to other works. On the contrary, confessing is the central act of the life of faith and as such must ever anew be realized in us. Can we live in faith except by "daily" being engaged in the movement of repentance, as Luther says in the first Wittenberg thesis? Can there be another "reasonable" service of God than that we claim for ourselves the service which God has done in Jesus Christ and thus let ourselves be cleansed of our sin by continually confessing it to him.

So understood, confession at first has nothing to do with pastoral care as a special undertaking; rather, it coincides with the daily confessing of sin and receiving of forgiveness out of faith in Jesus Christ within the church. It does not need to be justified by special texts of Holy Scripture. Holy Scripture as a whole testifies to the forgiveness of sin and the judgment on sin. Its message, therefore, is one great summons to evangelical confession. It stands as the one, great, and gracious commandment, as Jesus' summary of his whole message, at the beginning of the

Gospels: Because "the kingdom of God is at hand; repent, and believe in the gospel" (Mark 1:15). Now we understand why Jesus instructs us in the Lord's Prayer to call daily upon the Father in heaven and ask him to forgive our debts; why the apostolic letters constantly urge the churches to lay aside sin and to be cleansed by the blood of Jesus; why baptism and communion are instituted as the only true sacraments of penance, and the great penitential prayers of the Psalms are part of the liturgy of the church. (Cf. Walter Lüthi and Eduard Thurneysen, *Preaching, Confession, the Lord's Supper;* also the substantial essay on evangelical confession by W. Pfendsack in the *Kirchenblatt für die reformierte Schweiz,* 1945, Nos. 4 and 5.)

Confession is realized in the daily prayer of the individual, in his personal seeking and obtaining forgiveness. However, it is also realized in the corporate liturgical prayer of the worshiping congregation. The early church and again the renewed churches of the Reformation knew of no divine worship where sin was not audibly and publicly acknowledged and laid aside in a common confession. For every worship service was to become the place where the members of the congregation let themselves be called together into the presence of Jesus, their living Lord. Therefore, in the early church there was no worship without the celebration of communion, because communion is even more the place of Jesus Christ's presence, where his own are united with him in the eating and drinking of his body and blood. And how can we be united with him without accepting the forgiveness of sins? Prayer and partaking of communion are the first expressions of the ongoing confession of the church. (Cf. the discussion of worship in the early church in the important essay by Oscar Cullman, *Worship in the Early Church.*)

But is confession actually accomplished? Is this acknowledging and laying aside of the guilt of sin an ever new reality, either in the prayer of the individual or in the corporate confession of guilt before God? Would not the church look quite different if things were aright in this innermost respect? Referring to everything already said about the crisis and decline of spiritual life in the church, we assert: Crisis and decline exist because the movement of repentance in the Christian community is weakened, even well on the way to death. Repentance is the root from which the life of the community springs. Lacking repentance, this life is an illusion. As a cut flower may well keep its color and fragrance for awhile and yet must irretrievably wither, so all kinds of life impulses may be present in the church; yet if the thrust of true life from the power of forgiveness is missing, all these life impulses cannot hide the inner demise. Accordingly, the true movements for the renewal of the church were always penitential movements. The church cannot be renewed and kept alive by mere organizational or charitable endeavors; the church is renewed and kept alive again and again only by the spirit of repentance.

At this point pastoral care begins to operate. We recall what has been said about its task and basis. It is the extraordinary means given to the church so that it may lead its people to the use of the proper, ordinary means of sermon and sacraments to strengthen them, and thus awaken and sustain their inner life. Pastoral care is carried out in the form of a question to the individual, who thereby is shaken from the indifference of his unbelief and is called to repentance. This operation of pastoral care, however, is by nature once again nothing but a process of confession, though in a new shape and form reaching beyond what was previously presented. It is that shape and form of confession that comes first to mind when we talk of confession: confession as conversation, conducted by the pastor with an individual and by the individual with the pastor in order really and concretely to bring about repentance. Accordingly, confessing now means to confess his sin not only before God, but also before another person with the purpose and the goal of laying it down before God with the help of this neighbor. The previously developed form of confession is not abandoned or annulled, but rather enhanced by the confessional conversation with a neighbor. Confession is and remains first and last repentance before God, who is the Father of Jesus Christ and our

Father. It is realized first and last in personal prayer and in the prayer of the Christian community. Even pastoral confessional conversation will never be anything but an introduction to this proper and final form of confession. It takes place in order that the confessional prayer may actually happen. It is an auxiliary to confession, only an auxiliary, but as such it is necessary and indispensable.

The necessity of confessional conversation as the means for leading to confession is based on man's great pain in recognizing, disclosing, and exposing his own sin. Inhibitions in man work against the confession of sin. Man does not like to admit his sin. His pride, his self-righteousness rear up against it. Bent on mastering sin on his own, he objects to submitting to God and his grace. The struggle against grace, as we have repeatedly seen, constitutes the very nature of sin. Sinful man sins by wanting to lead the impossible life without grace of the individual who does not need God. Hence, sin shuts man off from God. It causes him to hide before him, to flee before him. This is expressed concretely by man's refusal to listen to the gracious summons of God's Word in Scripture and preaching, and to answer God in prayer. But this means that he no longer comes to repentance and to the realization of repentance in confession. For to repent and to confess would require man's opening himself to God and the end of his self-concealment.

The new life of him who seeks and finds the gracious fellowship with the Father in heaven begins with a great opening toward God and before God. The confessional prayer enacting repentance focuses on this seeking and finding access to God. Therefore, man strives against it, as long as he lives locked up in his sin. It belongs to the power of sin not to release man from this prison; sin intends to remain covered up; it hates to be disclosed. Were it disclosed, were it confessed and acknowledged, sin would end. It would lose its sovereign hold over man. Man would become free for grace. So seen, confession is the great counterattack against sin, the act of man's breaking out of his confinement. This is why man finds it so hard. This is why he avoids it as long as he can. Or we should say, as long as he must! For it is a must, something like a demonic spell which lies over him and prevents him from coming before God to surrender to his grace. If man would call upon God in the prayer of confession, this spell would be broken. But it shall not be broken! This is the dark will of the power from below to which we fall prey when we sin. Stubborn and fettered in dangerous deafness and mutism before God, I continue to sin. I keep my sin for myself, and while I keep it, it is kept; it cannot be forgiven me, and I drift toward the judgment and condemnation of my life. How shall I break out of my chains? How shall I be able to shake off the demonic grip of sin?

Now we understand the necessity and significance of the confessional conversation. The forgiveness of sins has long ago been established over me and lies ready for me. But it must now break through to me and seize me. Seized by it, I am safe. Precisely this happens in the encounter with someone else who approaches me from the Word of God, draws me into conversation, and thus becomes my neighbor who fetches me out of my prison. At last, I am decisively challenged in my flight from God by this conversation. I can no longer escape; I must abandon my flight. What I myself cannot bring about now occurs; I am made responsible, i.e., I am questioned by my neighbor about my sin, and I let myself be questioned about it. I can and I may draw my sin from its hiding place. It is called by its name. It becomes visible. This makes it possible to lay it down before God, offering it to him, and receiving his forgiveness. On the basis of this conversation, I can genuinely pray. Now I can finally confess; daily for myself and together with the worshiping congregation, I can truly call on God and come to feel his helping hand. In the strength of his Spirit, his life-giving Word enters my life, poor, but now open for God, freed from the spell and the hell of sin. This is the meaning and content of the confessional conversation. This service it renders to us.

The necessity for such pastoral confession can also be explained psychologically. The barriers erected by all kinds of inhibitions and fixations in man's mind and the releasing effect wrought by the skill of the psychotherapist, which loosens and drains off the inhibition by conversation, may be mentioned here. Correct as this is, it remains a preliminary observation. The origin and power of psychic inhibitions cannot actually be explained in a purely psychological view, as we already know. We understand it only if we recognize in the light of the Word of God the power of sin as the source of all psychic inhibtion and bondage. Likewise the release effected by the conversation with our neighbor receives its true foundation and force from the Word of forgiveness alone, which stands behind the conversation and makes it possible and fruitful.

We recall the things already said about the efficacy or inefficacy of human speech. Speaking, man awakes to his life as man who is an *I* that finds a *thou*, as man who may live in the bond of love with his fellow men. We cannot produce such speaking, nor the fellowship it engenders, out of our own resources. It is granted to us in the mystery of our being called by God in his gracious revelation. Only by God's drawing us into communion with him as he has himself become man in his Son and thus our true neighbor, human life together in love through common listening to one another and speaking to one another becomes both possible and real. That is to say, if a neighbor comes to talk to me and thus to become my helper, it is for the sake of forgiveness. God sends the neighbor and enables him to speak powerfully to me so that his words penetrate me and I can hear them as the Word concerning and releasing me. Its releasing power is attested when I finally speak myself and am fetched from my sinful confinement and lonesomeness. If this order of forgiveness did not exist, or did it not become effective in me, nobody who wanted to talk to me would be of any help. The other person would not become a messenger of relief to me; he would not reach me at all; his words would awaken no echo in me; I would remain stony and closed and ingrown. The great impact of the confessional conversation is manifest here. Immediately proceeding from the Word of God and leading to the Word of God, it is the place of a particularly authentic conversation from man to man. Nowhere else is man more truly another's neighbor than in the encounter and conversation of merciful confession.

Confession before God awakened by the Word of forgiveness is in both Testaments of Holy Scripture shown as the central act to be accomplished for obtaining grace. Confession before man is likewise found in numerous passages as the auxiliary for initiating this act. We think of the conversations between prophets and kings in the Old Testament; of the penitents' confession of sins before John the Baptist; of the confession of the prodigal son in the parable; of Jesus' conversations with the woman who was a great sinner, with the Samaritan woman, with Peter, with Zacchaeus, with the thief on the cross (Matthew 3:5; Luke 15:21; 7:36ff.; John 4:1ff.; Luke 5:8; 19:1ff.; 23:41-43); finally, of the concrete admonition to confession before others in the Letter of James (James 5:16). Most significantly, there reigns in the New Testament community a great opening and openness of the faithful before one another and for one another. It permeates all vital relationships and constitutes the *mystery of agape*, the new reality in which these people live. This openness before one another and for one another has its roots in the wholly new openness before God and for God as it is solely possible in repentance and confession. Because this new candor before God exists, these people can afford to be honest with one another, mutually confessing their sins, as the Letter of James says, in order to receive together the forgiveness of God. Because one recognizes and loves the other in Christ as his neighbor, there is the courage in each to be frank. And because one encourages the other to be frank, they can stay together in love. The root and fruit of confession are identical. (Cf. my study on "Evangelical Confession" in *Preaching, Confession, The Lord's Supper*.)

The pastoral counselor is therefore very definitely advised to make use of confessional conversation in his ministry. Pastoral care is not confined to confessional conversation, but it will always lead to it. Even though a long way needs to be traveled before one confesses his sin to the other, such confession remains the goal before us, as truly as all pastoral care is concerned with communicating the forgiveness of sins. The strength and resiliency of man's defenses against confessing must be fully reckoned with. There is a deep-seated softness and cowardice in man; he shuns the responsibility for his sinful action, excuses and hides himself. We must be prepared for strenuous conversations. We must not be dismayed and discouraged by closed doors. We must not cease to attend to the sinner and shall not regard a pastoral conversation as ended when it breaks off before it has turned into confessional conversation in some way. Any such conversation ultimately focuses on the return of the prodigal son to the father of which the parable speaks; but this return to the father is prompted by the recognition and confession of one's own guilt: "Father, I have sinned against heaven and before you." There is no clearer or stronger indication than the Parable of the Prodigal Son (Luke 15:11-32) of confession before another being commanded as a way to forgiveness.

We have described the necessity of confessional conversation. With like emphasis, however, we must now speak also of its limitations. Urgently as its practice is recommended, it is never to be considered as more than an auxiliary means apt to lead to confession proper, to confession before God. Here the deep, unbridgeable gulf separating evangelical confession from the Roman Catholic sacrament of penance opens up. In Catholic confession, the confessing before another and the awarding of forgiveness by this other person is not only an auxiliary, not only a way to the goal, but is itself fulfillment and goal. It not only leads on to Word and sacrament; it is itself sacrament. Evangelical confessional conversation, too, is a place where there is prayer, where confession is made before God. But this ends the conversation and the repentance accomplished before man; in Catholic confession, on the contrary, the conversation between confessor and penitent is itself confession proper, confession before God. Any distinction between the conversation before and with another man and the speaking of God to man and of man to God, breaks down; the speaking of the confessor coincides with the speaking of God. The Word of God does not only appear in the speaking of man by using the human words as announcement, as promise; the human words of the confessor are taken to be identical with the Word of God. The recipient of the confession is indeed the priest. As priest he stands where Jesus Christ the Son of God stands. He who confesses his sin to the priest confesses it to the divine authority itself. Consequently, the priest is able to do what only God himself does in the Son through the Holy Spirit: He forgives sin. His word is not only sign and instrument for God's Word; it is immediately identified with God's own authoritative Word.

We know that this denotes a fateful, though ultimately doomed, yet basically corrupting infringement of God's prerogative and majesty. The 16th-century Reformers perceived and sharply rejected this infringement. Their repudiation was not directed against confession itself, as long as it was rightly, i.e., evangelically, practiced. This certainly needs no further proof after everything that has been said. The battle against confession corresponds to the battle against the mass where not holy communion in itself, only its distortion and misuse, is attacked. Both misuses are very closely connected. The authorization of the priest to forgive sins in confession is a direct consequence of his authorization to perform transubstantiation in the mass. Singled out, ordained, daily repeating the sacrifice of Golgotha in the mass, the priest is also authorized to call to confession and receive confession. Furthermore, the receiving of confession is a prerogative which is solely his, the priest's. He alone may and can perform the sacrament of penance. Evangelical confession is not bound up with the office of the minister. On the contrary, all the faithful are called not only to repent as they acknowledge their sin and receive forgiveness, but also to call others to repentance, so that one may confess his sin to another. How could it be otherwise since evangelical repentance is the one work of faith in which all are engaged! This is why the Reformers removed the prerogative of the priest in confession and affirmed the priesthood of all believers. Therefore, the evangelical minister must not forget for a moment that as pastor he is nothing but the first member of his congregation, who precedes others in the act of hearing confession, but whom each member can follow and shall follow in the duty of pastoral care. It is indeed not he who forgives sins in the church. Rather, he has the task to assure the congregation of the heavenly Father's pardon. The more zealously he discharges his task, the more urgently he will summon the members of his congregation to the great, common obligation of pastoral confessional conversation with others.

This is not the place to show how the sacramental institution of confession developed in the Roman Catholic Church. One may consult the relevant literature of church history. A concise presentation is found in the treatise by W. Pfendsack already referred to. The development of confession into a sacrament is marked by the legalistic and compulsory character conferred upon confession, and the related application of casuistry in confessional practice. The priest becomes the judicial subject of a divine legal process in the course of which he hears the *confessio,* pronounces the *absolutio,* and imposes the *satisfactio* as well. Furthermore, there is a strong emphasis on the *actus poenitentiae* which is at the heart of the sacramental confession and must be accomplished by the penitent. Repentance is no longer the answer awakened in us by the Word of forgiveness and therefore in itself a sign of grace, but it represents the condition which must be fulfilled if forgiveness is to be granted. Finally, confession is characteristically established as secret, auricular confession to the priest. This makes it unmistakably clear that only the confession said to the priest is authentic.

The great attack of the Reformers was aimed at this sacramental confession. But numerous passages of their writings show that they did not want thereby to cut off confession in the form of the pastoral confessional conversation within the church. Of course, confession in worship and prayer was to replace the sacramental use of confession: "Thus, it is necessary," says the Second Helvetic Confession of 1566, "that we confess our sins to God our Father and be reconciled with our neighbor if we have offended him. . . . But we believe that this open confession which is done before God, whether in silence between God and the sinner or publicly in the church where the common confession of sins is made, is sufficient and that it is not necessary to confess our sins to the priest by whispering them into his ear and then hearing absolution from him with the priestly laying on of hands in order to obtain forgiveness. For there is neither instruction nor example for this in Holy Scripture" (Post. 14). Not without reason, then, the "open confession" becomes the prayer of the congregation every Sunday and the communion table is spread ever anew in the church. Likewise, pastoral confessional conversation is not rejected by the Reformers; on the contrary, it is recognized and upheld. They possessed knowledge of the Bible and knowledge of man enough to know about the necessity and the urgency of confessional conversation. They not only permitted but required it. Says Luther, "Beyond such public, daily, and necessary confession, this secret confession to a brother alone shall be used where something special troubles or tempts us, so that we are plagued and can neither rest nor find enough strength in our faith; let us complain of this to a brother, get advice, comfort, and strength when and as often as we will. . . . No one may require you to do this, but we say: Whoever is or would be a Christian, he has here true advice. Let him go and get the costly treasure. . . . Whoever goes to confession unwillingly and only for the sake of absolution may as well leave it off. We admonish, however: You shall confess and indicate your need, not as a work you do, but that you may hear what God has to say to you. . . . We do not say that one should see how you are full of filth and how your life reflects this, but we counsel and say: If you are poor and wretched, go and use the wholesome medicine. Whoever feels his misery and need will indeed have such desire for it as to hasten with joy. . . ." ("Brief Admonition to Confession," Larger Catechism of 1529.) And Calvin: "Nor is private absolution less efficacious or beneficial, when it is requested by those who need a particular remedy for the relief of their infirmities. For it frequently happens, that he who hears the general promises, which are addressed to the whole congregation of believers, nevertheless remains in some suspense, and his mind is still disquieted with doubts of the forgiveness of his sins. The same person, if he discloses to his pastor the secret distress of his mind, and hears this language of the gospel particularly directed to him, 'Be of good cheer; thy sins be forgiven thee,' will encourage his mind to an assurance, and will be liberated from that trepidation with which he was before disturbed." (Institutes III, 4, 14.)

We finally turn to the question as to how such true, evangelical confession is concretely accomplished in pastoral care. The following thoughts may guide us.

The strength and significance of every confessional conversation lies in the disclosure and revelation of sin in all its seriousness, whereby man knows that he is lost in his disobedience. Yet lost, he is now accepted by God. What is totally impossible from his own standpoint, namely his sonship before the heavenly Father, is now his inheritance through Christ. In the confession of his sin, he comes into this inheritance. And the pastoral conversation is the instrument which God will use to make it accessible to him. Sin is forgiven; the way is open. This is the message we have unreservedly to communicate in pastoral conversation. Evangelical confessional conversation is distinguished from Catholic confession precisely by the absence of requirements the fulfillment of which will bring about forgiveness. This has already been said. We emphasize that even confession itself represents no such requirement. It is to take place freely and without reservation. The one condition, if this is the appropriate word, is Christ's own sacrifice. His blood cleanses us of all sin. This means the exclusion of any human righteousness based on man's own work. Christ's sacrifice occurred, and it is all-sufficient. This must be proclaimed and accepted in confession. It only matters now that the sinner be directed through the call to confession to grasp the grace earned for him by Christ. This call will be serious, open, concrete, personal. For grace must intervene concretely and personally. This demands great care and circumspection in the course of the conversation. Man must perceive and participate in forgiveness in his quite specific entanglement with sin. The decisive help we have to render him in the confessional conversation will consist in preventing his escape, digression, hiding, and avoiding the attack of the Word of God. But we must beware of an imperious, domineering, legalistic, and manipulating approach. It will be part of the secret of such a conversation that we utterly respect even the sinful man. He shall know himself in God's hand, not ours. He shall not feel injured or violated. He shall come under the gracious dominion of the Word of forgiveness, not under ours.

It is not always easy to keep this respect for the sinner. It is often exceedingly tempting to use some kind of trick, so to speak, to push man to the wall and to make the kill. So much inner dishonesty, cowardice, and evil will come to light, so much self-justification, stubbornness, unwillingness to hear, rejection of all comfort, persistent bitterness and unbelief, that it may be infinitely difficult to persevere and continue to be patient and kind. Nevertheless, the great skill of sinful man in evading and obstructing proves the futility of each and every means of approach the counselor might use. Sinful man is so skilled, so cunning, so subtle, so strong, and so clever in his self-defense that no technique (not even the Jesuit!) will determine him to see and to confess his sin and to grasp the merciful comfort on his own. The Word of God alone is capable of this. And it *is* capable. It is our unique weapon. This knowledge will save us from the temptation to try to apply some human art or method of confession. The breakthrough to forgiveness can only be the work of free grace. Grace will fight and conquer. Our impatient pushing in pastoral conversation would only obstruct its way. Hands off! Let us instead set our entire hope on the Word of God! It promises us that there is not a single sinner for whom forgiveness is not in store. It makes its way to this defensive man, from conversation to conversation, without any human prompting, as long as we are ready to communicate it. Perhaps it lets us see little fruit or result and yet, to our astonishment and wonderment, never returns empty if we genuinely trust it. To trust it genuinely means to trust our partner in conversation, to reckon him to God from the outset, never for a moment yielding and following him if he thinks he can withdraw from the hold of God laid upon him, and not growing weary even though everything I say is apparently lost on him.

For example, we encounter people in pastoral care who are the victims of a severe disease, say alcoholism. It is tempting to call such addicts to reason with sharp words. Yet these victims can forego our harsh insistence on the corrupting effects of their addiction; they are already aware of the chains that bind them and of the necessity to shake them off if they are not to perish. It is not hidden from the alcoholic that he has gone astray. Yet his disease is only the symptom of a bondage that goes much deeper and may indeed be more or less hidden from him.

He who drinks is stuck with a difficult predicament, be it innate frivolity, the impasse of worries, or an unconquerably weak will. But even that is not the root of the evil. The evil proper is his attempt to help himself in ever-repeated, but fruitless, moralistic endeavors. Or perhaps even these have already ceased because he has mentally resigned and now is simply driven by his evil passion. He then says to himself, "There is no help for me, and I refuse to be helped anyway!" In any case, he does not cry out to God. He seeks no forgiveness. He knows nothing of repentance. But this is fighting against grace. And this is his sin proper. He fights against it like a prisoner who, although the door might open for him, prefers to remain in his cell. He will not and cannot avow his weakness. He will not and cannot capitulate. He will not and cannot confess. He resists by hiding all the more from God in his sin as in a savage defiance. This is the starting point for the confessional conversation. We must certainly talk plainly and unmistakably with this person, not simply of his alcoholism but of what lies behind it, his sin proper. Yet from the first word he must see the door that opens up forgiveness even for him. We must talk with him incisively and mercifully, mercifully and incisively, in the perspective of God and his grace, though with clear and concrete reference to the particular addiction in which his sin is clothed.

By far the most severe bondage, addiction, and sin we confront in pastoral care as soon as we press deeper is not alcoholism, by the way, not even the sexual problem in all its forms, but the addiction to mammon, the slavery of money, avarice. But even here, the underlying root is nothing but deep greed and its corresponding anxiety. Consequently, man attempts to create security by avarice and worry. He thinks mammon—money—offers and protects this security. But by concentrating on money, he loses sight of God, in whose hand we are solely protected and secure. Where he should stand, money now stands. Avarice is always idolatry (cf. Matthew 6:19-34). Many more people than we might think are infected by it. They come to us with apparently quite different concerns; they believe themselves far removed from any kind of idolatry; yet in fact what is at stake is their bondage to money. The confessional question, "Do you cling to money?" hits the mark all too often. Help does not easily come in these cases. One can be so exceedingly respectable and righteous, one can even be very "orthodox," "born-again," and "converted" and yet cling to money. Piety makes common cause with mammon, as Jesus warns in the Sermon on the Mount. His words are directed not to the people of the world, but to the church. We keep God before our eyes, but we do not look at him singlemindedly, eyeing money at the same time. We squint, and this squinting is the opposite of singlemindedness; the eye becomes "evil" (it becomes the "rogue," in Luther's translation), and darkness immediately descends on our whole life. What can be done here? Mammon has created for itself an almost impregnable position of power in the hearts and thoughts of men. As the Sermon on the Mount says, "the whole body" is full of darkness. That is, the darkness proceeding from mammon lies over all of man's doings; mammon overshadows and rules not only the personal life, but also economics, politics, and the entire social structure. If anywhere, it is visible here how the power of hell stands behind sin. Pastoral care is powerless as long as it does not get to the bottom of things and does not dare to oppose the power of hell by the power of grace. For the basis of man's enslavement to money is again the absence of grace wherein man in his avarice and anxiety perseveres, clinging to money as a substitute for faith. The basis of deliverance, however, is the forgiveness of sins. This forgiveness must be understood in all its power; it not only rescues the individual from the world, but also proclaims the Kingdom of God irrupting into the world and thereby saving the individual. There is enough evidence in the Gospels of its being capable even today as portent of coming redemption on the day of Jesus Christ to melt the ice of avarice and to free man from the subservience to mammon. The story of Zacchaeus (Luke 19:1-10) is a particularly strong promise of this, whereas the story of the rich young ruler (Matthew 19:16-26) depicts the sway of money over even noble and earnest men. Of what help is all generosity, all "good deeds," if one "has great possessions"? How great must be the victory of the Christ foretold in the forgiveness of sins if it can conquer even mammon and save the rich! How great is the task of pastoral care to prepare the way for forgiveness and call men to repentance!

This confessional conversation and nothing else must also determine our pastoral encounter with people in need of comfort. In fact, such people constitute by far the majority of all those who seek out our advice. They come to us not because of a particular sin they have committed. They come because they are afflicted and oppressed by perplexity, worries, and pain.

Concretely, they are caught in one of those psychic depressions of which we had to speak in our discussion of psychology and psychotherapy. They stand before a closed door which must open for them if their lives are to regain wholeness and strength. This door represents for one person another human being with whom he cannot get along, for another a deficiency of his character or his disposition which he is unable to alter. Others are locked up in a grief which they bear in their souls and cannot forget. Others are confronted with adverse circumstances getting in the way of their work, their mental development, their joy in life. Here belong the parents' problems of child rearing and the marital difficulties of husband and wife. Still others simply—and yet not so simply!—face physical suffering; it accompanies them day and night, a reminder of death which looms sooner or later. And who today is not up against the dark riddles the future holds, the heavy pressure, the bitter disappointments in the wake of war and the end of war, the great lack of truth, strength, help, and, last but not least, the manifest impotence, estrangement, and Babylonian confusion of tongues in the territory of ideology and faith? Any one of these afflictions may be brought up in the pastoral conversation.

These people need comfort in the proper sense of the word. When they come to the pastor, they expect an encouraging and liberating word. The question is raised as to whether we have to tell them something else than forgiveness of sins? Ought not the conversation whereby comfort is assured be of another nature than of a confessional conversation? The help provided by the confessional conversation lies in its leading to repentance. But does repentance really matter in the face of worry, pain, perplexity? Where is the sin to be forgiven? We answer with a counter-question: Must we not focus even in the face of anxiety, whatever name it bears, on the one help which is in Jesus Christ? But this help never bears another name than that of forgiveness. One has only to understand need and help deeply and vitally enough to know at once that all affliction is affliction of sin and all help is help of forgiveness.

Men are not distressed by just *any* thing, by one or another accidental evil. The closed doors whose final opening they await in their anxieties are ultimately the doors of God, "the gates of righteousness" as the Psalm says (118:19), the gates of true, victorious life from above. Therefore, in every instance, everything is at stake. If a person candidly perceives what troubles him personally, he actually faces the abyss that threatens everybody, the abyss not bridged by any progress or evolution, the abyss that separates us from heaven.

Consequently, no anxiety can be stilled except by the forgiveness of Christ. Behind even the smallest anxiety lies the one great quest, the quest for God and for reconciliation with him. Were we at peace with God—peace, as we have seen, is the center and content of forgiveness—we could deal with all our other needs. All, even the little, insignificant needs, burn so deeply because, preliminary as they are, they express the ultimate need. Only when the gates of God open is man helped. But what does this imply except forgiveness of sin? What separates us from God is never anxiety in itself, but the ever-fatal attempt to master it ourselves. Again we refer to what has already been said: Life's predicament rests on the lack of grace; in this affliction we are unable to see that one thing is needful in all that oppresses us. It is God's saving presence, the coming of his Kingdom. Lack of grace causes us consistently to avoid this one thing. Not without reason the passage on anxiety in the Sermon on the Mount ends on the decisive commandment, "But seek first his kingdom and his righteousness, and all these things shall be yours as well" (Matthew 6:33). This is nothing but a call to repentance. Therefore, even the comforting of the anxious must necessarily center on the disclosure of our lack of grace, our obduracy, our sin. To comfort always means to proclaim the "sole comfort" which in life and in death consists in the fact that Christ Jesus through his life and death has borne everything, and has taken care of everything for us. To comfort assuredly also means to communicate the "protection" which the sinner enjoys in the hands of the gracious God. Forgiveness in itself is at the same time ultimate consolation, because we are well taken care of in body and soul by the grace of Christ granted us through forgiveness. Repentance as the goal of confession consists in our no longer refusing to entrust ourselves to the hands of God in Christ, without reservation. The pastoral counselor has to dissuade the person seeking comfort from relying on any other help and salvation; he has to assure him, on the other hand, that no affliction is so great that this one comfort is not sufficient for it. Forgiveness is all and everything or it is not forgiveness.

Because forgiveness is the one and total act of God achieved in us, we are bound to say that forgiveness is a miraculous event. It is always the free work of grace which forsakes all human mediation. When a man bewails his sin, lays it down before God and is comforted, it is like a healing of the sick or a resurrection of the dead. Unexpectedly and mysteriously, neither to be precipitated nor to be stopped, forgiveness enters, to the thanks and joy of those who receive it. In confessional conversation the closed door may open, and a man may be released from the chains of sin and anxiety. We enter into conversation without knowing whether or how such an event will take place. We shall of course conduct the conversation in the expectation of success, and hence with all deliberation. We shall not retreat if the going gets rough; nor shall we be discouraged if "the gates of hell" inexorably close behind a man. On the contrary, we shall advance from moment to moment in the hand of him who is the Lord of this conversation. We shall wait and hope for the decisive clearing up of the sinful situation when the concealed, the hidden, and the restrained may be disclosed and laid out. But nothing can be forced. God acts and not the pastor. The latter is an instrument and nothing else. He commits both his fellow man and himself into God's mighty hand and lets God do to himself and to the other as he sees fit. Such an attitude of expectation encourages confession and with it prayer and forgiveness.

An example of such pastoral attitude is found in a letter of the younger Blumhardt. He intervened in a human predicament, for once not alcoholism or mammon or anxiety, but the magic power of erotism. The incident is reported in a small, but substantial book which Christoph Senft von Pilsach dedicated "to the memory of Christoph Blumhardt" (Berlin, 1925). Senft wrote:

> In the year 1901, I had an experience which had a tremendous impact on me. A friend of mine was exposed to a fearful crisis. He had married several years before as a very young man.

PASTORAL CARE AS CONFESSION 305

Although his marriage was by no means unhappy, he was suddenly seized as by a wild frenzy of his young blood with passion for another woman whom he violently desired. His marriage, blessed with children, was at the breaking point; insurmountable difficulties also barred union with the desired woman. Overcome by despair, he determined to commit suicide. My pleading was fruitless; even his own sister could not dissuade him from his fatal resolution. We were at our wits' end. He who has not lived through a similar nightmare can have no idea of it.

In great anxiety, I telegraphed and wrote to Bad Boll, and as with a thunder-clap, my friend's situation improved. His facial expression changed; soon he was again accessible to reasonable counsel, and gradually he himself, and later his marriage, was saved.

The answer from Bad Boll allows us to catch a glimpse of the work of a servant of God. It reads:

Dear Christoph!
I have received your telegram and your letter and take an earnest interest in the matter. Your friend does not yet know where he belongs; so he skips around with women. This is not love, but only abnormal feeling. He must be freed and lifted up; he must find himself before he can find a helper in a woman. Perhaps his wife had been a helpmeet, but he did not see it; and now the regret. Clarity and truth must reign in one's own heart, and clear relationships with other people will be the result. I hope it is not too late.
Yours, Christoph Blumhardt.

Not even a conversation took place here; but there was prayer that Christ may be able to do his work with the bound man. This work was done without any human participation except intercession. Yet notice the presuppositions of this pastoral care. With astonishing self-evidence Blumhardt proceeds on the assumption that only one thing can help this man: not lengthy counseling and arguments, but only the grace of Christ. He commits this man unconditionally into God's hand. He says of him, "Your friend does not yet know where he belongs; therefore, he skips around with women." This "he does not yet know where he belongs" quite certainly applies not only to his wife, to whom he has been unfaithful; Blumhardt means to say: He does not yet know that he, too, belongs to God. But he does belong to him. As soon as he acknowledges this, he will stop skipping around with women. To think and to speak in these terms means to reckon man to God; it means forgiveness, concrete forgiveness spoken to the specific situation of the sinner. Man's situation is grasped at the innermost center, and elucidated in a pastoral way. Of course, this case also had its very complicated psychological, perhaps even psychiatric, side; it offered material for extensive analysis. Yet the decision comes from quite another source: "He knows not where he belongs"—he must and he may, however, regain this knowledge. Blumhardt palliated nothing. He fearlessly calls sin by name and discloses it: "Clarity, inner truthfulness!" This is genuine pastoral care, pastoral care born of mercy; it lacks no firm grip, yet everything is placed entirely in the hand of the heavenly Father. And thereupon, deliverance happens as a miracle.

On the basis of the insight thus won into the nature of confessional conversation, its course and process is to be watched over and kept under control. The danger of losing control is ever present. Easily and almost imperceptibly, confession as the means in the hand of God becomes the means in the hand of the pastor who by his conversation undertakes to make the sinner confess. Perhaps he gets results this way. He shakes and overwhelms people and even achieves deliverance and healing. But they are paid for with a price too high for the holiness of God, who alone and himself intends to deliver and heal. Narrow and sharp is the dividing line between true and false pastoral care. We call the confession, brought about in this false way, a *forced* confession. It comes close to Catholic confession and partakes of all the objections and misgivings directed against it. Better no confession than one in which the pastor imposes himself as lord and master over the minds and consciences of men and thus usurps the place of him who alone wants to be and is the Lord of confession.

The danger of forced confession is most real when the pastoral counselor is a strong personality. He perhaps commands real inner strength; he has the gifts of knowing human nature and of dealing with people; he is an able and skillful partner in conversation. Even more, he is well versed in the Bible and has spiritual experience. All very well and not to be despised! But it is good and helpful only when it is coupled with the knowledge of the sole efficacy of grace. It immediately becomes highly dangerous if this knowledge is lacking; if the pastor, perhaps only for a moment, lives in the illusion that he himself is able, by virtue of his gifts, his strengths and methods, to lead the sinner to repentance and freedom.

A further danger, almost the trademark of forced confession, is the false personal fixation on the pastor or the no less dangerous partisan fixation on the group, fellowship, or sect represented by the pastor. If God's Word and grace alone are not allowed to rule in pastoral care, the pastor becomes the director of souls who subjects the penitent to his personal authority. A person entrusts himself to the pastor, who knows about the last secrets of his inner life, and now the person is chained to the pastor. The pastor has gained a new follower for himself or for his interpretation of the faith. The success of many a confessional and revival movement rests on the conscious or unconscious magic of such a following. A clever director of souls knows how to encourage it; yet such followings are a terribly fleshly, psychic phenomenon, however "spiritual" they may seem to be. We shall be bound by confession to God and not to men. We shall be called into the church and not into a movement, group, or sect. Freedom from all parties and "leaders" is a result and mark of true evangelical repentance and confession.

The deterioration from true confession to forced confession is foreshadowed in the outer, formal structure of confession. It transpires in the way of asking questions in the conversation, in the attempt to get men to confess. The mutual confession of several people, as practiced in certain revival movements must be mentioned here. People enter into a common confessional conversation or make their confession before a larger circle. Public or semi-public declarations of sins and confession of sins are made. Such a procedure rests on a perhaps well-founded psychological insight. One person carries the others along. The individual is exposed to a certain pressure. He sees and hears his neighbor at the point of laying bare the innermost questions of life, and now is encouraged to do likewise. But is this not one of those manipulations which, even though they may be fruitful, in fact violate man and prevent him from grasping free grace?

A further danger we have to beware of lies in the attempt to capture and to visualize all the details of our neighbor's sinful imprisonment. This can be threatening for both the counselee and the counselor since it actually has the effect of an exorcism of demons in which we no longer control the spirits we free. Also, our neighbor could thereby be thrown into shame and confusion and would shut himself off from us. It is usually sufficient briefly to mention and name the area of a person's aberration without exploring it to the limit. A warning must indeed be sounded against the agitation of the depths of sin. By neglecting to uncover all the details of sin, our conversation may look somewhat abrupt, not quite pursued to the end. So what? Let us not think we can ever remove sin entirely. Let us keep in mind that somebody else, Jesus Christ, removed it long ago. Suffice it, therefore, to invoke him and to leave everything to him. He judges and saves. Perhaps a complete confession of sin is not made at all; our neighbor leaves us without having laid bare his innermost soul. He will unburden himself before the Lord, into whose hand he has committed himself in the confession. Thereby everything happened that had to happen. Often, too, the counselee is driven by a truly morbid passion to pour out his heart; we do well to prevent such confessional passion since there burns a fire we had better not let flare up.

Finally, the shadow of spiritual narrowness and false seriousness is cast on any kind of forced confession. People cut themselves off; those who now regard themselves as born again separate from those who have not yet gone through the narrow gate of such confession. The regenerated are "inside," judging those who are still "outside" because they have not yet been converted in the same way. True confession, on the contrary, is free and broadminded and joyous in all the seriousness of the decision just taken. We recall the bright, almost worldly, aspect of repentance exhibited by the publican and sinner in the Gospels. The publican Matthew serves a supper to his companions and Jesus sits at their table while the pious and well-meaning people take offense (Mark 2:13-16). This also makes intelligible the uneasiness, reluctance, and objection of the so-called "children of the world" when they run into revival movements, awakenings, and evangelizations. True, their opposition stems from the evil defensiveness of the impenitent against the call to repentance. But this inner opposition is certainly not overcome by that joyless, Pharisaical, legalistic and oppressive pastoral care so preponderant in revival movements. It is not only the resistance of the evil world, but largely the graceless kind of pastoral care and proclamation of so many evangelists and preachers of awakening which barricades the way to true, liberating repentance.

The positive marks of true confession may be summarized by a few simple rules.

First: We shall enter into conversation with the *confident assurance* that under the power and protection of the grace of Christ the specific sin which keeps our brother or sister a prisoner will be called by name, disclosed, and pronounced forgiven. We therefore have to forsake all false uncertainty, shyness, and reticence in order to become entirely open and ready together with our neighbor for the work God wills to do in us. We must arm ourselves from the beginning with great mercy and complete fearlessness, in case our conversation must probe into very hidden depths of sin. But the sinful man belongs to Christ, and his grace has power to conquer all onslaughts and attacks of evil.

Second: In the confessional conversation, we must reach the point of communicating forgiveness of sins in specific and explicit terms. This communication implies what appears in the Roman Catholic Church under the concept of *absolution* as the concluding act of every confession. Such absolution must not be lacking in the Evangelical Church. Man's sinful situation is discussed and illuminated with the intention and expectation of being absolved by the proclamation of the Word of God. How is this absolution to be pronounced? Again, no technique or method can be specified. But this much is certain: Every true confessional conversation must climax in a word of comfort whereby the oppressed and enslaved sinner hears that his sins are forgiven him. Mere speaking, of course, is not enough. Everything depends on hearing what is said by God himself, who will use our human tongue for his own Word where and when he so chooses. Therefore, not much can be said about the form of this conversation. It is important that the *whole* conversation be made subservient to the speaking and hearing of what is said. From the beginning, even if forgiveness is not explicitly mentioned at all, every word, the whole attitude of the pastor, the manner and way of his speaking to his neighbor, must reveal that forgiveness, and forgiveness alone, matters. Then the right words will be given him to be credibly delivered to the other: With your sin and anxiety, you are in the hand of the Good Shepherd! This is absolution. It is evidenced when our partner leaves us with the certainty of that peace which passes all understanding, with the confidence that is helped and need not despair, that he must not throw away his life but, on the contrary, may take and will take certain steps into a new life.

Third: Since it depends entirely on God's own speaking, the conversation will have its end and its beginning in the *use of the words of the Bible.* Nothing in the conversation is not implicitly or even explicitly covered by biblical words. Therefore, in the course of confessional conversation, we shall open the Bible together. Along with reading the Bible we shall pray. Since God does everything here, we shall call upon him; our whole conversation will be borne by prayer. Pastoral care that is not imbedded in prayer is not pastoral care. We have already considered earlier how to initiate prayer.

Fourth: There is no confessional conversation without *admonition!* In the forgiveness of sins, we are addressed as new men. We are God's own. But does not the old man continue to live for himself and hence to be enmeshed in manifold sins? What we recognized and acknowledged in confession was precisely this quality of our life as the life of the old man. But now we are told that this old nature, while it still surrounds us, is overcome in Christ. This denotes in itself the outbreak of a fight, the fight of the new man against the old. We are summoned, awakened; we can no longer live unrestrained in the old vein. The impact of God's Word has been too strong; too inescapable the clasp of his hand. Our justification becomes sanctification. Insofar as pastoral care validates this assurance, which in itself is a claim, confessional conversation will be the place where we are summoned to such conflict: The conversation cannot come to an end without admonition.

Here is to be remembered everything that was said about the connection of gospel and law. The concept of obedience is to be accepted as the form in which faith is clothed. This obedience will never appear apart from faith; rather, it will be nothing but the sign of a man's coming to faith. Even when we impart instructions, we proclaim forgiveness. But this means that the obedience which we establish in the confessional conversation is obedience of the sinner. We know the great danger that threatens our pastoral care: the establishing of a law which man shall fulfill by himself. Were admonition to serve such a purpose, the conversation would be doomed. The test of genuine pastoral conversation will be admonition without any compulsion to perfectionistic, oppressive deeds of obedience, or to self-fulfillment of the law. "The righteous," i.e., the pardoned sinner, shall live his faith. And to live his faith means here: In an uninterrupted sequence of vital acts, he will take up the fight, unceasingly recognizing himself as a sinner, yet as a sinner fortunate enough to know his sin attacked, indeed conquered by forgiveness.

This signifies that admonition always takes the form of a promise. We shall say to a person: You not only must, but you *can* no longer continue in the wrong direction in which you previously went. Though still tempted to do so, you may now initiate a counter-movement which shows that you have been seized by the hand of God and torn away from sin. We must ponder and seek from case to case what this movement will be. Occasionally stern measures, perhaps in matters of money or against an overpowering passion, must be advised. We shall admonish earnestly and sharply, yet at the same time confidently and mercifully. The sign of joyful repentance will prevail. As long as this element of gladness and of promise is absent from the admonition, the admonition is not yet rightly administered.

Admonition will ultimately encourage man to cease living according to his own strength and devices and instead entirely to abandon himself to grace in every situation. Paradoxical as it may sound, it is still so: If I counsel abstinence to an alcoholic, it must, to be a truly evangelical instruction, imply that he live completely from grace! You no doubt are and remain a sinner, one who still thinks he can live without grace; withstand this tug toward the graceless life and avoid the tavern from now on as a sign of your new freedom in the strength of grace. It is impossible for you alone, but "with God all things are possible!" Let this be valid! Confirm it by gladly, if a thousand times unwillingly as far as your old man is concerned, shoving aside the corrupting glass. This is the only evangelical reason for abstinence. But it is a good reason. So interpreted, abstinence is not legalistic; it is a counter-movement indicative of the power of grace in the life of a captive.

Release, not a new legalism, must explain and sum up whatever instruction and admonition is expressed in pastoral care. Release, liberation, deliverance from severe bondage is implied by the tearing out of one's eye and the cutting off of one's hand in the Sermon on the Mount. The lonesome holding out on a difficut post, the persistence in a task almost beyond one's strength, as evidence, for example, in the faithful endurance of a wife at the side of a husband who makes life miserable for her, is advisable and successful only when it is done in the freedom of grace and in the obedience of faith. It must never be the weary, dogged dragging of a burden unwillingly borne; impossible as it may seem, it must ever again and ever anew be the free service a man takes upon himself because he himself has experienced the service of Christ in the forgiveness of sins.

Much the same may be said of a husband's persevering in a marriage with a woman who is not the helpmeet for him she should be. He clings to her; he does not leave her; he does not abandon her, not even when he is attracted to another woman who promises to give him what he cannot find in his own wife. The husband or wife who holds on in such a difficult marriage lets his partner, in spite of his perhaps almost unbearable rejection, continue to find grace, forgiveness, and mercy, since he knows about the grace which he himself has found before God. Such finding of grace before God suggests the advice to *live* according to such grace with his neighbor.

We think of the special emphasis placed in the Sermon on the Mount on the fifth petition of the Lord's Prayer: "For if you forgive men their trespasses, your heavenly Father also will forgive you; but if you do not forgive men their trespasses, neither will your Father forgive your trespasses" (Matthew 6:14-15). This sounds as if our forgiving represented the condition for God's forgiveness to us; it is, however, the establishment of divine forgiveness as the one great reality enabling people to live with one another. It is the establishment of love as the fulfillment of the law (Romans 13:10). This love is not to be likened to softness, or sentimentality. It is the love of Christ, the strength of our obedience. To be sure, love fulfills the "law." The law remains valid in all its austerity and sanctity. But love makes us understand the law, instead of only as a stern taskmaster, as a much-needed railing we can hold on to and along which we may find and tread our way in the strength of the grace of Christ. Admonition and obedience once again express precisely what pastoral care really intends, gives, and is. Tell me how you admonish, and I will tell you what kind of a pastoral counselor you are!

Fifth: All pastoral care will lead to the *church*. Where else can we find recognition of sin, assurance of forgiveness, comfort, admonition, instruction, and commandment, as described above, if not in the church which stands under the Word and lives from the Word? This is the Apostle's implication when very concretely he exhorts the Philippians to unite and liberates them from quarreling among themselves by evoking before them the vision of Christ's humiliation and calling them to peace (Philippians 2:1-18). The advice above all other advice to come from pastoral care is: Seek the brethern! Submit to the Word! Partake of the sacrament! If it does not lead to active membership in a congregation, pastoral care is done in a void. There is no isolated forgiveness and no isolated sanctification; forgiveness and sanctification exist only in the context of the Christian community, in whose center grace and obedience continually flow from the Word. Furthermore, flesh, sin, old man, lack of grace, and disobedience, or however we may name what must be overcome, it is an entity, it is the realm of darkness, the Bible calls it world. This realm is opposed to the other, new realm, announced, and not only announced but established, in the church. Pastoral care, like the total proclamation, helps spread this realm on earth. Therefore, it inescapably leads to the church. We must move away from the world toward the church if we are to receive help. This is tough for the old man; it goes against his grain. Nevertheless, this old man must be overcome, and we shall fail to vanquish and renew him except by instilling in him the humility and courage to join ranks with the church. He must become a member of that people which rises as one body with many members and enters into the new life under Christ its head.

Behind man's captivity to sin, the Holy Scripture sees an invisible dominion of evil spirits and powers. Yet in Jesus Christ, God masters even these hidden depths. Where forgiveness of sin exists, Satan's reign ends. He no longer may torment and seduce men. "One little word shall fell him." Because pastoral care announces this message, its work is to be understood as casting out demons and establishing the great hope in the final victory of Christ. In the power of this hope, pastoral care reaches into the spheres of bondage, superstition, and anxiety, as well as into the broad secular realms of politics and economics, in order to announce everywhere the message of the coming Kingdom of God and to sustain men.

15 Pastoral Care as Exorcism

Some last things often unexpressed, yet unforgotten, are now to be considered. They form the background of pastoral counseling. The forgiveness of sins has impressed us as the mighty act of Christ. Christ takes away sins. This work is the sovereign act which Christ does as the King he is. Forgiving sin, he re-establishes God's rule over fallen man. He gives God glory in a world which had forgotten this glory and subsequently sunk into guilt and pain and death.

In sermon, sacrament, and pastoral care the Word of God enters man's life and man comes again under the gracious hand of the Lord to whom he properly belongs. True, he had been under the hand of God all along, but he no longer knew it; he disregarded and resisted it. Therefore, God's hand could not prove merciful to him, but lay over him as the hand of wrath. Now everything changes; now the lost man returns at last; God becomes for him what he has been from the beginning: the Father visting man in his Son. In the light of grace through the incarnate Word even God's wrath and judgment, even man's condemnation, are now acknowledged and believed to be the one great work of this visitation. Something happens to us; God's own work is accomplished in man when we are baptized, when the gospel is preached to us, when we gather around the communion table, and when the Word of God encounters us in the very personal and arresting way of a pastoral conversation from man to man. This marks the state of life prior to faith, man's existence apart from forgiveness, outside Christ, estranged from the covenants of promise (Ephesians 2:12), the salvationless state, as more than a state of emptiness, of privation, of nonexistence. Even this state, the state of wrath, of yet unfulfilled forgiveness is mysteriously filled, occupied, and defined. It is in the proper sense of the Word "potent," i.e., governed by a power, the power which rules where God's reign is not yet re-established. It is the power of sin.

Sin is not only negative, nonexistent; sin is in its own way something extremely positive. It is a potency, a reign of its own. More precisely, the man of sin, the man without forgiveness, is disobedient to God, but his disobedience is not freedom; it is a kind of obedience, but a frightful obedience, the obedience of a serf, a slave, a captive, who must serve that evil lord whom we inevitably serve as long as we do not serve God. Neutrality is ruled out here. When the water is poured out, the glass is not empty; when there is no more water in it, air streams in. He who does not serve God serves—whom, then? We answer with Holy Scripture: Satan and his spirits. Only now it becomes unmistakably clear; forgiveness means not only that God's power takes possession of man's formerly empty life and that his peace fills it, but forgiveness is a change of regime. In order to give man his peace, Christ must first destroy the reign of the demons. In battle with them and in victory over them, he establishes God's reign in the forgiveness of sins. In this perspective, forgiveness is in fact a change of power: An old reign is overthrown, and a new reign is established. Assurance of pardon is ultimately to be understood as *exorcism*. Demons are cast out when God's

Word is forcefully proclaimed. (Cf. Mark 3:22-27; 4:15; Luke 10:17ff.)

But who is this counter-force? Who is Satan? Who is this Diabolos, the beguiler who confuses everything? Who are his helpers, the demons, the dark inhabitants of the intermediary world? Our first answer is that everything we may say on this subject must exclusively be drawn from the biblical testimony. Other sources, of course, abound, from which we get information and knowledge about the intermediary world or underworld in which the demons, the supernatural spirits and powers, have their being. *Vestigia diaboli* are plentiful and can be detected almost everywhere. There is no lack of extensive and even spirited and earnest attempts to grasp, interpret, and philosophically elucidate the dim mysteries of the supernatural. They have undergone varied formulation and manifold evaluation in the cosmologies of all times and places.

These extrabiblical sources flow muddily, however, and the indications they give of actual or supposed facts are contradictory. The magical picture of the world they project amounts to a *daemonologia naturalis,* a naturally elaborated theory about the supernatural world, which is as inadequate for the formation of spiritual knowledge and judgment as natural theology is for the perception of God and his world. Nevertheless, we must be well informed about it. For the magical picture of the world, by no means relegated to the museum, is still most vivid and haunts the minds and hearts of our contemporaries as it did a hundred or a thousand years ago. We constantly encounter it in pastoral care in the form of superstition, magic, and spiritualism, but also in much more subtle, scientific, and sophisticated disguises; we think of metaphysical systems, insofar as they develop a theory of the supernatural, but also of Anthroposophy and parapsychology as attempts at a science of the occult. (Cf. the detailed and complete *Handwörterbuch des Deutschen Aberglaubens* edited by Bächtold; the collection of documents about "cases from the supernatural realm" edited by Nielsen under the titles *Das Grosse Geheimnis* and *Das Unerkannte,* Munich, 1922 and 1923; and the anthroposophic writings already mentioned.) The pastoral counselor, however, is not concerned with metaphysical speculations, parapsychological experiments, and occult knowledge. Here as elsewhere, he is concerned with knowledge gained from faith. Insofar as we ought to know something about the world of the demons, the world of the *angeli mali*, we have no choice but to consult the Word of God. For our reflection upon what there is to the devil and his principality should not be prompted by our interest in demonology and magic; the one and only message of Christ and his victory over all dark powers in the forgiveness of sins must be our guide.

The Word of God speaks of Satan and his spirits exclusively in view of God and his Christ. The demons are mentioned only parenthetically, never as the main point, and they can nowhere claim an independent interest. For this would demand the turning of our attention away from God and his Christ. And this does not happen here for a moment. A preoccupation with demons, even if only temporarily disregarding God and Christ, would inevitably require more or less full attention, and this in turn would result in conceding them power, in being captivated and ruled by them. Where, in faith, Jesus Christ is in the center, this is positively excluded. The world of demons is brought up only as a shadow to reinforce the great light sent by God through Christ into the gloomy world. Because this light cannot be described without adding a word about the darkness which this light overcomes, the demons must be referred to. Because forgiveness is victory over the demons, they enter the vision of faith as a quite serious reality, yet one settled, overthrown, and dethroned in Christ.

This does not contest, but rather acknowledges, the actuality and dangerous impact of the demons. Because they have power, because they are dangerous, Christ must end their reign. Because there are "works of the devil," they must be destroyed, as a crucial passage affirms (I John 3:8). Because the "other gods" are a reality, the commandment goes out: "I am the Lord your God ... no other gods before me" (Exodus 20:2-3). The power and strength of the true God is described by proclaiming his subjugation of the false gods. They are no more than a gloomy foil of his radiant glory. They are the captives in Christ's triumphal march (Colossians 2:15). This is how they exist, how they are real, how they must be reckoned with; but they are no longer to be feared. If, however, we disregard even for a moment the fact that they are judged since Christ has taken the power from them, they immediately rise again with all their danger. Apart from Christ, the Devil is an unconquerable power. A fool is he who laughs at him! Without Christ, hell burns as deep as the abyss and as wide as the world, and there is no escape from it. Therefore, no dealing with it outside of faith! Therefore, away with curiosity about the demons! Not because they are imaginary figures or fakes, but because their "craft and power are great" as soon as Christ is left out, and meddling with them is dangerous. But in Jesus Christ, we may speak of them. It is like walking once again over the battlefield on which he has fought for us; at the sight of the enemy he strangled—the demons—we are amazed at the greatness of his victory. This is how the Revelation of John treats Satan and his spirits when it proclaims the subduing and binding of the Devil and announces the victory of the "Lamb," worthy "to receive power and wealth and wisdom and might and honor and glory and blessing!" (Revelation 5:12.)

In Holy Scripture, the description of the demons, the dark spirits, is the counterpart to the doctrine of angels, the good spirits. Both angels and demons belong to the invisible sphere of the created world; though supernatural, they are not uncreated, not divine, not beings existing from eternity. Just as man, a being who belongs to both spheres of the cosmos—the visible and the invisible—does not exist all by himself in the physical, visible world, but is surrounded by all things visible—animals, flowers, stones, and stars—he is likewise not alone in the invisible, spiritual world, but is surrounded by other spirits and beings. These fill and animate the realm of the invisible cosmos; like man, they are created by God and also summoned and called by God in a way hidden from us. A further affirmation is valid:

As man might and should be obedient to God's call and yet is disobedient, so the world of spirits is torn apart by sin and divided into the obedient and disobedient, into angels and demons. Classical dogmatics quite logically expounded the doctrine of the "good angels" and the "evil angels" (*de angelis bonis et malis*) in connection with the doctrine of creation. As part of the doctrine of creation, the doctrine of the good and the evil angels must in no way be understood as a contribution to a "biblical world view," as mythologizing theologians might call it. Even angelology does not propose anything but the gracious reign and power of God and his Son over all things visible and invisible. Neither angels nor demons as such are objects of faith; we believe only in the triune God, and in him as the Creator of the *"visibilia et invisibilia."* For the sake of this faith in the God who created both the visible and the invisible, Holy Scripture, especially the New Testament and dogmatics based on it, speaks self-evidently of the invisible world and of the existence of the indwelling spirits, forces, and powers. Why should these spirits, forces, and powers be denied? Yet not for a moment does the emphasis and interest center on the knowledge about invisible things, about angels and demons as such. The attempts of human curiosity to uncover mysteries which are hidden from our perception find no encouragement here, not even when they pretend to further a Christian view of the supernatural.

Consequently, books like *Ein Schimmer durch den Vorhang* written by the Danish theologian H. Martensen-Larsen with the subtitle "Of the Irruption of Supernatural Powers and Forces into Earthly Life," seriously as they are meant, seem to us at least ambiguous and certainly not helpful to a deeper understanding of faith. All that is befitting is the candid knowledge through faith of the reality of the supernatural, created world, and the further knowledge that the good spirits of that world, the angels, are obedient to God and serve him as his messengers "who do his word" (Psalm 103:20), whereas the evil spirits of that world, the demons, strive against God's will, yet are subject to God and, despite all the power still left to them, "shudder" before him (James 2:19). We may and we must count on an abundance, a host, of good heavenly beings (cf. Genesis 32:1-3), forces, and powers, serviceable to God and therefore helpful to us. If only we counted on them more consciously and more confidently! But there is no need for approaching them arbitrarily; we shall not call on them or show them the kind of honor and service due the triune God alone. Our salvation depends not on angels, but on Jesus Christ, who is raised above them all (cf. Hebrews 1:4ff.), but we may enjoy them and take comfort in them. With equal seriousness we must reckon with the dark forces, the demons, but also with the fact that they are captured and laid in chains by Christ. There is no need for meddling with them; in their presence more than elsewhere the commandment holds that God alone is to be loved and feared.

A well-developed and documented angelology is still missing in the contemporary dogmatics.* For the biblical theology of the Old Testament, consult L. Köhler, but especially W. Eichrodt (in his *Theologie des Alten Testaments*, Vol. II, ch. 18). Kittel's *Neutestamentliches Wörterbuch* has very little to say under ἄγγελος, δαίμων, and διάβολος. A significant contribution to the New Testament view of demons is found in Karl Heim's *Jesus the Lord*, chapters 9-11.

We shall inevitably encounter the demonic background of sin in conversation with those in need of pastoral care, as truly as sin brings with it bondage to the dark powers. From all that has been said, the counselor will have derived the clear advice to put himself in this encounter unequivocally and irrefutably on the ground of the biblical message. We must by all means avoid getting involved in philosophical conversation about supernatural things. We do well to put aside all interpretations and attempts to elucidate this background of sinful action, not only because the supernautral shuns actual observation and tested experience, but also because all these interpretations and clarifications ultimately aim at removing the responsibility for his

* *Translator's note:* The most extensive angelology has since been developed by Karl Barth, in *Church Dogmatics*, III, 3, 51.

sin from man and turning it over to the supernatural powers, which let the poor become guilty. These attempts only attenuate the inner situation and hinder man's repentance and thus his redemption; this is more true the more profound they are. Man all too readily tries to conceive and to analyze his sinful bondage to the dark power in terms of metaphysics or psychology, so as to reassure himself in the presence of the immense actuality of this power. He would like to conceive the inconceivable, as expressed by his surrender to his own sinful passion, in order to master it. But sin is mastered neither by philosophical nor by psychological conceptions, only by grace. Christ and his angels are our shield and buckler (cf. Psalm 90:1ff., 11ff.)

Once again, reference is made to Anthroposophy, which teems with spirits and beings of light and dark vesture and power; Rudolf Steiner's occult science teaches us how to perceive them and to relate to them so as to order and master our spiritual life with their help. Quite plainly the conclusion follows that knowledge about the spirits entails power over the spirits; though Steiner would deny it, this results in an admittedly sublimated, very spiritualized, yet unmistakable kind of higher magic. Likewise we refer once again to the much lower sphere of spiritualism and of the popular belief in spirits and demons with its accompanying fascination; it attracts attention since it in turn goes hand in glove with magic, crude this time, by virtue of which man hopes to gain control of the spirits and to make use of them. Finally, we cite the belief in fate, the fortunetelling and mastering of fate, as it is expressed by astrology and its seers.

Pastoral care has to warn against all these "magical arts." He who approaches occult science with the purpose of getting knowledge and help from it goes astray; he hopelessly entangles himself in a thicket and will cause confusion in his life and in that of others. Remember the warning against false gnosis in the apostolic testimony (Colossians 2:8; also the admonition to seek all knowledge in Christ, Colossians 2:3!). Particularly impressive in this context is Acts 19:18ff., where those who come to believe burn the books with whose help they had "practiced magic arts." These books must have been dream-interpretation books, zodiacal books, fortunetelling books, demon books. Away with them! it says here. Why should the whole intermediary world of spirits and demons still occupy and oppress us when access to the Father in heaven is now opened for us! What do we have to do with all the powers of fate when we have come under the power of Christ! This insight is of great importance for the church's preaching and pastoral care on the mission field, where the belief in demons is incomparably stronger than at home. There as nowhere will it be evident that we can prevail only by keeping strictly and exclusively to the line traced in the Scriptures.

The biblical testimony about these things shows the deeper understanding of grace and sin already presented. This is of special importance for pastoral care. Sin brings with it servitude to the power of darkness, while in receiving grace, man is liberated from it. This is expressed in Colossians 1:13, where it is said that man is redeemed because God in Christ delivers him from the dominion of darkness and transfers him to the Kingdom of his Son, and in 1 John 3:8, where Christ is hailed as he who in his work destroyed the work of the Devil. This view also underlies the Gospel reports about the healing of the possessed. Both of the sweeping New Testament passages cited above describe the occupation of our lives in sin by the powers from below as a total one. In special and marked cases, this occupation reaches a climax in the form of possession proper.

A possessed man is as if overrun, overpowered, swamped by the dark irruptive forces from the intermediary world. The consciously acting, thinking, and willing ego is completely shoved aside and actually eliminated. Of course, the possessed is not without consciousness; he thinks and talks, but actually not he himself thinks and talks, but "it" thinks, "it" talks in him and out of him. Something is in him which is no longer he himself, but has usurped his self by sovereignly and forcibly identifying itself with him. Psychologically, this strange and impenetrable process will be interpreted as a case of severe schizophrenia where the split goes deep enough to cause a more or less complete disintegration of personality. The ego has lost control over his life; the anonymous powers of the unconscious have occupied man and now pull him to and fro, as it is frightfully illustrated in the Gospel reports (cf. Mark 5:1-15; 9:14-29). But what does "interpret" mean here? The scriptural view of a real irruption of powers into man's life can never be explained away simply as mythology; behind the psychopathic phenomena a depth opens up which defies purely psychological considerations, yet need not be contested. When man says "yes" to sin, his life is subjected to a claim of far greater proportions than he could ever foresee or even suspect. His fetters can take various forms: passion, desire, addiction, neurotic compulsion, even subjection to ideas and mental influences of all kinds, and, in the most difficult and rare cases, possession proper, openly displayed in madness, mania, or depression.

We quite certainly have to beware of hastily coming out with a diagnosis of such morbid possession. Far from being an everyday phenomenon, it represents the most extreme and ultimate manifestation of the dark reign of evil. Above all, even when and where such possession is obvious, we must immediately consider the wholly other fact that Christ is the Lord even over the possessed. In order to perceive this, we are given the Gospel reports. They proclaim not possession but its conquest and healing. These reports do not intend to entice us to lose ourselves in reflection on the nature and the power of supernatural forces, but lead us to acknowledge the power of Christ. It may even be said that integral and final possession came to an end with the appearance of Jesus Christ on earth. Satan is already overcome and overthrown by Christ (cf. Mark 3:23-27 and Luke 10:18 ff.). We may count on the beginning of Christ's Kingdom and therefore also on the preservation and redemption of human life by him against all demonic irruptions. Even the sinner and unbeliever is protected and sheltered against them by the mighty hand of Jesus Christ. And the church is commissioned and sent to announce this protection and preservation and to make them effective in Word and sacrament. This is no weakening of what was said about the power of Satan and his spirits. Sin is certainly not to be joked about. Whether it is by avarice or sensuality or whatever inclination to evil—each time man succumbs to it in his separation from God's grace, a hidden door opens through which "the evil one" gains access to him. And yet we know that we are "freed from all power of the Devil." We know that when in the Lord's Prayer we pray with complete confidence for deliverance "from evil," we do not pray in vain, but are heard.

We may refer back to our discussion of psychotherapy and what has been said there about "forgiveness as healing." The demonological view of illness and sin in Holy Scripture is not to be regarded as surpassed by modern psychology and psychotherapy. Whatever psychopathic phenomena may come to light through psychological probing, they are not the primary cause according to biblical thought; they are the reflection and refraction of that metaphysical bondage to the powers of darkness to which sin has subjected man.

Without approving it, one may find it explicable when a psychiatrist writes: "Christ's miraculous healings of the blind and lame handed down in the New Testament, if they are historically founded at all, must have occurred primarily with hysterical patients"; and when he adds, "as is well known, in antiquity (and by the way, this is still the case today with all primitive peoples) mental illness, as well as epilepsy and hysteria, was attributed to possession by spirits; thence the casting out of spirits which Christ is said to have performed on the mentally ill"; when he also recalls in this connection with gentle mockery "the pastor Blumhardt, who even toward the end of the 19th century described a hysterical girl as possessed by the devil and healed her by spiritual procedures," and when he couples this event with the medieval belief in witchcraft (Rudolf Brun, *General Theory of Neurosis*, p. 17). Such affirmations betray the resentment of the modern, scientifically educated physician against the magic world view presumably underlying the New Testament reports. And yet these all too flippant remarks must be rejected as rash and unobjective. What is written in Ephesians 6:12 remains valid; it has to do neither with the medieval belief in witchcraft nor with the primitive ideas of antiquity, but it is to be understood spiritually and by faith: We "are not contending against flesh and blood, but against the principalities, against the powers, against the world rulers of this present darkness, against the spiritual hosts of wickedness in the heavenly places." But more important is the adjoining assertion (vss. 10-11, 13-19), that there is the armor of faith and prayer which equips us to be victorious in this battle. In the Bible the demonological view rests on, and is imbedded in, the *soteriological* view.

The biblical testimony concerning these powers allows a further insight. The history of the suffering, death, and resurrection of Jesus Christ, as well as the history of his preceding life leading up to the cross and to Easter day, is presented as a history of battle and victory, in which Jesus Christ conquers the powers of hell. On the road he travels from the throne of God to the manger, to the cross, to the resurrection and glorious ascension, he has received "the keys of Death and Hades" (Revelation 1:18). He has unmanned the powers. The forgiveness he achieved for us thus consists in an act of liberation. Jesus Christ releases us from the power of sin. Now it becomes unmistakably clear why forgiveness is the one and only act which saves us. Now it becomes unmistakably clear why every merely moral and psychological consideration and treatment of sin-bound man is insufficient. Only the grasping of forgiveness is sufficient. It is a new act of saying "yes"—saying "yes" no longer to sin, but to Jesus Christ, who absolves man and, by absolving him, enables him to share in the fruits of his battle and victory. In and with this assent to forgiveness, the dominion of the demons over us is broken. This is what saves us. True, sin may continue to hold us in its grip, but in effect its spell is taken from us, its chains are cut through. And the sinner's victorious comfort, as well as his signal liberation from concrete, evil bondages he may now lay aside, reveal that forgiveness occurred, that man exchanged the slavery of sin for the freedom of the child of God.

Once again, this in no way discredits the natural process of healing and means of healing. For the Christian, there is no contradiction between the healing by forgiveness and the healing by the physician. Rather, something like a promise of Jesus Christ lies on the hospitals and mental institutions, if only what happens there to the patients is done and accepted in the full knowledge that healing, though accomplished naturally, is ultimately a fruit of Christ's victorious mercy. If, for example, we today no longer mistreat the mentally ill as was still done in the Jewish and pagan world at the time of Jesus, or, to name a more recent example, as it is described in Gottfried Keller's *Grünem Heinrich* in the chapter about "Meretlein," then this, like every forward step in the art of healing and the tending of the sick, may be regarded as fruit and sign of this continuing mercy of Christ. Because Jesus Christ healed and still heals in the power of God, every human attempt at help and healing must be encouraged and may be a blessing.

For the pastoral conversation, bent on further spreading the victory and mercy of Christ, a final aspect unfolds here. It becomes a contest. Pastoral care is now to be considered a field where in the strength of Christ a real fight goes on against the powers from below. Spirits, "the world rulers of this darkness," are driven out by the Spirit of God, who through the Word intends to take possession of the life of fallen man. We are not engaged in an illusionary, intangible, airy, and vain enterprise, but we perform very hard labor when we enter into pastoral conversation. We do battle as mentioned in the passage from the Letter to the Ephesians (6:1ff.). We need not think of spectacular, dramatic outbreaks. On the contrary, responsible pastoral care proceeds very soberly, very undramatically. What is involved is not a psychic force we are to supply, but the plain communication of the Word with prayer and entreaty for the Holy Spirit. Bible and prayer and still more Bible and prayer are the weapons with which we fight here.

Where we rely on psychic dynamics and drama, allowing perhaps even for shrieking and conjuring, we are certainly involved again in the fatal attempt to engage the forces and powers on our own human strength. But this would not be pastoral care; this would resemble wicked spiritual magic. Of course, this also exists. However, it does not effect liberations, but only new bonds, much worse than the old. Pastoral care has indeed to do with exorcism, with casting out demons, but let us beware of pseudoexorcism!

A new seriousness will encompass the pastoral conversation. Easygoing and fashionable pastoral counseling has no right to existence. He who, scarcely converted himself, wants to convert others, who lines up case on case and boasts great numbers of successful pastoral treatments, only discloses his ignorance about the difficulty of the battle to be fought in true pastoral care. The reticence of a pastor like the elder Blumhardt, who agreed to minister to that tempted lady with whom he then was given the great experience of divine help in contending against the powers of darkness, remains impressive. He knew how utterly serious a risk we run each time we must wrestle for a soul in pastoral care. How shall we find the right words, how persevere, perhaps for years, if we lack such seriousness?

Such seriousness, such soberness and patience, but also true courage, confidence, and comfort, are imparted to us only when pastoral care is for us a seed of hope. This is the last thing we have to say. But the word hope must be understood here as it is understood in Holy Scripture: hope in the consummation of all things, in the actual, victorious end of the battle in the coming of the Kingdom on the day of Jesus Christ. The New Testament testimony never speaks of the battle against Satan and his spirits except to open up a view of this day, a view of the last things, the view of the end. The signs of the healing of the possessed are always signs of the promise of the Kingdom of God (cf. Luke 11:20). This Kingdom is in process, but only in process. The demons are conquered, but the full revelation of this victory is yet to come. "We are God's children now; it does not yet appear what we shall be" (1 John 3:2). Pastoral care also partakes of this "not yet." It must therefore include this eschatological perspective. All it does must be considered as preliminary, or better, as something anticipatory. Whatever happens in pastoral care is anticipatory in the sense that it points to that day when the final victory will be revealed. We press on in pastoral care as one presses on toward a goal that is certain but not yet attained. We need perseverance and must reckon with long delays. Therefore, our pressing forward is joined to a ceaseless waiting. For everything rests on faith, and faith is not yet beholding. He who wants to walk already by sight and anticipate what God can give only at the end is not fit for pastoral care. He will reach out for success close at hand and thereby defraud men of the great promise and hope which is given us in Christ as our only source of life.

Each pastoral conversation has an *immediate* goal which can and must be reached: to liberate a drinker from alcoholism, to lead a person from a sexual aberration back to the protecting and healing commandment, to give courage to the depressed, to prepare the dying for the end. A great thing, indeed everything that is required of pastoral care, is thus accomplished. Yet behind these immediate goals looms the *ultimate* goal of final redemption from all bondage, from all pain and death. And this is something else again. The reclaimed drinker is even in his health still imperfect. The traces of his sinful involvement continue to be visible in the form of various idiosyncrasies and weaknesses. If we release a person bound to his money from his captivity, we have certainly erected a sign for the victory of Christ over the power of mammon, yet complete victory is not yet at hand. Shall we then be idle? Shall we underestimate the sign because the reality behind it is yet to be revealed? Surely not! For we must now hear the corollary affirmation. Such signs point to the great shock which since Christ's resurrection from the dead shakes the foundations of this world still overshadowed by darkness, and promises its approaching end. Let us therefore not despise signs and immediate goals! The small achievement already contains the great victory. True, what occurs silently and secretly in pastoral care is but the deliverance of individual souls from worldly corruption. And yet, if here and there a human being awakens for God by our labor, it is more than an isolated event. Not only is one man saved, but, as this happens, God's cause advances in this world, and the kingdom of darkness diminishes. This we must see, and to this we must open the eyes of men. Only then have we helped them to find God. Just as pastoral care is truly a fight against demons, it is also as truly born from the hope for and certainty of the last things.

Hence, no one must be allowed to stay satisfied and self-content with what he receives when he first turns and repents. If he experiences true pastoral care, he cannot rest easy simply because his own little life has been cleared up and brought to peace. That salvation and truth were allowed to come to light in his life or in the life of his family must awaken in him the vision and hope of the great transformation of all things, which, far beyond his own personal affairs, shall one day take place on earth as truly as Jesus Christ has risen from the dead on this earth. The forgiveness of sins he has experienced is not exclusively meant for him, but is to be seen as a preliminary ray of the day of Jesus Christ which will dawn on all men. Each demonstration of God's help and redemption in which we share in pastoral care contains a summons to collaboration. This collaboration is faith and the hope born of it in the furtherance of God's cause not only in us but in the many around us whom we see lost and bound in their sins. It is a distinctive mark of genuine pastoral care that it calls those it reaches to such collaboration. The absence of this sign in our pastoral care must make us restless. True pastoral care has always a missionary dimension.

This dimension becomes apparent in our view of the personal in its interrelation with the whole of life, and of the predicament and redemption of the individual in their connection with the predicament and redemption of the social and political world around him. The sexual aberration in which a person is caught bids us attend to the sexual aberration that prevails around him. The alcoholism of a particular man leads us to pay attention to the whole problem of alcoholism; this in turn is bound up with the question of drinking customs and the financial power of the liquor industry. All these facets are indivisibly interwoven. The battle I fight by the Word of God in my own little life immediately points beyond itself to the great battle which rages all around the world for the sake of God's cause and Kingdom. This inescapably confronts me with tasks reaching beyond my personal sphere of life. The rich man whose eyes are opened in pastoral care to the danger of wealth must and will grow suspicious not only of his own possessions but of all possession. The social question is put to him and henceforth will never leave him alone. Likewise the poor, the deprived, the oppressed, must rethink this question in the light of the gospel with its special appeal to the poor.

The question of society, the questions of economics and politics, the questions of justice and of peace, are as relevant to pastoral care as they are to the broader realm of Christian witness. We stumble on them when we communicate God's Word and call men to repentance. A direct way leads from the turnabout of my life in the forgiveness of my sins to the great turning of all life for which the way is paved in Jesus Christ. A way leads from the justification of the sinful individual to the establishment of true justice for the sinful people, for state and society. A way leads from grace directly to the questions of human relations in the public sphere. There is not a sentence of the gospel of forgiveness which does not have an immediate social and political implication and significance.

Social and political questions must not, therefore, be evaded in pastoral conversation. Because the demons operate in the realms just described, and more still because the hope revealed to us in Christ of victory over the demons is not limited to the personal sphere but extends to the whole world, pastoral care will reach with its comfort and admonition even into this worldly territory. In so doing, it is not concerned with politics or economics as such. It is concerned with them for the sake of the souls of the people who are threatened by the powers at work in, and in control of, politics and economics. It must do so in order to strengthen the men entrusted to its care in the hope for Christ's victory over the kingdoms of this world. It will have a political and social concern because of the concreteness of its comfort and admonition. As a result, genuine pastoral care will bring forth people who by virtue of this hope and the admonition flowing from it are bold and willing to stake their lives wherever God's Word and Kingdom call them to serve and labor in the darkness of this world.

The stronger emphasis on the hope in and the prospect of the last things, along with the widening and extending of preaching and pastoral care to the great political and social questions beyond the mere individual in the witness of the church, is not primarily the merit of theological labor and research. Among scholars the eschatology of the New Testament is still reluctantly accepted or even considered to be a time-bound and thus obsolete notion. Preachers like the two Blumhardts, Hermann Kutter, and Leonhard Ragaz, again unlocked for us the door to faith in the reality of the coming Kingdom of Christ and reopened our eyes to the last things. They themselves were largely prompted by pastoral contact with people who suffered acutely from the life-destroying demonism of the powers of darkness.

In most recent times, the severe oppression of the churches on the part of the political powers in the countries conquered or threatened by Nazism engendered a new consciousness of the political responsibility imposed by the gospel. Think of the numerous incidents in the battle of the confessing church in Germany, Holland, Norway, and France, of the *Barmen Confession* or of Kaj Munk's sermons. Because this conflict confronted individuals man by man with decisions, pastoral counseling in turn had to deal with it anew. For example, the letters Karl Barth addressed during the war to the churches in Czechoslovakia, Holland, France, Norway, England, and Germany ought to be regarded as pastoral exhortations strengthening individuals to hold their ground politically as members of the church, admonishing and comforting them. They are printed in the collection,

Against the Stream. This collection of documents is preceded by the fundamental and important essay on *Church and State*, also published separately, in which the biblical-theological question of the indissoluble connection of gospel and politics, of church and true state is given a completely new orientation, centered in the message of Jesus Christ.

The pastoral counselor is the bearer and mediator of the message of forgiveness. He acts not in his own strength and judgment but as one who is called. In order to do so, he himself must be rooted in the Word and the church and live from faith in forgiveness. He shall not bind men to himself, but to the Lord of the church by leading them to the Word and by continually praying for them.

16 The Pastoral Counselor

Whoever engages in pastoral care must know that he occupies a special place. To use a picture, it is the place which lies between the Word of God and sinful man. The Word stands on the one side, the sinner on the other; the Word wants to cross over to speak to the sinner. This requires a bearer, a mediator. This bearer and mediator of the Word is the pastoral counselor.

In the evangelical churches, the churches of the priesthood of all believers, anyone can become a pastoral counselor. One does not need to be a minister. To be sure, since the minister by definition stands on this place of transmission, pastoral care will be one of his special and pre-eminent tasks. But whether minister or not, one must always take a special step to assume this place of pastoral care. The priesthood of all believers notwithstanding, pastoral care is not everyone's affair. An authorization and a corresponding commitment which rests upon an inner obligation are needed. Whoever accepts the charge of pastoral care steps out of the rank and file. This singling out, this special step, this authorization characterizes and sets apart the pastoral counselor as pastoral counselor.

We name this authorization the *call* of the pastoral counselor. This conclusively re-emphasizes what we have repeatedly encountered in explaining the basis, content, and practice of pastoral care: Pastoral care is a service which cannot be done in one's own strength and judgment. For what is to be communicated is indeed the Word of God. But this Word is free. It goes out where and when it pleases. And it is part of this freedom that God's Word not only elects him to whom it is directed, but also calls him whom it will use in the service of its communication.

The call to pastoral care is thus a special call going beyond the call to faith addressed to each member of the congregation. The minister, whose task of proclamation naturally includes the function of pastoral counseling, must be aware of this call in the first place. This call to the ministry and with it to pastoral care is to be dealt with in detail in pastoral theology. We refer to the pertinent textbooks, especially to what remains the standard work: Wilhelm Löhe's *Der Evangelische Geistliche*. Also the church member engaged in pastoral care with others, no less than the minister, has to examine from case to case whether authentic calling justifies his intervention. The priesthood of all believers cannot be construed to invite within the church the mutual practice of pastoral care, arbitrary and disorderly, because uncalled for.

Whether calling is present or not cannot be decided externally. We can only raise the question, whereas the answer is given in the secrecy of the decision of the Holy Spirit in man's heart. Nevertheless there are signs of the calling. They make evident the place of pastoral care and must not be lacking where true pastoral care takes place.

The first sign is that of a "charge." Again, it is the minister before others who has the credentials for pastoral care in that he is ordained and chosen as the shepherd of his congregation. But the same is true, if to a lesser extent, of the mutual pastoral care of the faithful. It is a "charge," though without a distinctive election or ordination, when a father and a mother counsel their children, or a husband counsels his wife, the wife her husband, the superior the subordinate, the teacher the pupil, the neighbor the neighbor, or whatever orders of life may dictate such human confrontation. All these cases have to do with a co-ordination of one person to another and a resulting encounter which is not simply of an accidental and arbitrary nature but, in faith, may be regarded as a sign of a commission and thus of an inner compulsion which does not simply exist in the imagination of the individual.

On the other hand, the so-called "pastoral gift" which many would claim for themselves is *not* a sign on which a calling can be based. The so-called specialists in pastoral care mostly turn out to be merely self-glorified and insidious counselors who cause more harm than good. We might even say that those with an authentic call and charge can be recognized by the fact that they know themselves as not especially qualified and equipped for it. They struggle against their task instead of rushing to it. They wish God would send someone else in their place. At any rate, this feeling of inadequacy of the pastoral counselor is not bad, but a good and positive sign. In spite of this feeling, an individual may, indeed he must, remain ready for the service of pastoral care. His resistance is overcome by the Word of God and he is urged into its service. Recognizing his feeling of inadequacy as an escape, he no longer shoves his own task off on others (say, on the minister), but becomes obedient to the inner calling and proceeds to fulfill it.

With this reservation, it will be a part of our calling to be equipped with certain gifts. We must have the ability to talk to people, to understand them, and to carry on an orderly conversation. This has already been dealt with. He who himself is inhibited and ingrown and has no knowledge of life will not be called. For he will not be able to loosen up the reserve of his neighbor and make him talk. Even among ministers there are those who had better keep away from counseling because they have not the gifts for it—which raises the question whether the ministry is the right place for them.

The decisive sign of the call, however, is the pastoral counselor's *own faith*. It is the root of that inner compulsion which operates in all true pastoral care. Its fruits are the zeal and the patience, the pressing forward and the waiting, the seeking out of the neighbor, the solidarity with him, above all the certainty in which we communicate the Word to him and which wins him for the Word. It can be a weak, a tempted, a struggling faith—and where is true faith ever without temptation?—but it must be faith: One's own knowing of grace and of sin, of repentance and regeneration, one's own praying and interceding. The lukewarm no more than the self-assured and the satiated are called. In the end this simply means: The pastoral counselor must on his part be a living member of the church which gathers around Word and sacrament and therefore lives from faith. One cannot be a pastoral counselor apart from the church. For what is the meaning and content of pastoral care if not the gathering of the lost into the people of God? And how can we gather if we live in the dispersion ourselves?

Furthermore, calling stands behind pastoral care; however, calling is not only calling *by* the Word, but it is also calling *for* the Word. The pastoral counselor, called to lead others to the Word, must himself be led by the Word, grounded and trained in the Word. Thus, *intimate knowledge of the Word of God* is the most important prerequisite for the counselor. He must be entirely at home in the Word. Again, this will apply to the minister before all others. He shall be a "scribe" in the good sense. Let us not shy away from the title of scribe. According to the words of Jesus himself, there are scribes who have been trained for the Kingdom of heaven (Matthew 13:52). Or, in other words, let us not shy away from being called theologians insofar as true theology is inevitably a theology of the Word. Of course, the ordinary church member without theological training is not excluded from pastoral care, but only when he grows up and lives in a congregation entrusted to a shepherd who on the basis of his studies is in the position rightly to teach the congregation, to impart true knowledge of faith to its individual members, and to equip them to render pastoral care to others.

An example: A dying man was brought to a clinic and died the same night. His wife was perplexed and desperate. She did not dare to summon a minister in the middle of the night. But she called a friend of her husband. He came and read John 11 with her and prayed. He told afterward how he had received solid instruction in his youth and remembered what is "the sole comfort in life and in death." Pastoral care in the church ultimately depends on the confessional stand, i.e., on the theology, of the minister who is in charge of the congregation. No true lay pastoral care can arise in the congregation on the basis of a minister's confused, shaky theology, stripped of confession and hence of assurance.

Well-founded knowledge of the faith is needed even to comfort a child. It is all the more indispensable in conversing with the adult of today, who is mercilessly adrift in his thinking and accordingly in his living. The Word of God needs to be interpreted and applied in order to bring clarity and direction into the human predicament. We are permitted to be its instrument, provided we first open and dedicate ourselves to the Word. This requires hours, days, years of continuous searching of the Scriptures. The argument that the daily tasks of the ministry leave insufficient time for study of the Scriptures simply does not hold. Strange practice of the ministry and of pastoral care which does not rest on *doctrine,* and is not constantly renewed by it! The Word of God has power over the spirits, but it can exercise its power only through him over whom it has won power. "The same must have conquered and unconditionally brought into its power all your thoughts, your will, and even all your emotions and feelings; then it also surrenders to your power, wholly and undividedly and without reservation, and permits your mortal tongue to perform eternal works." (A. F. C. Vilmar.)

Moreover, we pastoral counselors must have committed our own souls to care if we are rightly to render this service to others. Hence, *pastoral care to the pastoral counselor!* Let no one brush this aside as a superfluous requirement. The pastoral counselor must himself lead the way of repentance and confession. He must himself experience what it means to receive forgiveness of sins in pastoral conversation. The pastoral counselor, especially if he is a minister, must expose himself to a counseling situation. People can tell whether we talk to them out of our own knowledge of pastoral care. Only this makes us trustworthy to them.

Unfortunately, there are fewer pastoral counselors taken into pastoral care themselves than we might think. Conversely, there are ministers who had first to be released from their own deep entanglements and subsequently became true ministers and pastoral counselors. This, of course, must not be construed to mean that the pastor best assists those seeking help by laying before them his own salvation from sin and distress. This procedure sooner shakes than awakens confidence in the counselor's guidance. But it does mean that the task of the pastoral care of others discloses our own weakness. We experience defeats in pastoral care, and recognizing in them our inherent weakness and ineffectiveness, we seek a pastoral counselor for ourselves to receive his comfort and admonition and to return newly strengthened and equipped to our own pastoral counseling. Pastoral care rests on humility. And nothing is more humbling for us in a salutary way than a trip to our own pastor. He who has recognized that he himself is at his wit's end, that he is in constant need of grace, lives by grace, and must be referred to grace by a brother to whom he entrusts himself, will be able rightly to comfort, teach, and admonish others. We ministers should seek from one another and do for one another such brotherly service much more often.

The church suffers because this service is rendered so infrequently, because its ministers bypass each other in such an unbrotherly manner and pass up occasions for mutual service. How different would be the inner fellowship of the ministers of a church if they would undertake this mutual service! In this connection, a word is in order about the marriage of ministers and pastoral counselors. Has the pastor not in his wife the "helpmeet" to console, admonish, and comfort him? But, the counterquestion goes, is the pastor not obliged to strict discretion especially with regard to his wife, and could this discretion not be broken in conversing with her? The answer is that this obligation of silence undoubtedly exists with respect to the sins of others, but not with respect to his own weakness and sin. He detracts nothing from his own dignity; on the contrary, he shows true humility and is strengthened when he does not hide his inner distress from his life companion, but seeks her out and receives from her the assurance of the Word of grace which is valid also for him. True, he can do it only when he is united in faith with his wife. But is this not the self-evident presupposition of his marriage?

This leads us to a last point concerning the relationship of the pastoral counselor to his charges. Let the pastor not only proclaim forgiveness, let him not only teach forgiveness, but let him *live* from forgiveness with those entrusted to him. That is to say, let him reckon himself and them to God! This changes the initial contact into a relationship of final, mutual trust. The atmosphere of such trust must surround the pastoral counselor and the counselee. Only now true unburdening is possible. Such trust is more than mere sympathy. It can arise and exist even if what we call sympathy and human closeness is more or less completely lacking. It arises where, and only where, God's Word begins to reign over both, since both are addressed by it. Perhaps only one hears and understands it at first, but he hears and understands it forthwith also for the other, and therefore the other is also drawn into the reality of being addressed. And this provides the nurturing soil where trust grows as of itself and surrounds us like a new dimension, a new, spiritual realm of life, where we can breathe and now also talk with one another.

Admittedly, a danger crops up here, the danger of mutual dependency. Pastoral care must avoid dependencies which stand in the way of the one and only valid dependency, dependency on God. Both counselor and counselee must know: This is not a matter of human help. The pastoral counselor does not help. God helps. And this is so easily forgotten. Trust in God deviates into human, all too human, dependency where one puts his trust in another who, like him, is flesh. In the most common case the counselee is bound to his human pastoral counselor. The result is what in psychological terms is called a "transference."

A person clings in complete but purely human trust to the spiritual guide, instead of being led by him to God. He transfers all his feelings, hopes, desires, yearnings for redemption and liberation to the counselor. He sees in him something like an ideal, an embodiment of all the things he wishes to have and to become himself. He believes he can no longer live without him. The counselor becomes the helper and savior, whose constant and increasing guidance and direction is a must. It easily happens that the pastoral counselor in turn binds himself falsely to the person who approaches him in this way. He fancies to be the plainly indispensable guide of the one he guides, whom he must never let go and set free. Perhaps he actually delights in his dependency and trust. It pleases him if another person so completely gives himself into his hand. At this point, sharp vigilance and control over oneself and over the other are called for.

Every textbook of practical psychology abounds in examples of the fatal consequences of such transferences if they are not recognized and dissolved. Perhaps a certain transference is unavoidable. In psychotherapy, it counts as a necessary, technical means to be consciously employed in analysis, yet in such a way that the dissolution of the transference is just as consciously kept in view and aimed at from the beginning. There is no healing without unconditional release from the temporary dependency on the psychiatrist. In pastoral care, it can on occasion be an equally unavoidable process for the penitent to cling to his pastor as to a father who renders him the great and helpful service of leading him to the Word of God. But the pastoral counselor must be fully aware of what is going on and he must never for a moment take advantage of such transference of thoughts and feelings. He must guide his charge through this dangerous situation, and to guide here means to release him from the counselor in order to bind him to the only Helper, Saviour, and Lord, the Father in heaven.

No less than the one in need of pastoral care, the counselor himself, is threatened when such dependencies arise. He must beware of having his own human sympathy—which under the circumstances can be awakened very strongly in him—interfere with his pastoral care and of making a human friendship for himself out of every pastoral case. Sympathy and warm, hearty feeling for the fellowman will most certainly not be forbidden. It cannot be forbidden anyway. It is there, especially when we risk so much for a neighbor. Nevertheless, the counselor must be extremely alert not to seek something for himself, or else the Word of God is suppressed and overthrown, and pastoral care becomes an empty process and a sham.

What has just been said deserves special consideration when we engage in pastoral counseling with the opposite sex. Here particular vigilance and care are indicated. A self-evident and natural protection lies in the pastoral counselor's spiritually good and sound marriage. We have already asserted that he must never violate discretion, not even toward his own wife. We now must emphasize the decisive task of the pastor's wife to observe a likewise unconditional discretion and reticence and to repress any jealous impulse, however subtle. Those seeking pastoral care must find the pastor's house always open, even on the part of his wife, and be able to enter and leave in unqualified trust. What needs to be said further about this matter already belongs to the field of special types of pastoral care, which we do not wish to enter here. The real battle for keeping the relation to his neighbor pure must be fought in the pastoral counselor's own soul. It is the battle against his own instinctual nature, of which he always needs to be aware since it threatens to disturb and confuse the conversation. It is expressed in an unspiritual selfish curiosity about the neighbor and his fate. It is possibly disguised in the form of pity and compassion, hiding, however, an evil kind of curiosity about this neighbor's mistakes, errors, and temptations. Such curiosity may often lead to human closeness, but since it is too direct, it is not beneficial and can become an open gate through which something like a malevolent infection is communicated from the one to the other.

Only he who persists in prayer will win the battle for keeping the conversation pure. To pray means here that our listening to the neighbor, like our priestly speaking to him, is embedded in our listening and speaking to God. This prayerful hearing and speaking brings about the powerful protection, the great help, the liberating, purifying clarity which must surround, penetrate, and sustain the whole conversation. Then the demons are warded off, then the atmosphere is created for a mutual encounter without any false dependency, but in true unity before him who is the Lord of this conversation and wills our conversation to become the place where we may hear and transmit his gracious and saving call and word. All the wisdom we need in pastoral care is defined in the words of Ephesians 6:18-20:

"Pray at all times in the Spirit, with all prayer and supplication. To that end keep alert with all perseverance, making supplication for all the saints, and also for me, that utterance may be given me in opening my mouth boldly to proclaim the mystery of the gospel, for which I am an ambassador in chains; that I may declare it boldly, as I ought to speak!"

www.ingramcontent.com/pod-product-compliance
Lightning Source LLC
Chambersburg PA
CBHW052144300426
44115CB00011B/1518